EUROPEAN BANKING NATIONALISM

This book compares the different expressions of, and outcomes from, banking nationalism in two European countries to draw wider conclusions about the consequences for Banking Union in Europe and to show how national governments deal (or fail to deal) with international commitments.

It reveals how and why one case—Spain—managed to tackle failing banks within EU Banking Union regulations even before they became written in EU law, while the other—Italy—had more persistent problems. The book argues that Spain demonstrates a successful case of liberal economic nationalism, typified by aggressive, early state intervention to restructure Spanish banks, and help from the European Stability Mechanism even in the face of local political opposition. Italy, meanwhile, suffered from the weaker, delayed intervention which forced it to confront European institutions with demands for special treatment as a means of externalizing its own internal weakness.

This book will be of key interest to scholars, students and professionals in economic policy, Economic and Monetary Union and Banking Union in Europe, European and global governance, European/EU studies, European public policy, European public administration and EU law, as well as professionals working in the banking sector.

Shawn Donnelly is Assistant Professor of European Economic Governance at the University of Twente in Enschede, the Netherlands.

Gaia Pometto is an independent researcher based in Amsterdam, the Netherlands.

Routledge/UACES Contemporary European Studies

The primary objective of the new Contemporary European Studies series is to provide a research outlet for scholars of European Studies from all disciplines. The series publishes important scholarly works and aims to forge for itself an international reputation.

Series editors: **Eleanor Brooks**, *University of Edinburgh, UK*, **Ben Farrand**, *Newcastle University, UK*, **Helena Farrand Carrapico**, *Northumbria University, UK*, **Benjamin Martill**, *University of Edinburgh, UK*, on behalf of the *University Association for Contemporary European Studies.*

Domestic Politics and Norm Diffusion in International Relations
Ideas Do Not Float Freely
Thomas Risse

Euroscepticism as a Transnational and Pan-European Phenomenon
The Emergence of a New Sphere of Opposition
Edited by John FitzGibbon, Benjamin Leruth and Nick Startin

Global Power Transition and the Future of the European Union
Birol A. Yeşilada, Jacek Kugler, Gaspare Genna and Osman Göktuğ Tanrıkulu

The EU in the Global Investment Regime
Commission Entrepreneurship, Incremental Institutional Change and Business Lethargy
Johann Robert Basedow

The Dynamics of EU External Energy Relations
Fighting for Energy
Francesca Batzella

For more information about this series, please visit: www.routledge.com/Routledge-UACES-Contemporary-European-Studies/book-series/UACES

EUROPEAN BANKING NATIONALISM

State Power and Troubled Banks

Shawn Donnelly and Gaia Pometto

Routledge
Taylor & Francis Group
LONDON AND NEW YORK

UACES

First published 2023
by Routledge
4 Park Square, Milton Park, Abingdon, Oxon OX14 4RN

and by Routledge
605 Third Avenue, New York, NY 10158

Routledge is an imprint of the Taylor & Francis Group, an informa business

British Library Cataloguing-in-Publication Data
A catalogue record for this book is available from the British Library

ISBN: 978-1-032-36938-9 (hbk)
ISBN: 978-1-032-36940-2 (pbk)
ISBN: 978-1-003-33458-3 (ebk)

DOI: 10.4324/9781003334583

Typeset in Bembo
by Deanta Global Publishing Services, Chennai, India

1

ECONOMIC NATIONALISM AND BANKING UNION

Does economic nationalism pose a problem for Banking Union, and for the economy more broadly in Europe? If so, how strong is the problem, where does it come from, what specific pressures come to bear on European institutions, and can anything be done to mitigate it? One measure of economic nationalism revolves around the question of who is permitted to own and control banks in EU Member States. This question became particularly pressing for Europe in the aftermath of the Great Financial Crisis (GFC) of 2008, as state aid for banks spread throughout the European Union (and elsewhere), and is being repeated again during the Great Lockdown (2020–). State aid can keep national owners in control and make foreign investment or takeovers unattractive. How strongly is state aid motivated by nationalist impulses? Are there other impulses, such as protecting local varieties of financial capitalism, or even local varieties of capitalism more broadly conceived that limit economic and financial linkages across national borders? How have these linkages developed in the context of EU law and regulation to limit and roll back the increased tendency to national ownership after 2008?

The renationalization of finance in the EU after 2008—by which we mean the tendency of finance to retreat behind national borders (Jones 2015)—had the chance to decline in importance. But has it, and why or why not? This book identifies two countries hit hard by the Eurozone crisis (EZC) of 2010–2016, both within the single currency's southern periphery, that had different trajectories in response. Spain encountered a fast, deep crisis, and secured international support for rebuilding its banking sector, while Italy experienced a slower, but more punishing decline in banking that was more inward-looking and unable to secure international investment as part of the recovery plans. Are the two cases as different as they seem? And why is that so? Should we expect the same results in the context of the Great Lockdown (2020–2022)? This book compares the

DOI: 10.4324/9781003334583-1

combination of bank activity, central bank oversight, regulation and restructuring of the banking sector and finance ministry interventions through public support, state aid, restructuring and bank resolution in two Southern European countries hit hard by both crises to identify common trends, differences, as causes. We work from the premise that there must be different mechanisms at work in these two countries, both in the banking sector itself and within the institutions of the state, that account for the differences between them. We search for lessons that can be learned for policy makers and analysts alike.

The challenges investigated here take place alongside the ongoing construction of Banking Union in Europe. Banking Union (BU) was and continues to be a project to develop EU-level regulation and supervision of Eurozone banks, as well as the means to close banks in an orderly fashion while preventing one bank's failure from setting off a chain reaction through the single market (Howarth and Quaglia 2016a). It remains an incomplete project, primarily due to the lack of a European Deposit Insurance Scheme (Schnabel and Véron 2018; Schoenmaker 2018; Howarth and Quaglia 2018, 2021), and a complex one in which new European institutions and national authorities must work together to achieve resilience of the EU's financial system.

As a project, BU does not explicitly raise the nationalism question by demanding that international investors become partners in EU banks, but it does require banks generally to increase their capital reserves by attracting investment, which can be difficult if prospective investors are only sought within the national economy. This is doubly so in national markets where access to financial markets is fragile or tenuous, and where other national investors that might invest to assume ownership of a failing bank are themselves in a precarious position. Public policy in the form of state aid and supervisory forbearance, as well as corporate governance structures that hinder or deter foreign investors by protecting bank insiders, is therefore still possible. As we look for evidence of economic nationalism, our definition encompasses not only measures that are explicitly geared to exclude investors from other countries, but features of the country's variety of financial capitalism that preserve insider control of the bank, and links to local stakeholders like prominent families, city councils and other banks that outside investors find unattractive (Goyer and Valdivielso Del Real 2014). Given that investors are interested in return on investment and that they pay attention to corporate strategy, governance and investment portfolios, their willingness to invest in banks that are in financial difficulty depends on the likelihood of instigating changes to these factors. In this context, the difficulty of replacing bank management will have (inadvertently) nationalist effects.

The same potential support for economic nationalism is true for other connections and contracts that make it difficult to bring the bank back to financial sustainability. These are above all contracts with creditors that may have to be broken so that the bank's debts are reduced to a sustainable level moving forward. Both situations may be generated where failing banks have strong connections to city, regional and national governments, enterprises, community associations, foundations unions and retail customers that place expectations on them beyond profitability. In such cases, the roots of effective economic nationalism can be found in the everyday desire to protect and promote local communities, rather than outright nationalism per se. This is not an identification and promotion of large banks as national champions as economic nationalism typically focuses on (Epstein 2014), but rather the protection of smaller, regional banks as local champions. Where national institutions and governments are unable to square the demands of Banking Union with this local protection, we expect functional economic nationalism to follow communities, as governments protect the interests of their own citizens, rather than accept application of EU law. In this book, we suggest that Spain has had an easier time of squaring the circle than Italy, and has therefore been driven to defy EU law more strongly. We explore the reasons why it is found in institutional, political and socio-economic (variety of financial capitalism) characteristics.

Banking Union dates back to 2014, when the European Central Bank (ECB) began its duties as the direct supervisor for 128 systemically important banks. It took over this task from national authorities, which had been working collectively within the European Banking Authority since 2011, but had failed to catch significant shortfalls in a number of banks (Steffen 2014). The purpose was to increase the certainty that the banks were being investigated regularly and thoroughly and, among other things, made to increase their capital to compensate for a variety of weaknesses that plagued European banking since the onset of the Great Financial Crisis in 2008 (Wymeersch 2014). The most pressing of these weaknesses was that of non-performing loans (NPLs), which increased steadily in Europe as economic growth stagnated, and loans made to businesses and households fell increasingly into arrears (De Rynck 2016). Banks were expected to deal with this problem themselves by raising capital and writing off assets. These were unpopular for the banks, of course, and in some cases, their foot-dragging was tolerated by national supervisors who expected that once the economy eventually rebounded, the problem of NPLs would go away. Notable is that in 2014, the ECB undertook an Asset Quality Review of systemically important banks twice, before formally assuming responsibility from its national counterparts in November. Both in the spring and in the fall, half of all European banks which possessed insufficient capital were Italian (though the banks that had failed by the greatest margins were Greek and Cypriot), and only one was Spanish. This raises questions about both the banks and the bank supervisor, the Bank of Italy, as well as about the Bank of Spain as supervisor for the Spanish system.

The ongoing weakness of economic growth and employment in Europe after 2008, coupled with an even more pronounced downturn in Southern Europe, meant that European banks and the governments that had stepped in to salvage them from the wreckage of the financial crisis were still exposed to the possibility of bankruptcy. This in turn increased demands for mechanisms to ensure that this would not happen. To this end, European governments agreed in 2014 to the establishment of a Single Resolution Mechanism (SRM) that entered force in January 2016. The ECB, as supervisor, would decide if a bank was failing or likely to fail (FOLTF). If so, a new Single Resolution Board (SRB), located in Brussels, would decide whether a bank that was FOLTF should be closed and its remaining assets (such as mortgages, loans and government bonds) and liabilities (particularly bank accounts of depositors) transferred to other banks, who would ensure continuity of service. To ensure that there was enough money to do this, additional commitments were made to establish a Single Resolution Fund (SRF), into which European banks would pay, and which could be used to soften the negative impact of winding down the bank on other financial market participants (Howarth and Quaglia 2014; Kern 2015; Asimakopoulos 2018). In addition, a discussion ensued on whether and how to introduce a common system of deposit insurance that could be drawn on to assist with closed and restructured banks, minimizing the impact of failures on depositors and the broader economy. Agreement on this last component remained elusive (Donnelly 2018; Howarth and Quaglia 2018; Schnabel and Véron 2019).

As with Economic and Monetary Union (EMU), and EU politics more broadly, EU national governments had differing opinions on how much money to commit to the SRF, particularly how much money should cross national borders. Governments themselves stood back from contributing so that the fund is paid for by bank contributions, but Northern European governments in particular remained sensitive to burdening their 'own' banks with potentially paying for the failure of banks elsewhere. The result is that the fund remained limited in size. This in turn could only be sufficient if the financial requirements of resolving a bank were limited, meaning that it would not be sufficient (Asimakopoulos and Howarth 2022). This was to be achieved with an accompanying piece of EU legislation called the Bank Recovery and Resolution Directive (BRRD) that imposed losses on private creditors and shareholders in a resolution. To contrast with the practice of 'bailing out' insolvent banks with public money (as often happened in 2008), the new demand was dubbed a 'bail-in'. The fund might be called on, and national governments might eventually be called on after that to inject more cash into an insolvent bank as it was being resolved, but first the SRB would have to insist that the bail-in rules were respected. This would reduce the overall size of public money required to reach a satisfactory solution.

The EU instrument that incited pushback from the Italian government in particular, and which forms the starting point of our comparative study, is the BRRD, and in particular, the rules pertaining to bail-ins and state aid for failing banks. The entrance into force of the bail-in rule in 2016 was a game changer for European banks. According to the bail-in rule, before receiving support through government funds, an insolvent bank needs to increase its capital by reducing liabilities to creditors equaling at least 8% of its total liabilities (Official Journal of the European Union 2014). Designed to fight moral hazard by fostering investor's monitoring over the bank and to break the vicious cycle between sovereign and private debt (Gros and Schoenmaker 2014), the bail-in rule has encountered substantial opposition in certain Member States, with Slovenian subordinated bondholders going as far as to claim the rule was against the country's constitution, which eventually required the European Court of Justice to examine the case (Khan 2016; Guarascio and Sinner 2016). Similar cases have found their way to the courts in Portugal and Spain.

Italy, however, stands out for its official pushback against applying the bail-in rules. Compared to Member States such as Ireland, Germany and the Netherlands which were immediately affected by the financial crisis of 2008, Italian banks were hit only in 2011, when Italy's two largest banks lost 30% of their value (Howarth and Quaglia 2016; Di Quirico 2010). Thus, if the lower internationalization of the Italian banking system had at first spared them from needing state support, a combination of poor management, an overall increase of non-performing loans and a connection to Italian sovereign debt eventually hit several Italian banks. Four of these banks were bailed out in 2015, that is before the entrance in force of the much feared bail-in rule (Bodellini 2017). However, three more banks, namely Monte dei Paschi di Siena (MPS), and Veneto Banca and Banca Popolare di Vicenza (V&V) were not so 'lucky', and their destiny was to a large extent shaped by this new rule.

For European governments that had not already provided financial assistance to their banks, and aided their financial restructuring, the impending entry into force of the BRRD meant that they needed to do so before 1 January 2016. As with countries that had already completed the process, this meant creating special purpose financial institutions that absorbed non-performing assets, so-called 'bad banks', and then recapitalizing the banks with public money so that they could get a fresh start. To make matters more challenging, the introduction of the Single Supervisory Mechanism (SSM) came with an end to exceptional permission for state aid geared at recapitalizing banks in the wake of the Great Financial Crisis (GFC) of 2008. Henceforth, states could act as providers of patient capital only, rather than cash injectors. This meant they had to provide loans and charge interest at a rate the Commission found in line with normal market conditions.

The less constrained method of restructuring could be seen working early and vigorously in Spain. Spanish banks had gotten into trouble by lending too much to households in a property bubble that could not sustain a rise in unemployment during an economic downturn. The Spanish government created a body in 2009 designed to restructure banks, separating the good from the bad assets, selling the good ones to other banks, transferring the bad ones to a 'bad bank', bailing in creditors and winding down or writing off those NPLs over a longer period of time. Public money was used in the process, but the burden was shared between the public and private sectors. It was not enough to fully restore the banking sector to health, but it served as a first step, and as a role model for others. A number of European governments did likewise.

While Spain, along with many other EU governments, followed this model of using 'bad banks' to restructure failing banks between 2008 and 2016, Italy did not. Problems were known, and the Bank of Italy pursued changes to corporate governance at a number of Italian banks (the way in which banks are internally structured and function in accordance with principles of good practice; see Donnelly 2000; Aguilera and Jackson 2003), but financial reorganization remained absent. Both the government and the Bank of Italy denied a need to do so until shortly before the BRRD deadline, by which time Italian banks had intensified their links to local communities, ensuring widespread economic harm if the BRRD were applied. This put Italy in a special position of having particularly strong financial vulnerabilities, and a built-in incentive to push against European rules once banks got into trouble.

This is not necessarily a consequence of disproportionately poor bank strategy or public policy in Italy prior to the crash of 2008, but rather the reverse, which led to a relatively lower sense of urgency. Italian banks had not invested in complex American financial derivatives as in Germany or lent far beyond the capacity of borrowers to pay as in Spain so that a sense of urgency to offload toxic assets was not present as it was elsewhere (De Bonis, Pozzolo and Stacchini 2011). But while Italy's banks had fewer immediate problems in 2008 compared to their counterparts in Spain and Germany, for example, the prolonged Italian economic stagnation after 2008 led to a rise in toxic assets of their own: non-performing loans to households and businesses. This in turn squeezed banks' earnings and capital, leading them to look for new forms of investment to bridge what they saw as a temporary, cyclical downturn. They turned to their own customers, getting them to become investors more than depositors. Instead of savings accounts, depositors were encouraged to buy bonds from their banks, which would pay a higher rate of interest, and keep the banks solid. The Italian banking system therefore started with better cards than in Spain and elsewhere but lost strength and advantage over time and ultimately turned to measures that were unsustainable. By the time the government acted to intervene, the rule structure had changed at the EU level.

The way in which Italy and Spain handled the resolution of these banks is the starting point for the present research question on the existence, the form and the impact of economic nationalism. The main reason for pursuing this line of inquiry resides, on the one hand, in the way MPS' and V&V's crises were handled and, on the other hand, in the comparison with the resolution of banks in Spain, particularly the cajas (regional saving institutions) and Banco Popular. Not only does the use of state aid in the Italian cases appear to be in contradiction with the bail-in rule, but it also diverges from the way a similar crisis was handled in Spain. As we shall show, Italy was allowed to repeatedly support its banks without requiring investors to bail them in first. Spain, in contrast, prided itself on not using taxpayers' money directly in resolutions after 2010 and applying bail-ins even before it became a requirement under EU law, as well as after, when Banco Popular Español was first bailed in and later incorporated by Banco Santander (Banco Santander 2017; Il Sole 24 Ore 2017d).

Already at this stage of overview, then, there are questions about why Spain and Italy had differing capacities to restore their banking systems to health. Can it be reduced to the different behavior of banks, represented as a different variety of

CONTENTS

financial capitalism? Can it be explained by public sector differences: a weak state in Italy versus a far stronger state in Spain? Are there differences in state strength between the central bank and government? Can differences be explained by the conditionality of what eventually became the European Stability Mechanism, which played a role in Spain but not in Italy? Can it be explained by outright economic nationalism that was stronger in Italy than in Spain? This book suggests that while outright mercantilist banking nationalism protecting national ownership by any means necessary is less virulent than it once was, national governments can and do act in nationalist ways. This sometimes respects EU law, fitting our understanding of liberal economic nationalism. But it also sometimes extends to breaking EU law in the process when applying that law would create widespread economic loss large enough to unseat the government. In the comparison of Italy and Spain, it further argues that state strength is associated with more forceful interventions in banks that mitigate the depth and scope of societal damage (Donnelly and Pometto forthcoming). The role of the central bank, in particular vis-a-vis banks, and the degree of deference that the government pays to the central bank matter significantly. This book also points to the possibility that the European Stability Mechanism (ESM) has a positive impact on state strength, through its memoranda of understanding concluded with borrower governments, where the borrowing government was positively inclined to accept the advice.

This book is not just an exercise in the comparative political economy of economic nationalism in Italy and Spain, however. It is also a book about how European institutions react when banks fail and national governments seek to protect them and those who stand to lose from their closure. A comparative analysis of how the Single Resolution Board and European Commission interact with Italian and Spanish authorities is undertaken. It demonstrates the vulnerability of the SRB and Commission's powers when confronted with opposition from the national authorities of a member state.

Research questions, design and plan of the book

This book investigates the use of state intervention (or the lack thereof), including state aid for banks that are failing or likely to fail in ways that effectively keep ownership in national hands. As part of this investigation, it also examines the reasons motivating decisions by the governments of Spain and Italy on whether to bail in bank creditors. While this is a legal requirement under the BRRD since 2016, the practice precedes the directive and is thought to make the bank more attractive in the future to outside investors, wherever they may be. We want to explore the connections between whether the governments and regulators follow through on bail-ins and why, and what practical effect it has on bank ownership. More specifically, this study asks the research question:

> *To what extent did the Italian and Spanish governments act in ways that kept bank ownership national?*

We aim to understand whether Italy's opposition to the BRRD, and its prominent state interventionism even within the new, stricter legislative framework, might have been motivated by some form of economic nationalism, and how that differs from the Spanish case. It additionally tries to differentiate under what conditions economic nationalism tends to undermine or resist the application of EU law, to the extent it can be found to be present. In order to answer the main research question, the following set of sub-questions will be addressed throughout the course of this book:

1. To what extent were the Italian and Spanish governments able to keep their banking systems solvent?
2. Did the Italian and Spanish governments actively or effectively prevent the participation of foreign investors in the recapitalization of the banks?
3. Did the Italian and Spanish governments use state aid in order to protect investors?
4. What features of the financial system in Italy and Spain made restructuring more difficult or less?
5. To what extent, if at all, does state intervention in the case studies represent a case of economic nationalism?
6. How did the Italian and Spanish governments negotiate with the European Commission, the European Central Bank, the Single Resolution Board and the European Stability Mechanism in order to enjoy higher tolerance towards state aid?

The six sub-questions address relevant aspects of the case studies. Sub-question one, when placed beside the other sub-questions, invites connections between the resilience or fragility of banking systems and the practices they use to fund themselves, both in regular times and during periods of crisis. These connections are covered in the other sub-questions and in the analysis throughout this book and speak to the literature on varieties of financial capitalism. Sub-question two is concerned with finding out whether the Italian and Spanish governments or the banks refused to accept foreign investors which could have restored the banks to solvency without state-funded bailouts. The refusal of foreign investors strongly points to the government's will to keep banking ownership national on principle, or outright economic nationalism.

Sub-question three addresses another critical issue common to the Italian case studies: the high incidence of retail investors and even depositors who purchased their banks' bonds and shares, without realizing or being informed that they would be bailed in during a bank resolution. Since the bail-in rule requires investors to contribute to the bank's rescue, it is reasonable to explore the option that investors' protection might have been the reason behind Italy's opposition to bail-ins. But since this protection would prevent failing banks from being properly resolved or attract new private investors, it can effectively keep bank ownership national, even if that is not the intended outcome. This might be thought of as functional economic nationalism. We wish to be clear here that investor/depositor protection is not thought to determine functional economic nationalism. The practice was also present in Spain, but the use of state aid was not the same.

Sub-questions four and five are intended to differentiate between three kinds of economic nationalism based on different degrees and methods of state intervention, and to analyze Italy's and Spain's interventionism to keep banks solvent in this context to specify what is going on and the mechanisms involved. We identify mercantilist economic nationalism (EN), in which national ownership is promoted and protected regardless of international rules and obligations; liberal economic nationalism (LEN), which encompasses all those government interventions which aim to keep ownership national, within the bounds of international result and obligations to support national firms and/or prevent or contain foreign ownership and control (Helleiner 2002; Clift and Woll 2012; Donnelly 2018); and functional economic nationalism (FEN), in which government and banks retain corporate governance features allowing political influence of bank decisions (Levine 2004; Hopt 2013) and deploy state aid in the pursuit of local political goals, particularly for the protection of large societal groups connected to banks. The use of these tools is an important clue that can reveal the government's intentions and motivations and thus deserves special attention.

Finally, sub-question six delves into the negotiations between Italian, Spanish and European institutions that shed further light on the way that different manifestations of economic nationalism interact with EU bodies responsible for overseeing or approving the actions of national governments. It covers the issue of how active the respective national governments and regulators (bank supervisors, resolution authorities and deposit insurance corporations) are in dealing with fragile banks, in what way and in what kind of relationship with European institutions and law. We can distinguish between EN's principle of national mercantilism, in which ownership of banks is viewed through the lens of competing national ownership in a zero-sum world; LEN's devotion to national promotion in the context of international competition and commitments; and FEN's entanglement of national institutions that makes compliance with commitments difficult to sustain. These questions, which deserve dedicated research due to their complexity and relevance, are designed to shed light on Italy and Spain's behavior and, in general, contribute to the overall understanding of the case studies.

Societal and scientific relevance

As Europe continues to grapple with economic hardship, and political conflicts between North and South persist, it is helpful and useful to look for clues about what is most promising for recovery, and to understand the roots of entrenched conflict between EU Member States and the EU institutions and Eurogroup over the application of EU law. There is much at stake for the EU as a whole if the dynamics between Italy and the EU continue to drift further towards disintegration (Jones 2018, 2021), and equally much to learn from the relative successes of Spain. Banks, particularly local, alternative banks (Deeg and Donnelly 2016; Howarth and Quaglia 2016; Cassell 2020; von Mettenheim and Butzbach 2015), are proving to be critical in both the economic and social welfare of Member States, and in their ability to work with or against EU institutions and other Member States.

The treatment of banks is not the entire story—there are larger battles about the structure of EMU, the presence or absence of a Eurozone budget, and of coronabonds and recovery funds that affect the banks through their macroeconomic impact on overall economic conditions, and will affect their recovery, that are in large part beyond the scope of this book. These factors set parameters in which the urgency of dealing with banks, state aid and resolution in a particular way is paramount. We do not dispute those contextual factors here but maintain that there are critical differences between Spain and Italy in this context that require investigation to understand what works well and what works less well in the current system and its likely development into the future.

The same search for lessons applies to the manner in which EU institutions approach Member States in the completion of their tasks. As Donnelly and Asimakopolous (2020) argue, if the SRB and the Commission give way to economic nationalism, however motivated, they undermine the capacity of the EU to ensure financial sustainability and recovery. Merler (2017b) underlines as well that the allegedly inconsistent application of the BRRD across similar cases (Banco Popular on the one hand, and MPS and V&V on the other) casts doubts on the predictability of European legislations and Member States' equality before the law. Predictability, as opposed to arbitrariness, and equality before the law are among the main characteristics of the rule of law (Bingham 2010). It is therefore in the interests of anyone concerned with deepening the rule of law within the European Union to develop a better understanding of the events and to set the basis for further research, which will hopefully compare MPS and V&V's events with those of Banco Popular and others to come.

Scientifically, the present research undertakes a focused comparison of political economy and public administration in two large EU Member States, facing similar problems economically, legally and administratively, but with different political and administrative responses with lasting impacts. At the theoretical level, the research also attempts to investigate links between liberal intergovernmentalism, as a theory that roots national preferences in the interest of domestic interest groups and societal forces, with sociological institutionalism, that enquires into the normative features of national public policy rooted in institutionalized logics of appropriateness. This choice represents an attempt to move beyond rational choice assumptions, in an effort to test whether constructivist insights can enrich our understanding of EU-member state relations, by shedding light on national attitudes and tendencies towards EU commitments. Rather than focus on intersubjective norm development (Wiener 2006; Saurugger and Mérand 2010; Risse-Kappen 1996; Rosamond 1999, 2016), we focus here on the relative influence of national and local governments, banks and stakeholders in determining the degree of acceptance for liberal market arrangements or more protectionist attitudes towards the EU and its regulatory requirements in banking. If such links can be substantiated, this approach will contribute to the ongoing debate around the nature of the European Union, the relationship between European institutions and Member States and the role played by each of them.

In this context, this study aims to address the sources of various types of economic nationalism in two large EU Member States experiencing problems with bank solvency. Economic nationalism, which some had deemed anachronistic with the expansion of globalization and neoliberalism, made a noticeable comeback during and after the global financial crisis of 2008 and the Eurozone crisis that followed, after the 2016 elections in the United States, and again in the wake of the coronavirus pandemic. In these instances, observers were forced to notice that not only had economic nationalism not disappeared but it had been able to adapt to generally accepted rules and practices of a global, institutionalized economy, and to similar European constraints in the form of liberal economic nationalism (LEN) (Pickel 2003; Helleiner 2002; Deeg 2012; Donnelly 2018), and develop protectionist features under conditions of hardship. This book contributes to the EN literature by analyzing the Italian and Spanish case studies in depth with the aim of refining our understanding of the conditions that lead to it in its various forms.

The answers to our questions about the motivation of the Spanish and Italian authorities provide us with a better insight into the challenges facing the weakest financial and political link of the Eurozone, as Italy is closer to financial distress (being unable to borrow on financial markets) and subject to volatile outbursts of anti-European and anti-Eurozone temperament. They also give us a sense of when EU institutions work (or can work), and when they can't. Finally, the answers to these questions speak ultimately to how we should view the way that the EU works, particularly when confronted with controversy emanating from particular issues and countries.

The rest of the book is structured as follows. Chapter 2 outlines Banking Union, providing the context in which Italian and Spanish banks and authorities are required to work (or push back against). Chapter 3 examines the phenomenon of economic nationalism in its various forms, outlining a distinction between different types of economic nationalism and the room left open in Banking Union's institutions to exercise it. These types are economic nationalism, in which national ownership of banks is pursued on principle; liberal economic nationalism, in which national ownership of banks is pursued within the external constraints (in this case of the EU and the ESM); and functional economic nationalism, in which national ownership of banks is the default option for governments that find bank relationships and institutions. Chapter 4 binds together and makes new connections between European integration theory and theories of domestic preference formation that are rooted in sociological institutionalism, particularly the social institutions of financial systems. Chapters 5 and 6 apply the framework and present research on how Spain and Italy, respectively, have dealt with the problem of troubled banks. Chapter 7 concludes.

References

Aguilera, R.V., & Jackson, G. (2003). The cross-national diversity of corporate governance: Dimensions and determinants. *Academy of management Review, 28*(3), 447–465.

Asimakopoulos, I.G. (2018). International law as a negotiation tool in Banking Union; the case of the Single Resolution Fund. *Journal of Economic Policy Reform, 21*(2), 118–131.

Asimakopoulos, I.G., & Howarth, D. (2022). Stillborn banking union: Explaining ineffective European Union bank resolution rules. *JCMS: Journal of Common Market Studies, 60*(2), 264–282.

Banco Santander (2017). Banco Santander informs of the acquisition of 100% of the share capital of Banco Popular Español, S.A. Retrieved from Banco Santantaliante: santander.com/csgs/Satellite/CFWCSancomQP01/en_GB/Corporate/Shareholders-and-Investors/Corporate-Governance/Banco-Popular-Acquisition.html

Bingham, T. (2010). *The Rule of Law.* London, England: Penguin Press.

Bodellini, M. (2017). Greek and Italian 'lessons' on bank restructuring: Is precautionary recapitalisation the way forward? *Cambridge Yearbook of European Legal Studies, 19*(2017), 144–164. doi:10.1017/cel.2017.6

Cassell, M. (2020). *Banking on the State: The Political Economy of Public Savings Banks.* Columbia University Press/Agenda Publishing.

Clift, B., & Woll, C. (2012). Economic patriotism: Reinventing control over open markets. *Journal of European Public Policy, 19*(3), 307–323. doi:10.1080/13501763.2011.638117

Deeg, R. (2012). Liberal economic nationalism and Europeanization: The rise of Spanish and Italian banks. Paper presented at the Annual Meeting of the American Political Science Association, New Orleans, Aug. 30–Sept. 2, 2012.

Deeg, R., & Donnelly, S. (2016). Banking union and the future of alternative banks: Revival, stagnation or decline?. *West European Politics, 39*(3), 585–604.

De Bonis, R., Pozzolo, A.F., & Stacchini, M. (2011). The Italian banking system: Facts and interpretations. Economics and Statistics Discussion Paper 68, Universita degli Studi del Molise. Available at SSRN 2126074.

De Rynck, S.(2016). Banking on a union: The politics of changing Eurozone banking supervision. *Journal of European Public Policy, 23*(1), 119–135.

Di Quirico, R. (2010). Italy and the global economic crisis. *Bulletin of Italian Politics, 2*(2), 3–19.

Donnelly, S. (2000). Public interest politics, corporate governance and company regulation in Germany and Britain. *German Politics, 9*(2), 171–194.

Donnelly, S. (2018). Liberal Economic nationalism, financial stability, and commission leniency in banking union. *Journal of Economic Policy Reform, 20*(4), 159–173. doi:10.1080/17487870.2017.1400437

Donnelly, S., & Asimakopoulos, I.G. (2020). Bending and breaking the single resolution mechanism: The case of Italy. *JCMS: Journal of Common Market Studies, 58*(4), 856–871.

Epstein, R.A. (2014). Assets or liabilities? The politics of bank ownership. *Review of International Political Economy, 21*(4), 765–789.

Goyer, M., & Valdivielso Del Real, R. (2014). Protection of domestic bank ownership in France and Germany: The functional equivalency of institutional diversity in takeovers. *Review of International Political Economy, 21*(4), 790–819.

Gros, D., & Schoenmaker, D. (2014). European Deposit Insurance and Resolution in the Banking Union. *Journal of Common Market Studies, 52* (3), 529–546.

Guarascio, F., & Sinner, M. (2016). EU court says bail-in legal but bank rescues need not hit investors. Reuters. 19 July. Retrieved from: reuters.com/article/us-eurozone-banks-court/eu-court-says-bail-in-legal-but-bank-rescues-need-not-hit-investors-idUSKCN0ZZ0N8

Helleiner, E. (2002). Economic nationalism as a challenge to economic liberalism? Lessons from the 19th century. *International Studies Quarterly, 46*(3), 307–329. doi:10.1111/1468-2478.00235

Hopt, K.J. (2013). Corporate governance of banks and other financial institutions after the financial crisis. *Journal of Corporate Law Studies, 13*(2), 219–253.

Howarth, D., & Quaglia, L. (2014). The steep road to European banking union: Constructing the single resolution mechanism. *Journal of Common Market Studies, 52*, 125–140.

Howarth, D., & Quaglia, L. (2016). Internationalised banking, alternative banks and the single supervisory mechanism. *West European Politics, 39*(3), 438–461.

Howarth, D., & Quaglia, L. (2016a). *The political economy of European banking union*. Oxford University Press

Howarth, D., & Quaglia, L. (2018). The difficult construction of a European deposit insurance scheme: A step too far in Banking Union?. *Journal of Economic Policy Reform, 21*(3), 190–209.

Howarth, D., & Quaglia, L. (2021). Failing forward in Economic and Monetary Union: Explaining weak Eurozone financial support mechanisms. *Journal of European Public Policy, 28*(10), 1555–1572.

Il Sole 24 Ore (2017). Chi paga il conto del salvataggio del Banco Popular. *Il Sole 24 Ore*. 7 June. Retrieved from: ilsole24ore.com/art/finanza-e-mercati/2017-06-07/chi-paga-conto-salvataggio-banco-popular-172133.shtml?uuid=AENBqRaB

Jones, E. (2015). Getting the story right: How you should choose between different interpretations of the European crisis (and why you should care). *Journal of European Integration, 37*(7), 817–832.

Jones, E. (2018). Towards a theory of disintegration. *Journal of European Public Policy, 25*(3), 440–451.

Jones, E. (2021). Italy and Europe: From competence to Solidarity to competence. *Contemporary Italian Politics, 13*(2), 196–209.

Kern, A. (2015). European banking union: A legal and institutional analysis of the single supervisory mechanism and the single resolution mechanism. *European Law Review, 2*, 154–187.

Khan, M. (2016, June 19). EU court backs Slovenian bank 'bail-in'. *The Financial Times*. Retrieved from: ft.com/content/3d440752-571e-3bed-978d-ad125245052f

Levine, R. (2004). *The Corporate Governance of Banks: A Concise Discussion of Concepts and Evidence* (Vol. 3404). Washington D.C.: World Bank Publications.

Merler (2017b). Bank liquidation in the European Union: Clarification needed. Retrieved from Bruegel website: bruegel.org/2018/01/bank-liquidation-in-the-european-union-clarification-needed/

Mettenheim, K.V., & Butzbach, O. (eds.). (2015). *Alternative Banking and Financial Crisis*. London: Routledge.

Official Journal of the European Union (2014). Directive 2014/59/EU of the European parliament and of the council. Retrieved from: eur-lex.europa.eu/legal-content/EN/TXT/HTML/?uri=CELEX:32014L0059&from=IT

Pickel, A. (2003). Explaining, and explaining with, economic nationalism. *Nations and Nationalism*, *9*(1), 105–127. doi:10.1111/1469-8219.00077

Risse-Kappen, T. (1996). Exploring the nature of the beast: International relations theory and comparative policy analysis meet the European Union. *Journal of Common Market Studies*, *34*(1), 53–80. doi:10.1111/j.1468-5965.1996.tb00560.x

Rosamond, B. (1999). Discourses of globalization and the social construction of European identities. *Journal of European Public Policy*, *6*(4), 652–668.

Rosamond, B. (2016). Theorizing the European Union after integration theory. In M. Cini, & N. Pérez-Solórzano Borragán, eds. *European Union Politics*. Oxford: Oxford University Press, pp. 86–103.

Saurugger, S, & Mérand, F. (2010). Does European integration theory need sociology? *Comparative European Politics 8*, 1–18. doi:10.1057/cep.2010.1

Schnabel, I., & Véron, N. (2018). Breaking the stalemate on European deposit insurance. Bruegel blog post. https://www.bruegel.org/blog-post/breaking-stalemate-european-deposit-insurance

Schnabel, I., & Véron, N. (2019). Breaking the stalemate on European deposit insurance. in Pisany-Ferry, J. and Zettelmeyer, J., eds. *Risk Sharing Plus Market Discipline: A New Paradigm for Euro Area Reform?* London: CEPR Press, pp. 18–24.

Schoenmaker, D. (2018). Building a stable European deposit insurance scheme. *Journal of Financial Regulation*, *4*(2), 314–320.

Steffen, S. (2014). Robustness, validity and significance of the ECB's asset quality review and stress test exercise. SAFE White Paper 23. https://www.econstor.eu/bitstream/10419/103435/1/800968875.pdf

Wiener, A. (2006). Constructivism and sociological institutionalism. In Cini, M. and Bourne, A.K., eds. *Palgrave Advances in European Union Studies*. London: Palgrave Macmillan, pp.35–55.

Wymeersch, E. (2014). The single supervisory mechanism or 'SSM', part one of the banking union. National Bank of Belgium Working Paper, (255). https://www.econstor.eu/bitstream/10419/144467/1/wp255en.pdf

2

BANKING UNION

Until 2012, banking within the Eurozone was regulated through decentralized supervision and regulatory competition (De Rynck 2016). In the aftermath of the financial crisis of 2008, however, the will to boost Eurozone's financial stability and to break the vicious circle between sovereigns and banking failures (European Commission 2012) brought the Member States to agree in 2012 on the establishment of a European Banking Union, encompassing a Single Supervisory Mechanism, a Single Resolution Mechanism (agreed in 2014) and a financial backstop based on loans and conditionality: the European Stability Mechanism (Howarth and Quaglia 2016; Donnelly 2016; Official Journal of the European Union 2013). The financial backstop of first choice, a European Deposit Insurance Scheme, was proposed but not agreed.

Financial stability

In order to better understand the design of the European Banking Union, it is necessary to introduce the concept of financial stability, and some of the main tools that can be implemented in order to support it. Financial stability can be defined as a bank's on-going capacity to meet the demands of its depositors and creditors, including other banks. Banks' ability to lend each other money on a daily basis is a crucial aspect of financial stability (Donnelly 2014). Financial stability can be enhanced by taking a set of measures, including supervision, resolution, deposit insurance, and the establishment of a lender of last resort facility.

The first tool is *supervision*. Through supervision, the competent authority monitors a bank to ensure that its capital requirement, internal workings, and detection and elimination of toxic or non-performing assets meet sufficient liquidity and solvency criteria, with the purpose of supporting financial stability (Donnelly 2014). In order for supervision to be effective, supervisory authorities

DOI: 10.4324/9781003334583-2

need to have the power to enforce requirement compliance (Donnelly 2016; Véron 2012; Gren, Howarth and Quaglia 2015; Véron 2012; Wymeersch 2014; Lombardi and Moschella 2016). There is more than one manner to do this, either by combining supervision with central bank functions or not (Lombardi and Moschella 2016) or by combining supervision for different kinds of banks or not (Howarth and Quaglia 2016b), which can complicate negotiations on the exact form. However it is set, assertive supervision is considered essential.

Resolution, on the other hand, allows authorities to intervene in order to ensure the orderly closure of a bank (Howarth and Quaglia 2016). When initial interventions fail to restore an insolvent bank to health, a bank may be, and in Europe often was, usually wound down through normal insolvency procedures. However, certain banks are so large or so important that their closure under ordinary procedures would negatively affect financial stability. In this case, resolution intervenes to preserve the critical functions of the bank and limit negative impacts on the economy (European Court of Auditors 2017; Howarth and Quaglia 2014; Culpepper and Tesche 2019).

Lastly, a *deposit insurance* scheme sets out to reimburse a bank's depositors up to a given amount in case of failure. Deposit insurance schemes aim to prevent 'bank runs', that is to prevent depositors from withdrawing their savings fearing a collapse. By preventing bank runs, deposit insurance schemes enhance financial stability (Financial Stability Board 2012). Key features of effective deposit insurance include broad protection of depositors to drive down the likelihood of a bank run, with best practices including between 90% and 95% of depositors; proper information provided to depositors, which ensures their awareness of the fact that they will be reimbursed, once again with the purpose of avoiding bank runs; and timely intervention, that is the ability to reimburse depositor within a week (Donnelly 2016). Deposit insurance schemes can be funded ex ante, that is by collecting fees from banks through the years in order to prepare for a potential crisis, or ex post, that is when the crisis occurs. Ex ante-funded deposit insurance is desirable because it reduces the chances that taxpayers will be called upon to support a bank, and because it discourages moral hazard, and promotes depositors' monitoring of the bank's activity (Donnelly 2016). In either case, however, deposit insurance schemes need to be able to access a solid financial backstop in order to be credible (Van Rompuy 2012). No matter how well prepared, deposit insurance is not sufficient in case of a systemic crisis. Banks need therefore to be able to access an open-ended public financial backstop that is able to support failing banks and prevent the crisis from further affecting financial stability (Brandt and Wohlfahrt 2019; Donnelly 2016, 2018b).

The three pillars of Banking Union

As Schoenmaker (2013) has pointed out, the international banking system produces a 'financial trilemma' among three elements: financial stability, cross-border banking and national financial policies. These three elements are unable to coexist. One has to give in. The burden of ensuring financial stability, whether through supervision, regulation or financial support, can fall on national authorities, but only if banking (and potentially bank ownership) across borders is restricted. Similarly, opening up national banking systems to investment from outside would establish cross-border banking that requires European rather than national provisions. Howarth and Quaglia (2016b) note additionally that Eurozone membership exacerbates this dilemma even further by restricting government intervention and national financial policies while banks are still effectively national in nature.

Banking Union sets out to improve financial stability by harmonizing and Europeanizing bank regulations, resources and institutions within the euro-area. The original layout of the Banking Union as envisaged by the European Commission included five components: a single framework for banking supervision; a single resolution authority; a common deposit insurance scheme; a common backstop for temporary financial support; and a Single Rulebook for on bank capital and liquidity (European Council 2012b, c). Of these, the first three components: supervision, resolution, and deposit insurance, were considered the three indispensable pillars of the Banking Union (European Commission 2017a).

However, the supply of these mechanisms was highly uneven and incomplete. The Single Supervisory Mechanism (SSM) is the only one which has proved to have strong supranational powers, although still partially relying on national supervisors. A key component of the SSM is the Single Rulebook (Verdun 2016). The Single Rulebook consists of a set of rules that aims to harmonize supervision and resolution practices of EU banks. It applies not only to euro-area countries but to all EU Member States (European Banking Authority n.d.; World Bank Group 2017; Howarth and Quaglia 2016).

The Single Resolution Mechanism (SRM), on the other hand, still relies heavily on national discretion for both the drafting and execution of resolution plans and lacks sufficient resources to work autonomously (Véron and Wolff 2013; Kudrna 2012; Donnelly 2018; Donnelly and Asimakopoulos 2020; Culpepper and Tesche 2019). Finally, the European Deposit Insurance Scheme (EDIS) has yet to be agreed upon, leaving deposit insurance an exclusive competence of the Member States, harmonized by the Deposit Guarantee Scheme Directive (2014/49/EU) (Howarth and Quaglia 2018).

Instead of EDIS, a common backstop for temporary financial support was established through an international agreement under the name of the European Stability Mechanism (ESM). Due to its international rather than supranational nature, the ESM is not considered part of the Banking Union (Germain and Schwartz 2014), though it is formally linked to it since 2018 as an institution that can provide a line of credit to the SRM under specific circumstances.

The remainder of this chapter focuses on the structure of Banking Union. In order to do so, the next three sections introduce each of the three pillars of Banking Union individually, emphasizing their purpose; the role of negotiations in shaping the outline of each pillar; and the institutions involved and their workings. Each section concludes by drawing a set of expectations for the case studies.

The Single Supervisory Mechanism

The Single Supervisory Mechanism (SSM) was established in October 2013 and entered into force on 4 November 2014 (Official Journal of the European Union 2013). The SSM transferred banking supervision for systemically important banks from the national to the supranational level, with the purpose of ensuring consistent prudential supervision throughout the euro-area (De Rynck 2016; European Central Bank n.d.). The activity of the European Banking Authority, which had relied since 2011 primarily on the exchange of information, regulatory advice and mutually conducted stress tests had not proven up to the task of ensuring rigorous supervision in times of crisis (de Larosière Group 2009). The European Banking Authority (EBA) furthermore attracted the criticism that supervisors continued to act on a 'narrow national perspective', which rendered the system unable to 'respond to the challenges of a globally integrated market, for which the EBA had been established in the first place (Allen et al. 2011; Financial Services Authority 2009; Padoa-Schioppa 2007). In response, supranational supervision was introduced in order to curb national supervisors' forbearance and to prevent moral hazard, a desire voiced especially by Germany (Howarth and Quaglia 2016: 89).

German national preferences significantly shaped the delivery of the SSM. Germany's concern with moral hazard, which was backed up by other Northern European countries such as the Netherlands and Finland, was not limited to supervision, but also to the introduction of the European Stability Mechanism, which was announced on the same day as the SSM (Howarth and Quaglia 2016). As Minister of Finance Schäuble made clear, Germany's approval of the establishment of the European Stability Mechanism and its use as a financial backstop for Banking Union was conditional on the creation of centralized supervision (Schoenmaker and Véron 2016). It should therefore not come as a surprise that the SSM was the first pillar of the Banking Union to be established. Germany's position was held so strongly that, in the words of European Central Bank (ECB) President Draghi, the SSM was 'an essential precondition for the other pillars of Banking Union' (European Central Bank 2016c).

The difference in treatment towards systemically important banks and smaller banks was also influenced by German demands. More specifically, it was influenced by the difference between Member States' banking systems, and the governments' will to shape the new supervisory system to their advantage. Within the German banking system, *Landesbanken* (regional banks) and *Sparkassen* (savings banks) are numerous and cover a significant portion of the market (European Banking Federation n.d.). Finance Minister Schäuble, reluctant to allow the ECB to directly supervise local banks, therefore opposed full supranational supervision (Epstein and Rhodes 2016). On the other hand, direct supervision over all

European banks was favored by countries such as France, the Netherlands, Italy, Spain and Luxembourg (Howarth and Quaglia 2016a; Lombardi and Moschella 2016). Among these, France, whose banking system was dominated by large banks, viewed the difference in supervision between large and small banks as unequal treatment (Howarth and Quaglia 2016b).

The negotiations resulted in a compromise between the two coalitions. Germany reached its goal of maintaining national supervision over less important banks, but the ECB obtained the power to take over supervision of any of the 6,000 euro-area banks if it considers it necessary (Epstein and Rhodes 2016). Curiously enough, Germany's goal to defeat supervisory forbearance was hindered by its own demand to keep small banks under national supervision, which proved to be, as will be discussed in the following section, the main obstacle standing in the way of a thorough and consistent supervision over all euro-area banks.

The SSM therefore provides for *direct ECB supervision of the Eurozone's largest banks*. Within the SSM, euro-area banks are divided into European systemically important banks (E-SIBs), and smaller, less important banks (European Central Bank n.d.; European Central Bank 2016b). The first group falls under the direct supervision of the ECB. The ECB exercises its supervisory capacity through the Supervisory Board. The Supervisory Board is composed of a Chair, a Vice-Chair, four members of the ECB and one representative per euro-area country supervisory authority (European Central Bank n.d.). The number of E-SIBs has varied across the years, with 128 banks being directly supervised by the ECB in 2014 (European Central Bank 2014), and 114 in May 2021 (European Central Bank 2018). Each E-SIB is supervised by a Joint Supervisory Team (JTS). With a staff composed of both national and ECB supervisors, JTSs have the goal of facilitating the sharing of information and enhancing the consistency of decision-making (Schoenmaker and Véron 2016; Transparency International EU 2017).

The ECB has proven to possess the power and the will to perform strong direct supervision upon the E-SIBs (Donnelly 2018). Compared to national supervisors, the ECB has been more intrusive, performing more frequent on-site visits and asking more questions during investigations (Schoenmaker and Véron 2016). However, National Competent Authorities (NCAs) still play an important role in the supervision of systemically important banks: NCAs are the first line of communication with the banks and are in charge of providing EU institutions with data and developing resolution plans (Donnelly 2018). Given NCAs' inclination towards national forbearance, their involvement in systemically important banks' supervision calls the quality and cross-case consistency of implementation into question.

Smaller banks are supervised by National Competent Authorities (NCAs). Due to a matter of resources and competence, most euro-area countries choose to establish their NCA within the national central bank (European Central Bank n.d.). In this context, the ECB is in charge of monitoring the supervisory work of NCAs over smaller banks and effectively acts as a supervisor of national supervisors (Lackhoff 2013; Howarth and Quaglia 2016b). Furthermore, the ECB ultimately retains the power to supersede NCAs and take over banks' supervision (Epstein and Rhodes 2016). If the NCAs' role in the supervision of systemically important banks leaves room for discretion, its role in the direct supervision of less important banks is even more subject to loose implementation of European regulations and potential supervisory inconsistency across countries. The ECB and the NCAs are required to cooperate in good faith and exchange information, but the boundaries and obligations between the two are blurry, giving way to a complex dynamic, involving a considerable amount of discretion and unpredictability (Gren 2017). As Schoenmaker and Véron (2016) note, national authorities are more subject to political pressure to pursue, for instance, perceived national interests over rigor. As a result, the considerable autonomy granted to NCAs may result in supervisory forbearance.

From this structure, we should expect banking supervision to create more room for forbearance at the national level, at least with regard to less-systemic banks. The ECB can be expected to rigorously supervise E-SIBs, to engage in repeated on-site visits and detailed investigations and to make politically independent decisions. However, the NCAs' involvement in tasks such as the provision of data to the ECB allows them room for discretion. As a result, a certain amount of variance can be expected in the implementation of supervision across countries. Supervision of less important banks, on the other hand, is not enhanced by ECB presence. NCAs' history of supervisory forbearance therefore casts serious doubts over the quality and impartiality of their supervisory performance.

Single Resolution Mechanism

The second tool for boosting euro-area financial stability to be included in the Banking Union is resolution. A resolution regime represents a political solution to distributive questions concerning the costs of a bank failure. Therefore, if during the financial crisis the bill was largely given to taxpayers, the Single Resolution Mechanism (SRM) was established with the purpose of making shareholders and bondholders responsible for the costs. By transferring the costs of a bank failure from state funds to a bank's stakeholders, the SRM set out to break the negative feedback loop between banks' and sovereign failures, therefore ultimately boosting financial stability (Howarth and Quaglia 2016).

The SRM was established in 2014 and became fully operational in January 2015, except for the bail-in rule, which was enforced in January 2016. The SRM functions through the Single Resolution Board (SRB) and the National Resolution Authorities (NRAs). The SRM is regulated by the Banking Recovery and Resolution Directive (BRRD) and by Regulation (EU) No. 806/2014, also referred to as the Single Resolution Mechanism Regulation (SRMR), as well as by Commission-delegated regulations and the European Banking Authority (EBA) standards and guidelines (European Court of Auditors 2017).

However, beyond the sheer success of establishing a common resolution authority of any sort, the SRM lost several of its initial features through the heated negotiations that preceded its creation, resulting in a mechanism that fell short of what many had hoped for (Donnelly 2016; Donnelly and Asimakopoulos 2020). In order to better understand the SRM and its limitations, the following sections will explore the role of national preferences, and especially of German demands, on the final design of the SRM. In addition to that, a brief legal explanation is introduced that partially explains the lack of substantial empowerment of the SRB.

National preferences on resolution were strong and divergent, making it difficult to reach an agreement on strong institutional powers. Although plans for centralizing resolution were in the making since the autumn of 2008, the first proposal for the BRRD was put forward by the Commission only in 2012. On the one hand, this delay can be attributed to the fact that the Commission wanted to make sure the plan would be in line with newly set international standards. On the other hand, however, the resolution was a delicate subject for Member States and was thus subject to extensive consultations, which took place on several occasions between 2009 and 2011 (Howarth and Quaglia 2016). Welcoming the Commission's proposal, France, Italy and Spain insisted on the need to create a complete Banking Union in order to break the negative feedback loop between sovereign and banking crises and therefore supported the establishment of an SRM (Szago 2013; Rajoy 2013). In the same way, the Dutch government was in favor of the creation of the SRM, and together with the three main Dutch banks it advocated in favor of the complete independence of the mechanism (Netherlands Government 2013). On the other hand, Germany's position was dictated by concerns of moral hazard by banks and governments elsewhere, particularly in Southern Europe. The moral hazard concerns brought Germany to support the BRRD and the bail-in rule, which they urged should enter into force, as was eventually decided, in 2016 rather than in 2018. Meanwhile, Germany's will to protect its own cooperative and savings banks (see above) was mirrored in the final compromise by allowing the NRAs, rather than the SRB, to be responsible for less important banks (Howarth and Quaglia 2016).

Beyond the role of Germany's demands, however, the delegation of resolution powers to a new body was limited by the Treaty on the Functioning of the European Union (TFEU). Under the TFEU, agencies cannot be endowed with tasks that involve a 'margin or discretion' and only EU institutions, such as the Commission or the Council, can decide on matters of resolution. These limitations explain why, under the SRM, the Commission and the Council ultimately retain the power, for instance, of vetoing SRB decisions (Lintner 2017).

The BRRD constitutes the EU legal framework for dealing with banking crises (Bodellini 2017) and therefore sets out the scope and consequences of resolution. As for all the other elements of the Single Rulebook, the BRRD applies not only to euro-area countries but to all EU Member States (European Banking Authority n.d.; World Bank Group 2017). Consistent with the overall objectives of resolution, the BRRD has the goal to promote the orderly resolution of failing banks while avoiding significant adverse effects on the financial system and to allow for banks to continue performing their critical functions. Another priority of the BRRD is that of breaking the negative feedback loop between private debt and sovereigns, especially by avoiding the use of taxpayer money in tackling failing banks. At last, the BRRD also sets out to protect insured depositors, client funds and client assets (Art 31 BRRD). In order to reach these goals, the BRRD sets the rules for the prevention, early intervention and resolution of failing banks within the EU (European Council n.d.).

Overall, the BRRD sets a framework for crisis prevention and preparation, in order to avoid last-minute, uncoordinated and ad hoc measures, as was the case during the financial crisis (Lintner 2017). Therefore, the BRRD's scope is not limited to the very last phases of a crisis but includes measures that call for early intervention through the implementation of recovery plans for troubled banks or of other measures aiming to stabilize the bank (European Council n.d.). Furthermore, under the BRRD, the default option for banks that are failing or likely to fail is to go through normal insolvency proceedings. This can be changed only if the competent resolution authority decides that normal insolvency proceedings are likely, in the specific case of a specific bank, to negatively affect financial stability. In this case the bank is put through resolution procedures (European Commission 2017b).

Single Resolution Board

The SRM deals directly with E-SIBs and relies heavily on the input of national resolution authorities. The Single Resolution Board (SRB) is the resolution authority for significant banks and cross-border banking groups supervised by the ECB, whereas the NRAs are responsible for the remaining, less important banks (Single Resolution Board n.d.). Unlike the ECB, the SRB has proven unable to be a strong, centralized authority, lacking both the autonomy and the means to do so. By design, the most important decisions concerning resolution are left to the ECB and the Commission, whereas the Council and the Commission retain veto power on certain crucial aspects of resolution. Therefore, rather than being a strong, independent authority able to centralize euro-area resolution, the SRB is a system of coordination of national resolution authorities, which relies on the Commission and the Council for the most critical decisions concerning financial stability (Mayes 2018; Donnelly 2018).

The Board's tasks are shared with the ECB and Commission. First of all, the decision to deem a bank failing or likely to fail (FOLTF) is left to the ECB. As a matter of fact, as stated in article 18 of the SRMR, the SRB can declare a bank FOLTF only in specific situations, and only if the ECB does not react within three days (Lintner 2017). Once a bank is declared FOLTF, the SRB is in charge of assessing whether winding the bank down under normal insolvency proceedings would have negative effects on financial stability (European

Commission 2017b; World Bank group 2017). If it decides that a resolution is necessary in order to protect the public interest, the SRB produces a resolution proposal, which includes the actions the bank should take in the context of resolution (European Commission n.d.). Nevertheless, the Commission has the power to object to or amend the proposal within 24 hours and ask for the Council's involvement. In case of objection, the SRB has eight hours to modify the resolution proposal. However, the final decision rests upon the Council: if the Council decides to veto the resolution procedure, the bank will be wound down under normal insolvency proceedings (Lintner 2017).

Apart from tasks directly related to resolution decisions, the SRB is also in charge of drafting the recovery plans for the banks within its remit, in consultation with the NRAs, which are later to be assessed by the ECB (European Commission 2017b); developing a framework for assessing whether a bank is failing or likely to fail (Véron 2018); administering the Single Resolution Fund, although, since these decisions directly concern financial stability, the Council has the right to veto on them (Lintner 2017); and ultimately ensuring consistency and harmonization within the SRM (European Court of Auditors 2017).

On top of the severely limited autonomy granted to the SRB, the European Court of Auditors' (2017) report underlined a set of shortcomings in the fulfillment of the SRB tasks. These shortcomings can be attributed to the fact that the SRB was set up from scratch in a short period of time and entrusted with considerable responsibility while still in a 'start-up phase'. In addition to that, the board was largely understaffed and overall lacked the necessary resources needed to perform its tasks (European Court of Auditors 2017). This led to situations in which the SRB had not yet completed the resolution plans for the banks within its remit, and plans submitted in 2016 did not fully meet the Single Rulebook requirements (European Court of Auditors 2017). The creation of proper resolution plans is important for systemic financial stability because it has the potential to avoid lengthy resolutions through a court-order liquidation and allows for banks to be resolved through an orderly administrative process instead (Véron 2018).

The SRB was not entrusted with the responsibility of developing a framework for assessing whether a bank is failing or likely to fail (European Court of Auditors 2017). This role was given to the European Central Bank in its capacity as bank supervisor. In regard to this specific issue, concerns have been raised as to whether or not the SRB actually played its role in the precautionary recapitalization of Monte dei Paschi di Siena (Véron 2018). Assessing whether or not a bank is failing or likely to fail is of critical importance because it can determine whether or not it will be wound down. The lack of clear criteria upon which to base such a decision threatens to result in arbitrary and inconsistent decisions across similar cases (Merler 2017). The European Court of Auditors' (2017) final worry concerned the lack of an efficient and timely flow of information from the ECB to the SRB, as well as the lack of a clear division of tasks between the SRB and NRAs once the ECB declared that a bank was failing or likely to fail. This in turn has created space for national authorities to exercise great discretion in the handling of resolutions. In Italy, this has led to questions about the legality of the financial assistance provided to banks, and the application of resolution rules, particularly those involving private bail-ins of creditors and major depositors.

While resources have improved in the time since then, *national resolution authorities remain the principal actors within the SRM*, based on the division of tasks between them and the Board. Under the SRM, each Member State is required to establish a National Resolution Authority (NRA). Each NRA is in charge of drafting resolution plans for the banks within its remit and of assisting the SRB in drafting resolution plans for the remaining banks (Magnum and Mesnard 2016). They are also empowered to intervene in the affairs of potentially troubled banks by requiring measures that ameliorate restructurings, such as appointing special figures and temporary managers. These are above and beyond other changes that the ECB as the single supervisor or national supervisors as part of the SSM can demand, such as increasing capital, increasing capital that can be easily bailed in during a resolution and forcing changes to the bank's board of directors (European Council n.d.).

In addition, the NRAs are in charge of executing the resolution plans for E-SIBs and cross-border banking groups when required by the SRB and of providing the SRB with information regarding the banks (Magnum and Mesnard 2016). As far as resolution decisions are concerned, each NRA can decide autonomously whether or not to resolve a given bank, as provided under the BRRD (Lintner 2017). The resolution of banks under the NRA's remit occurs under normal insolvency proceedings (Single Resolution Board n.d.). Where this happens, however, the SRB is given the task of confirming that the bank in question is indeed a less-systemic institution that can be resolved in this way. As a result, the SRM is constructed in such a way that preserves considerable national discretion in developing and implementing responses to troubled banks.

Single Resolution Fund

A third element of the SRM is the Single Resolution Fund (SRF). The Single Resolution Fund was established through the SRM Regulation, and it has the purpose of providing temporary support in case of bank resolution, stakeholder compensation and recapitalization (European Council n.d.). The SRF is funded through annual contributions of the 19 euro-area Member States, with the goal of reaching an amount equal to 1% of all covered deposits within the Banking Union by 2023. The SRF cannot be used to recapitalize banks or cover their losses. However, in exceptional circumstances, the fund can be used to contribute to a credit institution under resolution, provided that the contribution does not exceed 5% of the bank's total liabilities and that a bail-in of at least 8% of the bank's risk-weighted assets has taken place (Single Resolution Board n.d.).

The SRF is controlled by an intergovernmental agreement, though it is designed to be used within the SRM. This feature ensures that money from the fund can only be used under exceptional circumstances. The SRB makes a recommendation of how much money would be required from the fund to prevent a closure of the bank from creating a domino effect of insolvencies throughout the financial system. That recommendation goes to the Commission, which presents it to the Council, which then approves (or not) the release of funds on the basis of a vote, with Member State votes weighted by their contributions to the fund. This means that the proper functioning of the SRM depends on an intergovernmental agreement in which Germany retains more influence than it would in the Council, and without the normal accountability of the fund to EU institutions (Fabbrini 2014; Asimakopoulos 2018) or any access to a further public backstop (Brandt and Wohlfahrt 2019). These have implications for the design of the case studies undertaken below. Due to limitations in its design, the SRB's decision-making and action rely on the NRAs, on the Commission and on the Council. As far as the determination of banks which are failing or are likely to fail, the SRB is expected to follow ECB indications. All in all, the SRB is a weak institution, unlikely to play a central role in the case studies.

In contrast, national resolution authorities and other political actors have more freedom of action when dealing with banks that are in financial distress, even before the point at which they are deemed failing or likely to fail. This also has implications for the degree of attention paid to one case study compared to another. Where bank problems are persistent, politicians remain attached to state aid as a means of ensuring local ownership, and where EU institutions fail to alter this dilemma, there is very likely to be a great deal of back and forth between local, national and European institutions as well as the banks themselves. Where the national government is more strongly committed and able to resolve distressed banks, the case studies are bound to be less detailed and involved. As Chapter 3 will discuss, some forms of economic nationalism provide more observation points than others when resolving a bank.

The European Deposit Insurance Scheme

The original design of Banking Union was supposed to entail a third, unrealized pillar: the European Deposit Insurance Scheme or EDIS (European Council 2012a). During the financial crisis, and until 2014, deposit insurance was regulated through the DGS (Deposit Guarantee Schemes) Directive of 1994 (94/19/EC), which introduced minimum harmonization among national DGS. This directive required all Member States to cover at least 90% of deposited capital, for a minimum of €20,000 per person. This minimum was however exceeded by most Member States (Howarth and Quaglia 2018). The Directive left room for a considerable amount of variety among Member States. For instance, Member States could choose whether to protect deposits per depositor, per account or 'per depositor per institution', and whether to fund the DGS ex ante, that is to collect premium in preparation for a possible crisis, or to fund it ex post, that is to collect resources from surviving institutions in the event of a bank's failure (Howarth and Quaglia 2018).

However, the global financial crisis underlined the importance of a strong deposit guarantee in improving financial stability (Financial Stability Board 2012). As a result, several international and European observers supported the idea of establishing a common European Deposit Insurance Scheme (International Monetary Fund 2012; Van Rompuy 2012; Constancio 2014). The Van Rompuy's report (2012), for instance, commented that the establishment of a European Deposit Insurance Scheme would 'strengthen the credibility of existing arrangements and serve as an important assurance that eligible deposits of all credit institutions are sufficiently insured'.

Critically, though, Member States were split in their position towards the EDIS: France, Italy and Spain expressed their support for the project, which they saw as a necessary step towards completing the Banking Union (Szego 2013, 7; Rajoy 2013), whereas Germany and Austria strongly opposed the idea. When the establishment of the EDIS was first proposed by the Commission in 2010 (European Commission 2010), Germany and Austria immediately rejected it. Germany's opposition in particular pushed the EDIS out of the agenda until 2015, when the Commission made one last attempt at presenting a draft proposal (Howarth and Quaglia 2018), which until the time of writing, however, has yet to be agreed upon (Donnelly 2018a).

Opposition to the EDIS was mainly motivated by the fear that the costs of bank failures or insolvency would fall on those countries with more stable banking systems, and by concerns for moral hazard. The first set of concerns was expressed by Germany, the Netherlands, Austria and Finland, which feared that in a European Deposit Insurance Scheme, benefits and costs would be unevenly distributed. In addition to these countries, non-Eurozone Member States, such as the UK and Sweden, saw no benefit in joining such a scheme: being outside the Eurozone, their central banks already provided them with a fiscal backstop (Howarth and Quaglia 2018). The concerns of moral hazard, on the other hand, were expressed mainly by Germany. Although other Member States such as the Netherlands had made similar statements (Government of the Netherlands 2012), Germany engaged in a full-frontal opposition, supported by all German political parties (Koalitionsvertrag 2013) and voiced most notably by Minister of Finance Schäuble (Howarth and Quaglia 2018).

Although Member States opposing the EDIS explained their opposition based on the two reasons discussed above, Howarth and Quaglia (2018) convincingly argue that the underlying reason for this position can be ultimately found in the difference between national banking systems, which in turn substantially shaped national preferences regarding Deposit Guarantee Schemes. In Germany and Austria, multiple DGS and institutional protection schemes were in place, most of which were funded ex ante (Howarth and Quaglia 2018). German banks therefore opposed the creation of an EDIS, both because they feared it would harm the existing protection schemes (Handelsblatt, 7 November 2012; Kaiser

2012) and because, just like Minister Schäuble, they did not trust ex post funded DGS, which were in use in other Member States, such as the UK, Italy and the Netherlands (Howarth and Quaglia 2016).

Due to the failure to establish a common deposit guarantee scheme, deposit insurance remains an exclusive competence of Member States under the *DGS Directives*, which set out minimum standards for coverage and speed of repayment. Instead of a common deposit insurance scheme, the EU upgraded minimum standards on national deposit insurance instead. At the outset of the Great Financial Crisis, national systems had a minimum coverage of €20,000 in line with a 1994 minimum standards directive. In the context of the crisis, this limit was found to be too low to keep capital flight at bay and increased. Directive 2009/14/EU upgraded the minimum coverage to €100,000 and mandated that depositors be repaid within 20 days. The 2009 innovation effectively brought the coverage of other national systems up to the levels provided by Italian deposit insurance coverage (Howarth and Quaglia 2016; Demirguc-Kunt, Lane and Laeven 2014). Further amendments to the Deposit Guarantee Schemes (DGS) Directive took further steps to implement additional recommendations from the global standard-setting body, the International Association of Deposit Insurers. Directive (2014/49/EU) lowered repayment times to one week, tackled the issue of ex ante funding with an obligation for national systems to build up reserves over time and set out a legal framework for deposit insurance to be used during bank resolutions. These last components replicated the use of deposit insurance in some countries for this purpose and constituted part of the construction of the Single Resolution Mechanism. Prior funding by banks would be used to help soften the financial contagion of bank resolutions in the same country as the failing bank. However inter-state loans across national systems remained voluntary, with the risk that the Member States which were most in need might lack sufficient funds (Donnelly 2016). Furthermore, following German requests, certain types of banks, such as credit unions, cooperative and saving banks, are exempted from these requirements.

The 2009 and 2014 DGS Directives posed no real challenge to Italian interests or expectations. But the new EU rules regarding the use of deposit insurance in cases where the bank had not yet collapsed were unclear, especially before and during a resolution. In Italy, the main deposit insurance system is a private fund fueled by bank contributions and frequently used under the direction of the Bank of Italy to partially recapitalize banks in the event of impending insolvency. This potential restriction proved to be a point of legal contention between the Italian and European authorities in a number of cases outlined below. Spain found itself with most other European countries in two respects. It had to increase deposit insurance coverage from 20,000 euros to 100,000, gradually begin ex ante funding of the system and decrease the waiting time for a payout, from 20 days to 7 days (Fondo de Garantía de Depósitos de Entidades de Crédito 2014).

Room for economic nationalism in Banking Union

In conclusion, Banking Union is incomplete, leaves several crucial tasks within the remit of national institutions and overall falls short of its original design and of the suggestions of experts (Donnelly 2016). The flaws should not eclipse the fact that supervision has been established with unquestionably strong and effective powers. It is what happens when a bank is failing or likely to fail that is more problematic. As seen throughout the chapter, the gaps in the architecture of Banking Union can be largely attributed to negotiations between Member States (see Howarth and Quaglia 2016). The point has therefore been made that the deficiency in the current state of Banking Union is motivated by intergovernmental politics designed to retain significant rights and responsibilities for the Member States (Donnelly 2018). This is compatible with the expectation in work on Economic Nationalism, that nation-states intervene in the market to provide national firms or banks with comparative advantage in an otherwise liberal globalized economy (Clift and Woll 2012; Deeg 2012).

Based on the assumption that Member States are, at least in part, driven by some form of economic nationalism, the following chapter theorizes (varieties of) economic nationalism, presents how state aid is regulated under the BRRD and explains how countries can exploit the loopholes in the law to their advantage and where the line lies between exploiting loopholes and breaking EU law.

References

Allen, F., Beck, T., Carletti, E., Lane, P., Schoemaker, D., & Wager, W. (2011). *Cross-Border Banking in Europe: Implications for Financial Stability and Macroeconomic Policies.* London: CERP.

Asimakopoulos, I.G. (2018). International law as a negotiation tool in banking union; the case of the single resolution fund. *Journal of Economic Policy Reform, 21*(2), 118–131.

Bodellini, M. (2017). Greek and Italian 'lessons' on bank restructuring: Is precautionary recapitalisation the way forward? *Cambridge Yearbook of European Legal Studies, 19*(2017), 144–164. doi:10.1017/cel.2017.6

Brandt, F., & Wohlfahrt, M. (2019). A common backstop to the single resolution fund. *Journal of Economic Policy Reform, 22*(3), 291–306.

Clift, B., & Woll, C. (2012). Economic patriotism: Reinventing control over open markets. *Journal of European Public Policy, 19*(3), 307–323. doi:10.1080/13501763.2011.638117

Constâncio, V. (2014). Banking union and European integration. Speech at the OeNB Economics Conference, Vienna, May 12. Retrieved from: ecb.europa.eu/press/ key/date/2014/html/sp140512.en.html

Culpepper, P.D., & Tesche, T. (2021). Death in Veneto? European banking union and the structural power of large banks. *Journal of Economic Policy Reform,* 24(2), 134–150.

De Larosière Group (2009). The high-level group on financial supervision in the EU. Retrieved from: ec.europa.eu/internal_market/finances/docs/de_larosiere_report_en.pdf

De Rynck, S. (2016). Banking on a union: The politics of changing Eurozone banking supervision. *Journal of European Public Policy, 23*(1), 119–135.

Deeg, R. (2012). Liberal economic nationalism and Europeanization: The rise of Spanish and Italian banks. Paper presented at the Annual Meeting of the American Political Science Association, New Orleans, Aug. 30–Sept. 2, 2012.

Demirguc-Kunt, A., Kane, E., & Laeven, L. (2014). Deposit insurance around the world: A comprehensive database. *Deposit Insurance Around the World: Issues of Design and Implementation.* IMF Working Paper 14/118. https://www.imf.org/external/pubs/ft/wp/2014/wp14118.pdf

Donnelly, S. (2014). Power politics and the undersupply of financial stability in Europe. *Review of International Political Economy, 21*(4), 980–1005.

Donnelly, S. (2016). Expert advice and political choice in constructing European banking union. *Journal of Banking Regulation, 17,* 104–118. doi: 10.1057/jbr.2015.13

Donnelly, S. (2018a). *Power Politics, Banking Union and EMU: Adjusting Europe to Germany.* London: Routledge.

Donnelly, S. (2018b). Advocacy coalitions and the lack of deposit insurance in Banking Union. *Journal of Economic Policy Reform, 21*(3), 210–223.

Donnelly, S., & Asimakopoulos, I.G. (2020). Bending and breaking the single resolution mechanism: The case of Italy. *JCMS: Journal of Common Market Studies, 58*(4), 856–871.

Epstein, R.A., & Rhodes, M. (2016). The political dynamics behind Europe's new banking union. *West European Politics, 39*(3), 415–437.

European Banking Authority (n.d.). The single rulebook. Retrieved from: eba.europa.eu/regulation-and-policy/single-rulebook

European Banking Federation (n.d.). Germany's banking sector: Facts & figures. www.ebf.eu/germany/

European Central Bank (2014). The list of significant supervised entities and the list of less significant institutions. Retrieved from European Central Bank website: ecb.europa.eu/pub/pdf/other/ssm-listofsupervisedentities1409en.pdf

European Central Bank (2016b). Caught in the middle? Small and medium-sized banks and European banking supervision. Retrieved from European Central Bank website: bankingsupervision.europa.eu/press/speeches/date/2016/html/se160222.en.html

European Central Bank (2016c). *ECB Annual Report on supervisory activities 2015.* Frankfurt: Germany.

European Central Bank (2018). List of supervised entities. Retrieved from: bankingsupervision.europa.eu/ecb/pub/pdf/ssm.list_of_supervised_entities_201802.en.pdf

European Central Bank (n.d.). Single supervisory mechanism. Retrieved from: bankingsupervision.europa.eu/about/thessm/html/index.en.html

European Commission (2017a). *Report from the Commission to the European Parliament and the Council on the Single Supervisory Mechanism established pursuant to Regulation (EU)* 1024/2013.

European Commission (2017b). State aid: How the EU rules apply to banks with a capital shortfall: Facttalia. Retrieved from: europa.eu/rapid/press-release_MEMO-17-1792_en.htm

European Commission (2012). A roadmap towards a banking union. Communication from the commission to the European parliament and the council. Retrieved from: eur-lex.europa.eu/legal-content/EN/TXT/?uri=CELEX:52012DC0510

European Commission (2010). State aid: Commission approves Spanish recapitalisation scheme for credit institutions. Press release IP/10/70. 28 January. https://ec.europa.eu/commission/presscorner/detail/en/IP_10_70

European Council (2012a). Roadmap for the completion of EMU [press release]. Brussels: 14 December 2012. Retrieved from European Council website: consilium.europa.eu/uedocs/cms_data/docs/pressdata/en/ec/134320.pdf

European Council (2012b). The European council agrees on a roadmap for the completion of economic and monetary union. Retrieved from Eurtalianuncil website: european-council.europa.eu/home-page/highlights/the-european-council- agrees-on-a-roadmap-for-the-completion-of-economic-and-monetary-union?lang=en

European Council (2012c). Conclusions on completing EMU. Retrieved from European Council website: consilium.europa.eu/uedocs/cms_data/docs/pressdata/en/ec/134320.pdf

European Council (n.d.). Single rulebook. Retrieved from: consilium.europa.eu/en/policies/banking-union/

European Court of Auditors (2017). Single resolution board: Work on a challenging Banking Union task started, but still a long way to go. Retrieved from European Court of Auditors website: eca.europa.eu/en/Pages/DocItem.aspx?did=44424

Fabbrini, F. (2014). On banks, courts and international law: The intergovernmental agreement on the Single resolution fund in context. *Maastricht Journal of European and Comparative Law, 21*(3), 444–463.

Financial Services Authority (2009). The turner review: A regulatory response to the banking crisis. Retrieved from Financial Services Authority website: fsa.gov.uk/pubs/other/turner_review.pdf

Financial Stability Board (2012). FSB publishes peer review on deposit insurance systems [Press release]. Retrieved from: fsb.org/wp-content/uploads/pr_120208.pdf

Fondo de Garantía de Depósitos de Entidades de Crédito (2014) Frequently asked questions. https://www.fgd.es/en/PreguntasFrecuentes.html

Germain, R., & Schwartz, H. (2014). The political economy of failure: The euro as an international currency. *Review of International Political Economy, 21*(5), 1095–1122.

Government of the Netherlands (2012). Kabinetsreactie op het voorstel van de Europese Commissie voor de oprichting van een Europees resolutiemechanisme. Retrieved from: eerstekamer.nl/eumobiel/behandeling/20130909/brief_regering_kabinetsreactie_op_2/info

Gren, J. (2017). The politics of delegation in European banking union: Building the ECB supervisory oversight capacity. *Journal of Contemporary European Research, 13*(2), 1109–1124.

Gren, J., Howarth, D., & Quaglia, L. (2015). Supranational banking supervision in Europe: The construction of a credible watchdog. *Journal of Common Market Studies, 53*, 181–199. https://doi.org/10.1111/jcms.12271

Handelsblatt, November 7, 2012

Howarth, D., & Quaglia, L. (2014). The steep road to European banking union: Constructing the single resolution mechanism. *Journal of Common Market Studies, 52*, 125–140.

Howarth, D., & Quaglia, L. (2016a). *The Political Economy of European Banking Union*. Oxford: Oxford University Press.

Howarth, D., & Quaglia, L. (2016b). Internationalised banking, alternative banks and the single supervisory mechanism. *West European Politics, 39*(3), 438–461.

Howarth, D., & Quaglia, L. (2018). The difficult construction of a European deposit insurance scheme: A step too far in Banking Union?. *Journal of Economic Policy Reform*, 21(3),190–209.

International Monetary Fund (2012). IMF calls on eurozone to take determined action in response to crisis. Retrieved from: imf.org/external/pubs/ft/survey/so/2012/int071812a.html

Kaiser 2012

Koalitionsvertrag (2013). Deutschlands Zukunft gestalten Koalitionsvertrag zwischen CDU, CSU und SP 18. Legislaturperiode. Retrieved from: bundesregierung.de/Content/DE/_Anlagen/2013/2013-12-17-koalitionsvertrag.pdf?__blob=publicationFile

Kudrna, Z. (2012). Cross-border resolution of failed banks in the European Union after the crisis: Business as usual. *Journal of Common Market Studies*, *50*(2), 283–299.

Lackhoff, K. (2013). How will the single supervisory mechanism (SSM) function? A quick overview. *Journal of International Banking Law and Regulation*, 29(1), 13–28.

Lackhoff 2013

Lintner 2017

Lombardi, D., & Moschella, M. (2016). Domestic preferences and European banking supervision: Germany, Italy and the single supervisory mechanism. *West European Politics*, *39*(3), 462–482.

Magnum, M., & Mesnard, B. (2016). Single resolution mechanism: Main features, oversight and accountability. Retrieved from European Parliament website: europarl.europa.eu/RegData/etudes/note/join/2014/528749/IPOL-ECON_NT(2014)528749_EN.pdf

Mayes, D.G. (2018). Banking union: the disadvantages of opportunism. *Journal of Economic Policy Reform*, *21*(2), 132–143.

Merler (2017). Bank liquidation in the European Union: clarification needed. Retrieved from Bruegel website: bruegel.org/2018/01/bank-liquidation-in-the-european-union-clarification-needed/

Official Journal of the European Union (2013). Council regulation (EU) 1024/2013. Retrieved from: eur-lex.europa.eu/legal-content/EN/TXT/?uri=celex:32013R1024

Padoa-Schioppa, T. (2007). *Letter to Fernando Teixeira dos Santos, President of the ECOFIN Council*, 26 November, Italian Ministry of Economy.

Rajoy, M. (2013). Discurso del presidente del Gobierno en la inauguración de la reunión del Grupo de Reflexión sobre el futuro de la Unión Europea Palma de Mallorca. July 19, Madrid.

Schoenmaker, D. (2013). Governance of International Banking: The financial trilemma. Oxford University Press.

Schoenmaker, D., & Véron, N. (2016). European banking supervision: The first eighteen months. Retrieved from Bruegel website: bruegel.org/wp-content/uploads/2016/06/Blueprint-XXV-web.pdf

Single Resolution Board (n.d.). The SRB in the banking union. Retrieved from: srb.europa.eu/en/content/srb-banking-union

Szego, B. (2013). Esame degli atti comunitari COM (2013)266 (Proposta di direttiva sui conti di pagamento) e COM(2013)520. Proposta di Regolamento sul Sistema Unico di Risoluzione. Retrieved from: bancaditalia.it/pubblicazioni/interventi-vari/int-var- 2013/Audizione-Szego-17-10.pdf

Transparency International EU (2017). Two sides of the same coin? Independence and accountability of the European central bank. Retrieved from: https://transparency.eu/wp-content/uploads/2017/03/TI-EU_ECB_Report_DIGITAL.pdf

Van Rompuy, H. (2012). *Towards a Genuine Economic and Monetary Union. [Four Presidents' Report]*. EUCO 120/12, PRESSE 296, PR PCE 102. Retrieved from: europa.eu/rapid/press-release_PRES-12-296_en.pdf

Verdun, A. (2016). Economic and monetary union. In M. Cini, & N. Pérez-Solórzano Borragán (Eds.), *European Union Politics* (pp. 295–307). Oxford: University Press.

Véron, N. (2012). *Europe's Single Supervisory Mechanism and the Long Journey Towards Banking Union* (No. 2012/16). Bruegel Policy Contribution.

Véron, N. (2018, January 15). *Bad News and Good News for the Single Resolution Board.* Bruegel. Retrieved from: bruegel.org/2018/01/bad-news-and-good-news-for-the-single-resolution-board/

Véron, N., & Wolff, G.B. (2013). *From Supervision to Resolution: Next Steps on the Road to European Banking Union* (No. 2013/04). Bruegel Policy Contribution.

World Bank Group (2017). Bank resolution and "Bail-In" in the EU: Selected case studies pre and post BRRD. Retrieved from: pubdocs.worldbank.org/en/120651482806846750/FinSAC-BRRD-and-Bail-In-CaseStudies.pdf

Wymeersch, E. (2014). The single supervisory mechanism or 'SSM', part one of the banking union. National Bank of Belgium Working Paper, 255. https://www.econstor.eu/bitstream/10419/144467/1/wp255en.pdf

3

ECONOMIC NATIONALISM AND EU STATE AID RULES

Economic nationalism: mercantilist, liberal and functional

Before discussing liberal economic nationalism, it is worth presenting economic nationalism as a mercantilist policy without the liberal qualifier. Economic nationalism can be defined as the will to protect and promote the national economy and to prevent it from helplessly fluctuating with the ebbs and flows of the international markets (Pryke 2012; Hobsbawm 1992; Pickel 2003; Harmes 2011). It is tightly related to the concept of nation-state as a champion of national concerns, whether they be related to the prestige of the country generally or the prospects for private enterprise (Nakano 2004; Helleiner 2002). This stood in contrast, and often in opposition, to liberal expectations for open borders and free trade inherent in the rise of globalization and neoliberalism in the 1980s.

Liberal expectations were followed up during that era with the establishment of international rules, practices and agreements to facilitate cross-border investment and ownership, with much of the heavy lifting being done by national governments in search of attracting (international) investments (Held and McGrew 2007). The United States and the United Kingdom were early, voluntary converts to the liberalization of financial, production and trade flows enabled by reductions and transformations of tariffs, trade and regulatory policy. The European Economic Community followed the Single European Act of 1986, coupled with transition periods for new Member States to open their economies to richer, incumbent Member States. Germany intensified its liberalization trend in the aftermath of reunification to help foster investment. The newly established European Union set out to complete the single market following the principles of liberalization after 1992 (Jackson and Deeg 2012). Overall, the perceived demise of economic nationalism was at its peak during the 1990s when the alleged success of neoliberal policies brought scholars of diverse backgrounds to accept the

DOI: 10.4324/9781003334583-3

'apparently unstoppable rise of economic imperatives, heralding the demise of politics' (Clift and Woll 2012).

Despite all this, predictions of the demise of the state and of national varieties of capitalism might have been premature (Hall 2018). Nation-states might still have a reason to engage in some form of economic nationalism that circumvents international commitments and rules, as well as the supervision of supranational institutions. After all, international and European rules have frequently been built with the consolidation of the nation-state in mind (Milward, Brennan and Romer 1992). In a globalized economy, however, politicians are still faced with the paradox of having to pursue democratic pressures emanating from the economic interests of their nation while being very limited in their actions due to the economic and legal interconnectedness of markets (Crouch 2008; Putnam 1988). This latent conflict became ever-more acute when the Global Financial Crisis hit in 2008, sending national economies sprawling. National governments had additional reasons to protect national companies and banks, even through new and untested measures. In this instance governments adopted measures aiming to stimulate consumption, prop up credit markets and prevent the overall failure of the national and international financial system by using quantitative easing, issuing state guarantees, taking on large chunks of private debt and so forth (Grossman and Woll 2014; Clift and Woll 2012; Epstein 2014; Donnelly 2011).

It is therefore important to notice that state intervention per se is not necessarily a symptom of mercantilist economic nationalism but can also be largely found in internationalized, neoliberal economies. Although neoliberalism is founded on the conviction that state intervention in the market is to be avoided because governments do not dispose of enough information to be able to manipulate the market in a virtuous way (Hayek 1944), liberal markets actually 'need constant state intervention' (Polanyi 2001) as governments respond to the ongoing instability of liberal policy and institutions (Schmidt and Thatcher 2014; Hall 1986; Wade 2004; Joerges, Stråth and Wagner 2005; Donnelly 2011; Weiss 2018; Jessop 2017). Within this book, state interventionism per se will not be considered economic nationalism, whereas protectionism will. This protectionism might be directed at market share, but we focus here on company ownership (in the case of fragile banks, of viability together with ownership by investors of the same nationality).

Before deeming a case of state intervention in the economy a symptom of economic nationalism, the observer needs to analyze the scope and purpose of such intervention. Both state interventionism and protectionism provide national firms and banks with subsidies or support of different kinds. Nevertheless, while simple state intervention is limited to providing help to national companies to keep them alive, protectionist policies also actively aim to: (1) harm foreign investors or competitors, or at least put the national in an advantaged position (offensive action) and (2) protect the company from foreign acquisitions (defensive action) (Clift and Woll 2012). Specifying this allows us to avoid false findings of economic nationalism where other motivations dominate.

Liberal economic nationalism

As others have observed, economic nationalism has been able to survive and adapt to neoliberalism and the rule structures in which it operates (Pickel 2003; Helleiner 2002). In doing so, analysts differentiate economic nationalism from liberal economic nationalism (LEN) as a form that has acquired a new set of tools to pursue national goals in a liberal setting. LEN is liberal in that it 'fosters market competition and cross-border openness' but is nationalistic, because it does so in order to 'enhance the competitive advantage of domestic firms vis-à-vis non-domestic competitors' (Deeg 2012). Another aspect of liberal economic nationalism that sets it apart from traditional economic nationalism is its adherence to prevailing international institutions and agreements regulating trade and investment. Gaps and gray areas are exploited, but hard rules are not normally breached. This feature takes on importance in comparing Italy and Spain.

Clift and Woll (2012) argue that, just as with protectionism, LEN policies aim to favor domestic firms and hinder foreign ones, albeit through different measures that are not explicitly mercantilist, including the selective and strategic combination of privatization and liberalization with features that tie national firms to other national companies. An example that Clift and Woll proffer is the state-promoted hard core of interconnected French companies that together can share capital and above all ownership control in ways that keeps companies French despite the theoretical liberalization of capital and ownership. It is worth adding that the authors also consider protectionism and LEN as points on a continuum that can coexist under certain circumstances rather than as clearly divided categories. We build on this by distinguishing between traditional economic nationalism (nationalist by design and unrestricted in the mercantilist sense), liberal economic nationalism (nationalist by design but restricted by commitments) and functional economic nationalism (nationalist by default, due to incompatibilities between international commitments and domestic institutions that the state cannot overcome).

A further contrast in the behavior of the state under LEN and its differences with other forms of economic nationalism lies in the nature and extent of its form of state intervention. In the LEN model, the state is proactive in setting out the terms for companies to exist and compete in the marketplace, and in providing state aid guarantees for the survival of strategic sectors as a lender of last resort, but more at arm's length to particular companies than is the case for mercantilist economic nationalism. States lose the capacity to direct economic activity within the country if they ever had it (Hall 1986), and they refrain from shutting down trade and investment or taking over the means of production through state-owned enterprises as an outright economic nationalist state would do.

The boundaries of what is considered liberal economic nationalism and what is not are best illustrated by the European Commission's attitudes towards state aid and other forms of ownership preference, particularly in the rescue of banks. State aid for banks is permissible to preserve the banking system as a whole, as is evidenced by the Commission's series of Banking Communiqués that followed the Great Financial Crisis in 2008 and extended through 2013. This was considered an intervention that was required to respond to a general economic disturbance, and therefore in the general public interest. But there were also limitations claimed in principle that became more pressing over time. First and most important in the short term, banks receiving aid would not be permitted to take over banks in other EU Member States. This would have exploited state backing to engage in mercantilist economic nationalism, unleashing an arms race, or an all-out ownership war in the single market that was not intended. There was also to be a time limit for support in principle, with the Commission undertaking regular reviews to determine when state aid should end and 'return to normal' commence. Finally, there should be a plan for after the initial emergency when state aid would be permissible to make up for market failure only (European Commission 2013). This would mean that governments could lend to banks when capital markets failed to invest, despite the banks being fundamentally sound. This is a formula that the Commission's Directorate General (DG) Competition eventually deployed to determine the line between the permissible and the banned. Note that in the absence of resources at the EU level to ensure the survival of banks, it relies on national resources and therefore reinforces (liberal) economic nationalism, with national governments at the sharp end of decisions to offer aid, and the European Commission ensuring these methods to not violate the principles above.

Functional economic nationalism

If liberal economic nationalism finds ways to ensure national ownership by design in a formally liberalized, open, competitive environment, and mercantilist economic nationalism explicitly rejects these restrictions, there are other situations in which local and national companies, followed by local and national governments, act in ways that keep outside investors away (both national and foreign). This leaves the state as an actor of last resort that intervenes nationally, and with respect to EU institutions and law in ways that are effectively nationalist, without the principled attachment to national ownership. *Local institutions and practices that keep bank ownership national and hold the state hostage* are ones where local banks and councils are intertwined in ways that complicate efforts to reduce the incidence of non-performing loans (meaning solvency problems become structural), and where bank customers and banks are intertwined in ways not covered by deposit insurance (meaning resolution and deposit insurance systems do not function to detach the management of a failing bank from its impact on the local community).

These are necessary, but not sufficient characteristics to incite a different kind of economic nationalism. They can be found in Spain and in Germany (Cassell 2020) as well. Three additional factors play a supporting role and are visible in a comparison of Spain and Italy. One is *state assertiveness*—the willingness of the state to intervene to clean up banks in trouble. As we will show below, this is stronger in Spain at a very early stage, in ways that outstrip the efforts of Italian authorities, who are active at the same time, but with less vigor. This not only means nipping problems in the bud (stronger state intervention vis-a-vis bank, and earlier) but also taking advantage of a window of opportunity in EU law and state aid control that allowed for vigorous, interventionist state involvement in supporting banks and restructuring their assets, and recapitalizing them in 2009 that were illegal by 2016.

The second is *external reinforcement of state assertiveness*. The Spanish government's capacity to clean up its banking sector is partial until after 2012 when it enlists financial support from the European Stability Mechanism (ESM) tied to conditions to further restructure the entire savings bank sector in the country. This outside support, as we show, was crucial to saving the country's LEN model and strategy. In Italy, the picture is quite different, with a national government reluctant to work with the ESM in any way. The consequence is that when Spanish authorities confronted bank resolution problems, they were able to overcome political, social and legal resistance to the logic of crisis combined with conditions for aid set outside the country. These were very considerable, as Spanish cajas were responsible for housing and social issues of local councils that went back to the establishment of the system and were heavily laden with the logic of appropriateness that was hard, indeed impossible to break through even after the 2008 crisis and its aftermath. This was never an option in Italy, given the more insular approach taken by national authorities, coupled with their inability to resolve the problem within the bounds of EU law. The result is an incompatibility of domestic institutions, both private ones in the banking sector, and public ones in finance, regulation and supervision authorities that could not break through local arrangements as Spain did after 2012. We call this deep-rooted incompatibility of local institutions, EU law and weak national public institutions functional economic nationalism.

The third condition is the degree and direction of *bank marketization* (national dependence on local or international investors). Marketization internationally should increase the incentive for state institutions to resolve banks quickly and thoroughly, while domestic marketization should lower it. Looking at international marketization, Hardie and Howarth (2013) focus on the transformation of banks (and other financial institutions), particularly with regard to fragility. Particularly, the marketization of banks on either side of the balance sheet can render banks unstable over time and lead to higher political demands for intervention. This intervention, whether nationalist or not, would normally be unattractive to outside investors (unless already present, and they are not discriminated against by the form of support). This can be detected in both Italy and Spain, but at different points in time, with differing characteristics and different effects. Marketization (in Italy) takes place at a rather late stage in the 2010s and takes the form of making domestic depositors bondholders. This renders the banks more fragile, and more politically important. Marketization in Spain happens earlier as banks liberalize and expand in the late 20th century, using foreign investment capital in the process. This means that banks become more fragile during downturns, but also that foreign investors become more politically important in ways that is not the case in Italy. In Italy, the reverse is true: banks need to service local depositors and businesses who hold bank bonds and resist initiatives that hurt them under EU law. A key indicator of state response is the use of state aid in bank resolutions. This is discussed in the next section.

Economic nationalism, state aid and patient capital

EU law distinguishes between state aid that is permissible for a Member State (and therefore compatible with liberal economic nationalism) and that which is not. In European Union law, illegal state aid is defined in Article 107 of the Treaty on the Functioning of the European Union (TFEU). Article 107(1) defines state aid as

> any aid granted by a Member State or through State resources in any form whatsoever which distorts or threatens to distort competition by favoring certain undertakings or the production of certain goods [...], in so far as it affects trade between Member States.

As a consequence of state aid, in which a government provides financial support to a bank in the form of capital injections or subsidies unavailable to others, the firm or bank in question receives a competitive advantage compared to the other firms or banks in the market. Therefore, state aid is normally equated with unreconstituted economic nationalism and disallowed. DG Competition can launch investigations, order the repayment of economic advantages and levy fines directly.

However, EU state aid law and policy allow for state aid in a series of prespecified, exceptional situations. One example of this is a financial crisis, where the Commission can determine that a general economic disturbance is at work which requires emergency financial support for companies and banks for a limited period of time. In other cases, the Commission can determine the general economic and public interest in promoting the research and development of strategic technologies that companies would otherwise not develop. The latter is of little import here. The former, however, is illustrated in the Bank Communiqués issued by the Commission's Directorate-General for Competition between 2009 and 2013 (European Commission 2013), which permitted national governments to support their banks due to the grave, systemic consequences of bank failure in the wake of the crisis. The main provision is that companies in receipt of such assistance do not use it to take over companies in other Member States. This would go beyond the purpose of rescuing critical infrastructure and go into the realm of distorting competition. The Great Lockdown of 2020–2022 presents another example of this willingness to admit state aid for limited purposes of meeting an emergency for a limited time.

In a third area, however, state aid is permitted to rescue banks and effectively keep them national, or delay the moment of closure, provided that the banks have reasonable prospects for returning to profitability after a severe external or internal shock. The fact that the rules permit state aid even when the given crisis or exceptional situation involves just one Member State is consistent with liberal economic nationalism, given that state aid is provided within a set of parameters monitored and applied by the European Commission. A more specific example of LEN and state aid within the financial sector is the provision of patient capital to insolvent banks. The term patient capital, also known as long-term capital, refers to the provision of economic resources on market basis, thus with low interest rates, to be returned in the long term (Deeg, Hardie and Maxfield 2016).

Patient capital can be provided by private firms as well as by the government. An example of government provision of patient capital can be found in the UK, where the necessity of state support of start-ups through patient capital has been publicly supported by business (UK Industry Panel 2017). State provision of patient capital also applies to the banking sector to help them weather economic shocks, particularly downturns affecting more than one financial institution. Following the same logic as the one used by the UK towards start-ups, governments provide patient capital to insolvent banks that would otherwise be unable to access loans on the market, and in doing so act as lenders of last resort (Iftinchi 2017; Donnelly 2018).

One of the main purposes of the Bank Recovery and Resolution Directive (BRRD) is to heavily reduce the use of state aid within the EU (Donnelly 2018). In order to do so, the BRRD builds on Article 107 of the Treaty on the European Union, according to which any sort of state aid which threatens to distort competition must be avoided. In order to prevent the use of state aid, under the BRRD banks reporting a capital shortfall are urged to raise capital on the market or from other private sources before the point of insolvency is reached (European Commission 2017). In addition, the BRRD introduces the bail-in rule (below), which makes the use of state aid even less accessible.

However, both in the TFEU and in the BRRD, a set of exceptions are made to this general disposition that aims to account for natural, social or economic calamities. In particular, Article 107.3(b) of the TFEU allows for state aid when it aims to 'remedy a serious disturbance in the economy' of a Member State. In the same way, the BRRD allows for state aid in exceptional situations, such as in the case of a systemic crisis, or of a severe disturbance to the economy. The reason behind this requirement is that the BRRD aims to allow for emergency intervention to prevent a systemic crash, but also curb the occurrence of moral hazards. It therefore stipulates that state aid needs not be used unless strictly necessary.

Therefore, state aid is allowed only in extraordinary circumstances. During a serious disturbance of the economy, other credit institutions are likely to be short of liquidity, and therefore the state needs to act as a lender of last resort. Furthermore, in this case, precautionary recapitalization does not foster moral hazard, because a severe disturbance of the economy is likely to be beyond the control of a bank's board (Olivares-Carminal and Russo 2017).

Critically, however, the criteria for determining a serious disturbance of the economy are not clarified within the BRRD. Although crisis management legislations need to leave enough room for discretion to allow for each case to be tended to in its specificities (Véron 2017), the haziness around such a critical term makes the territory surrounding precautionary recapitalization more uncertain that it is desirable (Olivares-Carminal and Russo 2017). These loopholes tend to the necessity of crisis management legislation to retain enough flexibility to be able to respond to the circumstances of different scenarios (Véron 2017).

A secondary consequence of such loopholes is the room left to Member States to lobby European institutions in order to satisfy their nationalistic goals. State aid is still allowed under the BRRD, under specific conditions, namely:

- In the context of a *resolution* procedure, conditional to burden-sharing and compliance with the bail-in rule.
- Is in the form of *emergency liquidity assistance (ELA)*, provided by national central banks.
- In the case of a systemic financial crisis, through the *public equity support tool* or through the *temporary public ownership tool*, and still conditional to burden-sharing and compliance with the bail-in rule.
- In case of a serious disturbance of the economy, under the form of a *precautionary recapitalization*, and solely conditional to burden-sharing.

Due to the fact that its use is conditional to the truly exceptional nature of a systemic crisis, the public equity support tool and the temporary public ownership tool have not been used since the entrance into force of the BRRD. The bail-in rule, emergency liquidity assistance and precautionary recapitalization, on the other hand, are relevant both for the case studies at hand and for the new resolution regime as a whole. The following paragraphs will therefore focus on them.

Bail-ins as private sacrifices

State aid is possible under the BRRD, but only after a bail-in has taken place. If a bank's shortfall persists and the bank is put through resolution procedures, the Member State can decide to provide it with state aid by notifying the Commission. Nevertheless, the provision of state aid is conditional on burden-sharing. This consists of the conversion of subordinate bonds into shares, which reduces the bank's liabilities and increases its capital, as well as a forced reduction in the value of bonds and other outstanding debts the bank owes. Unlike liquidation, a bail-in typically aims to keep the fundamental functions of the bank working (Bodellini 2017). Nevertheless, it can be used to make it cheaper and less risky for another bank to take over the sick bank's business, in whole or in part.

The bail-in rule requires creditors and shareholders to bear losses for a minimum of 8% of the bank's core equity capital before the bank can resort to other funds, such as resolution funds. The BRRD aims to protect natural persons and small- and medium-sized enterprises holding accounts of up to €100,000, which are put at the end of the bail-in sequence and possibly exonerated from it. Compliance with the bail-in rule is a precondition for accessing state aid or Single Resolution Fund (SRF) funds during a resolution procedure (European Council n.d.).

The bail-in rule fulfills two goals: on the one hand, it aims to break the vicious circle between private and sovereign debt, while on the other it aims to curb moral hazard by motivating investors, creditors and depositors to hold the bank accountable for its actions (Gros and Schoenmaker 2014). More pragmatically, due to its high cost for shareholders, creditors and investors, the bail-in rule has the effect of motivating banks to seek private capital rather than immediately recurring to state aid failing banks. The bail-in rule therefore drastically changed the European financial framework, especially with regard to investors. For the first time, investors are called upon to bear the costs of a failing bank, with the possible—and intended—effect of moving investors away from risky deals. Lastly, by making state aid conditional to a bail-in, the bail-in rule curbs the overall use of taxpayers' money in banks' failures, with what was intended to be positive effects for financial stability.

Despite its potential benefits, the point has been made that the bail-in rule could actually foster the very financial distress it is meant to prevent. If writing down the bank's liability results in a transfer of insolvency from the bank to its creditors, or if a significant portion of the liabilities is held by other banks, a bail-in can create or accelerate contagion and generate a domino effect (Avgouleas and Goodhart 2016). This issue is addressed by Article 44 of the BRRD, which allows resolution authorities to exempt some liabilities from bail-in if at risk of generating financial instability. In addition to that, Article 8 of Commission Delegated Regulation (EU) 2016/860 requires that in such delicate situations resolution authorities meticulously assess the interconnectedness of the credit institution and exclude risky liabilities from the bail-in process (Bodellini 2017). Another problematic aspect regards the limited use of resolution funds. Under Article 44 of the BRRD, a bank can resort to a resolution fund only if a bail-in for a minimum of 8% of the liability has previously taken place, and the fund can cover only up to 5% of the liabilities. This rule can be problematic if the bank finds itself in the particular situation described above, that is in case a bail-in would risk triggering contagion (Bodellini 2017; European Council n.d.).

ECB-centric tools: emergency liquidity assistance and precautionary recapitalization

Similar to provisions in state aid law that provide tools for liberal economic nationalism, the European Central Bank (ECB) also has mechanisms, or a key role in permitting mechanisms to keep distressed banks afloat. Emergency Liquidity Assistance (ELA) is issued by a (national or European) central bank to a commercial bank to provide it with liquidity under exceptional circumstances, where banks cannot access financial markets normally to refinance themselves (European Central Bank n.d.). The bank receives cash (liquidity) on the basis of illiquid assets on the bank's balance sheet, giving it (and investors, governments and regulators) time to seek a solution during a crisis. In order for ELA to be carried out, the ECB must be notified two working days before the provision of state aid (European Central Bank 2013). Examples of ELA can be found in a number of banks studied in this book, including Banco Popular in Spain, and the Veneto and Vicenza banks in Italy. On 19 January 2017, the Bank of Italy received the Commission's approval to provide Veneto Banca and Banca Popolare di Vicenza with state aid in the form of public guarantees on subordinate bonds (Banca Popolare di Vicenza 2017a; Gruppo Veneto Banca 2017; Corriere del Veneto 2017). ELA was also provided twice by the Bank of Spain to Banco Popular ahead of closure (Buck and Brunsden 2017).

The ECB defines precautionary recapitalization as an exceptional measure that provides the injection of state funds into an insolvent bank in case of serious disturbance to the economy (European Central Bank 2016a; Official Journal of the European Union 2014). Through precautionary recapitalization, Member States provide the insolvent bank with patient capital (Donnelly 2018). In order for precautionary recapitalization to be lawful under the BRRD, Article 32 requires a set of conditions to be met:

- The bank must be solvent and therefore deemed not to be failing or likely to fail.
- The precautionary recapitalization must be approved under the EU state aid framework, the amount of capital provided to the bank through the precautionary recapitalization must be limited to covering the shortfall assessed by the competent authority and it must not confer an advantage upon the institution (proportionate).
- The precautionary recapitalization needs to address a severe disturbance in the economy of a Member State in an effort to preserve financial stability, and it must be of temporary nature (Véron 2017).

These terms build on the Banking Communications for the European Commission which first set out the admissibility of state aid in 2009. Aid was required to be precautionary and temporary and not confer advantages over competitors. This meant that it would end at some point. This later favored the use of contingent convertible bonds that can be bailed in at a future date. By 2013, it was also clear that private investors would have to ultimately bear the brunt of the adjustment costs, reducing state aid in the process (European Parliament 2017). In short, precautionary recapitalization, which required the prior authorization of the ECB and the Commission, would remain the only option available to Member States which allows them to provide banks with capital without performing a bail-in (Olivares-Carminal and Russo 2017).

The decision about a precautionary recapitalization involves a number of steps. It starts with the question of whether a capital shortfall can be addressed through private investors. If the answer is yes, then a solution is deemed to exist without any need to consider bail-ins or state aid. If private investors cannot be found, the ECB must then determine whether the bank is failing or likely to fail (FOLTF). This is effectively a determination of whether the bank has passed the point of no return or not. If it is not FOLTF, then a precautionary recapitalization using state aid as patient capital is possible. This is typically the case if the bank holds enough good assets to be profitable in the long term (solvent) but lacks capital in the present moment (liquidity).

If the ECB decides that the bank is FOLTF, then the use of state aid depends on further steps. The case is handed to the Single Resolution Board, which then decides whether a resolution is in the public interest. If it is deemed to be in the public interest, i.e. if the Board decides that the bank is systemically important, then the BRRD applies, and a bail-in must be implemented. The Single Resolution Fund may also be tapped to soften the knock-on effects of the bail-in on other financial institutions. Likewise, national state aid may be considered, but only after these two steps have been taken.

If the Board determines that the bank's resolution is not in the public interest, then national bankruptcy law and procedure for winding down companies apply. Crucially, this means that the BRRD does not apply, bail-ins are not mandatory and state aid may be applied in the process, subject to review by the European Commission. In cases where state aid is contemplated like this, it is primarily deployed to clean up the bank's finances before another bank takes it over. There are good reasons to ask whether international investors would be satisfied with the results of such a procedure, even with the provision of state aid, given that bankruptcy proceedings can be complicated and take years of court time. This points to effectively keeping bank ownership national.

State aid or patient capital? A loophole

Precautionary recapitalizations provide a last-resort means for countries to avoid a confrontation over state aid rules when a bank is in financial trouble without closing it, subject to conditions. As explained above, when banks present a capital shortfall, they are urged to recapitalize on the market or from private sources. However, Member States are also allowed to satisfy the bank's need for capital themselves, as long as the capital supply is in line with market conditions. This means that loans are made for a finite period, and at a fictional interest rate that a bank would have to pay in the absence of financial distress (Hadjiemmanuil 2017; Novkovic 2021). In practice, the Commission has granted permission for loans made for five-year periods, at interest rates payable elsewhere in the Eurozone. An example of this has taken place in Portugal in March 2017 when the government recapitalization of the fully state-owned bank Caixa Geral on market terms was not considered state aid (European Commission 2017e).

It is worth noticing that, although this kind of state intervention is not considered state aid under EU law, it fits the definition of patient capital provided by Deeg, Hardie and Maxfield (2016). Therefore, this can be considered the first way through which Member States can support their banks without breaching EU law. As we outline below, the manner in which national governments provide state aid and then negotiate conditions with the European Commission is linked to the kind of economic nationalism (or liberalism) that prevails in national policy. The next section discusses these policy types and the way they deal with banks and European institutions. These differences have a great impact on the state's capacity to provide financial stability in the banking sector, and within the context of Banking Union's rule structure. While the Spanish state is relatively strong vis-a-vis its own banks and can pursue a liberal economic nationalism that works within European rules relatively easily. Where it has found itself encountering difficulties, it has reached out to the European institution that strengthens the autonomy of the state towards the banks, the ESM. In contrast, the Italian state is entangled much more densely with banks in its own variety of financial capitalism and is reluctant to strengthen its hand by leveraging demands from European institutions. This makes it difficult to apply EU law and raises the benefits of negotiating with EU institutions regarding exceptions, modifications and inconsistencies in application. In other words, EU institutions do little to strengthen the state and the prevalence of functional economic nationalism.

Conclusions and propositions

Based on the discussion above, we can underpin the following propositions that we expect to apply to the study of how bank resolutions are implemented differently between Spain and Italy, with the potential for lessons that can be applied to other times and countries.

Proposition 1: Banking Union mechanisms provide room for state aid, and therefore economic nationalism.

Proposition 2: Economic nationalism can be mercantilist, liberal or functional, depending on (1) the degree of state assertiveness in supervising and resolving banks and (2) the degree and direction (local or international) of bank marketization.

Liberal economic nationalism should be highest where state assertiveness is strongest and bank marketization internationally oriented. Functional economic nationalism should be most prevalent where state assertiveness is lower and bank marketization is domestically oriented.

The next chapter reviews and further develops the theoretical landscape in which comparative political economy drives the successes and failures of the European political economy. In this case, the goal is to understand the attitudes of national governments towards the Single Resolution Mechanism, their willingness and capacity to implement it, what they do when they encounter resistance from domestic banks and how that response reverberates back onto the functioning of Banking Union institutions.

References

Avgouleas, E., & Goodhart, C. (2016). An anatomy of bank bail-ins why the Eurozone needs a fiscal backstop for the banking sector. *European Economy*, (2), 75–90.

Banca Popolare di Vicenza (2017a). Press release 19 January 2017 [Press release]. Retrieved from Banca Popolare di Vicenza website: popolarevicenza.it/BpVii-web/data/BpVii-comunicato/comunicati-stampa/eng-nodiscl/2017/Press_release_20170119/allegato/19_01_2017-European_Commission_assessment_on_state_aid_rules.pdf

Bodellini, M. (2017). Greek and Italian 'lessons' on bank restructuring: Is precautionary recapitalisation the way forward? *Cambridge Yearbook of European Legal Studies, 19*(2017), 144–164. doi:10.1017/cel.2017.6

Buck, T. and Brunsden, J. (2017). Emergency funds failed to save Banco Popular from death spiral. *Financial Times*, 8 June. https://www.ft.com/content/6f32eca2-4c62-11e7-a3f4-c742b9791d43

Cassell, M. (2020). *Banking on the State: The Political Economy of Public Savings Banks*. New York: Columbia University Press/Agenda Publishing.

Clift, B., & Woll, C. (2012). Economic patriotism: reinventing control over open markets. *Journal of European Public Policy, 19*(3), 307–323. doi:10.1080/13501763.2011.638117

Corriere del Veneto (2017). Banche venete, sì alle garanzie sui bond: L'Ue autorizza lo «scudo» dello Stato. *Corriere del Veneto, 20* January. Retrieved from: corrieredelvenettaliaiere.it/veneto/notizie/economia/2017/20-gennaio-2017/banche-venete-si-garanzie-bond-l-ue-autorizza-scudo-stato-2401220419083.shtml

Crouch, C. (2008). Economic patriotism and the paradox of neo-liberal democracy. Paper presented at the First Economic Patriotism Workshop, Warwick University, 13–14 February.

Deeg, R. (2012). Liberal economic nationalism and europeanization: The rise of spanish and Italian banks. Paper presented at the Annual Meeting of the American Political Science Association, New Orleans, Aug. 30-Sept. 2, 2012.

Deeg, R., Hardie, I., & Maxfield, S. (2016). What is patient capital, and where does it exist? *Socio-Economic Review, 14*(4), 615–625. doi:10.1093/ser/mww030

Donnelly, S. (2011). The public interest and the economy in Europe in the wake of the financial crisis. *European Political Science, 10*(3), 384–392.

Donnelly, S. (2018). Advocacy coalitions and the lack of deposit insurance in Banking Union. *Journal of Economic Policy Reform, 21*(3), 210–223.

Epstein, R.A. (2014). When do foreign banks 'cut and run'? Evidence from west European bailouts and east European markets. *Review of International Political Economy, 21*(4), 847–877.

European Central Bank (2013).

European Central Bank (2016a). What is a precautionary recapitalisation and how does it work? Retrieved from European Central Bank website: bankingsupervision.europa.eu/about/ssmexplained/html/precautionary_recapitalisation.en.html

European Central Bank (n.d). Single Supervisory Mechanism. Retrieved from: bankingsupervision.europa.eu/about/thessm/html/index.en.html

European Commission (2013). Communication from the Commission on the application, from 1 August 2013, of State aid rules to support measures in favour of banks in the context of the financial crisis ('Banking Communication'). https://eur-lex.europa.eu/legal-content/EN/TXT/HTML/?uri=CELEX:52013XC0730(01)&from=EN

European Commission (2017). State aid: Commission approves aid for market exit of Banca Popolare di Vicenza and Veneto Banca under Italian insolvency law, involving sale of some parts to Intesa Sanpaolo [Press Release]. Retrieved from: europa.eu/rapid/press-release_IP-17-1791_en.htm.

European Commission (2017e). State aid: How the EU rules apply to banks with a capital shortfall – Factsheet. Retrieved from: europa.eu/rapid/press-release_MEMO-17-1792_en.htm.

European Council (n.d.). Single rulebook. Retrieved from: consilium.europa.eu/en/policies/banking-union/

European Parliament (2017). Precautionary recapitalisations under the bank recovery and resolution directive: Conditionality and case practice. https://www.europarl.europa.eu/RegData/etudes/BRIE/2017/602084/IPOL_BRI%282017%29602084_EN.pdf

Grossman, E., & Woll, C. (2014). Saving the Banks: The Political Economy of Bailouts. *Comparative Political Studies, 47*(4), 574–600. doi:10.1177/0010414013488540

Gruppo Veneto Banca (2017). *Press release 19 January 2017.* Retrieved from Gruppo Veneto Banca website: gruppovenetobanca.it/documents/17503/1443157/19.01.2017+PRESS+RELEASE.PDF.

Hadjiemmanuil, C. (2017). Limits on State-funded bailouts in the EU bank resolution regime. *European Economy* 2016 (2), 91–115.

Hall, P.A. (1986). *Governing the Economy: The Politics of State Intervention in Britain and France.* Oxford: Oxford University Press.

Hall, P.A. (2018). Varieties of capitalism in light of the euro crisis. *Journal of European Public Policy, 25*(1), 7–30.

Hardie, I., Howarth, D., Maxfield, S., & Verdun, A. (2013). Banks and the false dichotomy in the comparative political economy of finance. *World politics, 65*(4), 691–728.

Harmes, A. (2011). The rise of neoliberal nationalism. *Review of International Political Economy, 19*(1), 59–86. doi: 10.1080/09692290.2010.507132

Hayek, F. (1944). *The Road to Serfdom.* Chicago: University of Chicago Press.

Held, D., & McGrew, A.G. (Eds.). (2007). *Globalization Theory: Approaches and Controversies.* Cambridge: Polity.

Helleiner, E. (2002). Economic nationalism as a challenge to economic liberalism? Lessons from the 19th century. *International Studies Quarterly, 46*(3), 307–329. doi:10.1111/1468-2478.00235

Hobsbawm, E. (1992). *The Age of Extremes The Short Twentieth Century, 1914–1991.* London, England: Michael Joseph.

Iftinchi, V. (2017). State aid and the financial sector: the evolution of the legal framework of State aid law. In *Research Handbook on State Aid in the Banking Sector.* Cheltenham: Edward Elgar Publishing.

Jackson, G., & Deeg, R. (2012). The long-term trajectories of institutional change in European capitalism. *Journal of European Public Policy, 19*(8), 1109–1125.

Jessop, B. (2017). The future of the state in an era of globalization, in Pfaller, A. & Lerch, M., eds. *Challenges of Globalization* (pp. 13–26). London: Routledge.

Joerges, C., Stråth, B., & Wagner, P. (Eds.). (2005). *The Economy as a Polity: The Political Constitution of Contemporary Capitalism*. London: Routledge Press.

Milward, A., Brenner, G. and Romero, F. (1992). *The European Rescue of the Nation State*. London: Routledge.

Nakano, T. (2004). Theorising economic nationalism. *Nations and Nationalism, 10*(3), 211–229. doi:10.1111/j.1354-5078.2004.00164.x

Novkovic, K. (2021). The developments of the precautionary recapitalization rules: from its inception to the recent amendments and the Covid 19 pandemic. Master thesis, Università Ca' Foscari Venezia.

Official Journal of the European Union (2014). Directive 2014/59/EU of the European Parliament and of the Council. Retrieved from: eur-lex.europa.eu/legal-content/EN/TXT/HTML/?uri=CELEX:32014L0059&from=IT

Olivares-Caminal, R., & Russo, C. (2017). Precautionary recapitalisations: Time for a review? In-depth analysis. Retrieved from European Parliament website: europarl.europa.eu/RegData/etudes/IDAN/2017/602089/IPOL_IDA(2017)602089_EN.pdf

Pickel, A. (2003). Explaining, and explaining with, economic nationalism. *Nations and Nationalism, 9*(1), 105–127. doi:10.1111/1469-8219.00077

Polanyi, K. (2001). *The Great Transformation: The Political and Economic Origins of our Time*. Boston: Beacon Press.

Pryke, S. (2012). Economic nationalism: Theory, history and prospects. *Global Policy 3*(3). 281–291. doi:10.1111/j.1758-5899.2011.00146.x

Putnam, R.D. (1988). Diplomacy and domestic politics: The logic of two-level games. *International Organization, 42*(3), 427–460. doi:10.1017/S0020818300027697

Schmidt, V.A., & Thatcher, M. (2014). Why are neoliberal ideas so resilient in Europe's political economy? *Critical Policy Studies, 8*(3), 340–347.

UK Industry Panel (2017). Patient Capital Review. Retrieved from UK Government website: http://www.gov.uk/government/uploads/system/uploads/attachment_data/file/661397/PCR_Industry_panel_response.pdf.

Véron, N. (2017). Precautionary recapitalisation: time for a review? Retrieved from European Parliament website: europarl.europa.eu/RegData/etudes/IDAN/2017/602089/IPOL_IDA(2017)602089_EN.pdf

Wade, R. (2004). *Governing the Market: Economic Theory and the Role of Government in East Asian Industrialization*. Princeton: Princeton University Press.

Weiss, L. (2018). *The Myth of the Powerless State*. Ithaca: Cornell University Press.

4

INTERESTS, INSTITUTIONS AND IMPLEMENTING EU LAW

This chapter aims to build a theoretical framework that can be used to understand and explain why Spain and Italy have had such different experiences and outcomes in resolving insolvent banks. The goal is to make it sufficiently generalizable to apply elsewhere. In the process of sorting out a model we find most promising, we refer both to integration theory and to comparative political economy. To be clear, we are not primarily interested in how institutions are established when looking at the integration literature, but in what those theories tell us about what to expect after institutions are established. This chapter sorts out why we settle on a mix of sociological institutionalism as the preferred means of understanding and explaining state behavior. We take the primary assumptions about politically involved actors, their motivations and behaviors during the integration process to extrapolate their comportment after the establishment of EU institutions, programs and procedures. We then move on to the comparative theory that rounds out our ability to understand and explain the activity of both state and private actors.

Integration theory

Neo-functionalism and intergovernmentalism, together with variations on these two grand theories, constitute the two main theoretical approaches to European integration that most analysts refer back to when looking at questions of integration. These theories set expectations on actors' behaviors and generally serve as a backbone for European studies research (Rosamond 2016). Beyond the creation of institutions, they also lay the groundwork for expectations on whether the governments of EU Member States can be expected to respect legal obligations determined by EU legislation, whether they have the effective room to engage in competitive economic nationalism, and whether they are likely to use it. Getting

DOI: 10.4324/9781003334583-4

to the point where such explanations can be offered requires an investigation of the primary assumptions and models used to predict behaviors. We use them here to underline portable, testable hypotheses while keeping an eye on the empirical lessons of bank supervision and resolution in Italy and Spain.

Neo-functionalism

Neo-functionalism generates optimistic expectations of Member States, private sector and EU institutional behavior in two different ways. First, it expects all of these actors to work together to create new EU institutions in response to new problems that affect the entire Union (Haas 1958; Jensen 2016). Second, it expects the actors to respect EU law and institutions, together with the obligations they carry with them. These expectations accept the self-interested nature of interest groups, national governments and even EU institutions but expect them to compromise with each other in ways that generate new institutions and adjust existing behavior to meet the obligations they already have. Difficulties in doing so are expected to lead actors to agitate for change, lobbying EU institutions together with like-minded allies organized into cross-border networks and EU-level lobbies.

This process is expected to happen through three phenomena: elite socialization, supranational interest groups and the spillover effect. The *elite socialization* hypothesis postulates that, after spending a considerable amount of time involved in European decision-making, national leaders develop loyalty towards the EU. Once such loyalty is developed, they are expected to promote collective European solutions to common interests in their country of origin. As they do so, the incentive rises to emphasize integration that agrees on leveraging technocratic expertise and avoids politicized approaches and issues, where competing values and interests might block progress (Haas 1958). The *supranational interest group* hypothesis postulates that interest groups will organize at a European, cross-country level and lobby their country of origin for more integration once they realize the advantages of doing so over lobbying only their national governments. This allows competitive businesses to secure better access to markets, but also unions and other stakeholders to promote a level playing field across EU Member States in public policy and regulation. As interest groups gravitate to the European level, they sustain societal support for an increase in supranationalism (Stone Sweet and Sandholtz 1997). Lastly, the *spillover* hypothesis expects political cooperation among Member States, plus new EU institutions, powers and resources to expand beyond public policy areas that have already been Europeanized to include ones that remain in the national realm. The outcomes of the spillover effect are the generation of new, common goals, the transfer of sovereignty from the national to the supranational level and better coordination of national and European public policy (Schimitter 2005).

Neo-functionalism identifies three types of spillover: functional, political and cultivated spillover. Functional spillover occurs when Member States' collaboration on one issue requires further collaboration in order to fully achieve the original goal. An example of functional spillover is the single market, where the original goal of facilitating trade has led to the adoption of regulations at the European level to ensure minimum standards and coordination across national administrations (Jensen 2016). Political spillover takes place when national governments realize that a given issue cannot be addressed at the national level due to the transnational nature of the problem and therefore requires a supranational approach (Turkina and Postinikov 2012) and is closely related to the elite socialization hypothesis (Jensen 2016). Finally, cultivated spillover concerns the role of supranational institutions in promoting integration. This follows the neo-functionalist belief that, once created, supranational institutions are not under the control of Member States but act as policy entrepreneurs in the pursuit of ever-closer integration (Haas 1958).

A critical component of neo-functionalist models stems from expectations of path dependence and increasing returns at the European level. Path dependence refers to how political actors, bureaucrats and interest groups stick to commitments made in the past, particularly institutionalized ones that lock them into a restricted set of policy options into the future. Even if they perceive disadvantages to their current arrangements, they are likely to eschew radical departures and prefer an evolutionary change that respects inherited structures. This path dependence may rest on material calculations, in which the benefits of continuing on the same path are called increasing returns, based on the design of public policy and institutions with particular foundations in mind, and can be considered as positive feedback processes (Pierson 2000). They may also have an ideational component, in which political actors heavily discount proposals to move in another policy direction, based on the previously established policy paradigms. Either way, the expectation is that, once committed, Member States and other actors faced with a poorly functioning EU policy area should be expected to conflict over how it should be adapted, rather than scrapping it altogether or withdrawing as a Member State.

As Niemann and Ioannou (2015), Verdun (2015) and Schimmelfennig (2015) underline, some European leaders explicitly acknowledge path dependence in critical cases at the core of the EU's development. In the case of EMU and eventually Banking Union, German Finance Minister Schaüble warned that the collapse of the euro would destroy much of what the EU had achieved (Wittrock 2011). Even more explicitly, Spanish Prime Minister Rajoy argued that Member States could not just abandon the euro and its consequences just because the obligations it imposed were inconvenient (Rajoy 2013). This ultimately means that Member States are not in full control of the integration process or its consequences. While Schmitter (2005) sees the further delegation of powers as the most convenient solution, and the most likely outcome given the presence of non-state actors (Risse-Kappen 1996) and European institutions (Jensen 2016), others see intergovernmental negotiations constrained by a common desire to make existing agreements work, which leads them to develop Banking Union to save EMU, albeit with strong intergovernmental input. If this is the case, then we should expect the Italian and Spanish governments to accept their legal obligations under EU law, having negotiated and accepted the terms of the agreement. While looking for ways to bend the law is conceivable, breaking it (Donnelly and Asimakopoulos 2020) is not expected.

Scholars embracing neo-functionalism explain the establishment of Banking Union as a response to functional dissonances, amplified by the occurrence of the economic crisis (Epstein and Rhodes 2016). These authors underline the necessity of creating more and stronger institutions, particularly supranational ones to deal with evolving challenges (Sadeh 2019), as well as supranational interest groups' and supranational institutions' proactive role in giving momentum to the maintenance of the euro in the most critical phases of the crisis, including open advocacy in favor of a complete Banking Union in several occasions, nudging elites towards maintaining the euro and increasing integration.

In particular, Niemann and Ioannou (2015) underline the ECB's proactive role in implementing several monetary policy measures to address the secular weakness of economic growth in the Eurozone and openly advocating in favor of a complete Banking Union. In addition to that, the authors argue that, despite initially taking on a rather passive role, the Commission and the Parliament successfully pushed in the direction of delegating supervisory and resolution powers to the EU level. Epstein and Rhodes (2016), meanwhile, emphasize the ECB's and the Commission's role in promoting Banking Union, and how supranational institutions managed to achieve a further step towards an ever-closer union. Furthermore, they point out how analysts tend to stress Germany's victories in the Banking Union's negotiations and to forget all the concessions that Germany and its allies were forced to make as a result of supranational pressures produced by a coalition of supranational institutions, Member States and private actors.

Neo-functionalism links path dependence and increasing returns to European integration with the Commission and ECB guiding and socializing other actors to go down the path. This phenomenon is rather clearly observable in the development of Banking Union, where the existence of the common market first motivated Member States to create a common currency, which in turn created the need for the harmonization of economic policy at first, and later for the establishment of common institutions such as the Single Supervisory Mechanism (SSM) and the Single Resolution Mechanism (SRM) (Zimmermann 2016; Epstein and Rhodes 2016).

Nevertheless, the neo-functional approach downplays the role of Member States in ways that fail to fully account for their behavior, and which, we argue here, also discount path dependency at the national level, which can lead to conflict over potential collective decisions, and even foot-dragging over implementation. Neo-functionalist literature on Banking Union acknowledges but underplays the prominent role of intergovernmental negotiations to supply new institutions for EMU. For Niemann and Ioannou (2015), the Commission played its most 'proactive role once the heads of state broadly agreed to move ahead with further integration'. Germany's commitment to making EMU work was present, but its reservations on Commission and ECB proposals were non-trivial and crucial to explaining the form of EU institutions moving forward. This finding of institutional activism is supported and extended to include the Council by Nielsen and Smeets (2018). The next section looks to intergovernmental theory in search of tools that give greater weight to these nationally defined parameters.

Intergovernmentalism

In contrast to neo-functionalism, intergovernmentalism assumes that Member States are powerful, rational actors that largely control the integration process and only enter into arrangements that are compatible with domestic politics. Some smaller countries might find themselves outvoted in areas with qualified majority voting, but larger countries like Spain and Italy should be able to represent themselves to meet domestic needs. This assumption is only qualified when specific circumstances render countries vulnerable to non-agreement, which weakens their bargaining positions. Drawing from realist international relations theory, intergovernmentalism regards nation-states as self-interested, rational actors that are fundamentally interested in maximizing power resources, paying attention to relative gains (how international cooperation influences a country's position in the international system relative to others) and retaining sovereignty (Hoffman 1966; Cini 2016). Countries are only expected to engage in international organizations if it allows them to strengthen, and not lose grip of, their control over domestic affairs (Milward et al. 1992; Keohane 1984; Moravcsik 1993).

Member States are expected to create and use European institutions as agents to better achieve goals without losing sovereignty, creating a principal-agent dynamic that arises between themselves (principals) and EU institutions (agents) (Pollack 2002). In this dynamic, Member States delegate tasks to EU institutions but pay close attention to their original mission and monitor the agent's behavior to avoid a growing gap between their preferences and that of the agent. As a consequence, the design of international institutions needs to reflect states' goal of safeguarding and strengthening sovereignty (Pierson 1998).

In a scenario with such strong-willed and powerful Member States, European institutions are primarily conceived as instruments used by Member States to facilitate the achievement of their goals in the international arena, and there is no transfer of power or sovereignty towards supranational institutions (Keohane and Hoffman 1991). Countries build and make use of international institutions because they provide them with a set of benefits: they drive down transaction costs, reduce information asymmetries, monitor compliance and reduce the chances of withdrawal (Pierson 1998). This has two implications: that governments willingly choose to support European institutions (so they know what they are getting into in advance) and that they are expected to retain some room for domestic design and implementation after EU law and institutions are established. Major changes are not foreseen until a change in government has taken place, reflecting a considerable shift in societal (reflecting economic) preferences.

Classic intergovernmentalism views European cooperation as possible, but pragmatic: Member States understand that it is more convenient to solve common problems with common solutions (Cini 2016). As a consequence, countries must have a clear benefit from cooperation that offsets any costs and are expected to use what power they have to strike convenient deals. This may involve threats of unilateral action in the absence of a deal or in withdrawal from the negotiating table or existing institutions. An example of the latter can be found in the empty chair crisis of 1965.

All in all, intergovernmentalism paints a much less idealistic image of European integration than neo-functionalism: from the intergovernmentalist perspective, Europe is not bound to an ever-closer union, but to a collection of collaborations based on mutual benefits that are shaped by international power dynamics. In other words, according to this theory, there is nothing intrinsically different in the EU that distinguishes it from other international organizations. The institutional bargains only go further than cooperation and delegation found elsewhere as long as Member States are willing to support them (Moravcsik 2018).

Although it is not often used in its original form in current literature, intergovernmentalism has been able to adapt through the years, and to transform into two varieties of intergovernmentalism, which are still widely popular: liberal intergovernmentalism (LI) and new intergovernmentalism. These two versions of intergovernmentalism have been used as a basis to analyze the establishment of Banking Union. Therefore, the next two sections provide an overview of both LI and new intergovernmentalism.

Liberal intergovernmentalism

Just like classic intergovernmentalism, liberal intergovernmentalism (LI) builds on the assumption of rational state behavior (Cini 2016). According to LI, European integration is a set of rational choices made by rational leaders in response to international interdependence (Schimmelfennig 2015). On top of that, however, LI sets out to address issues of preference formation (the national interest); of relative power and asymmetrical interdependence in determining whose interests are likely to prevail in international negotiations; and to explain the establishment of supranational institutions (Moravcsik 1998). In order to do that, LI offers a tripartite explanation of integration, composed of economic interests, determined domestically and negotiated internationally; relative power between countries, which is shaped by asymmetrical interdependence; and an interest in ensuring credible commitments to collective action, the need of which may result in the establishment of supranational institutions.

These three factors are posited to be responsible for the form, substance and timing of the most important steps in the integration process (Moravcsik 1998).

Overall, LI considers the EU to be a 'successful intergovernmental regime designed to manage economic interdependence through negotiated policy coordination' (Moravcsik 1993), and one that has reached a stable equilibrium, in which the Member States have reached the outer limits of cooperation they are willing to agree to.

LI understands national governments to be playing a two-level game when dealing with the outside world, similar to the one described by Putnam (1988): governments first define their interests domestically (level I) and then engage in international negotiations to satisfy those interests (level II). In this two-level game, LI sees the economic and commercial interests of Member States as the main drivers of integration, and the raison d'être behind the most important negotiations in the history of the European Union (Moravcsik 1998). Within the European integration process, preference formation can be thought of as a demand for cooperation, whereas the international negotiating table can be seen as the supply for integration (Moravcsik 1993).

On the national-level (level I) liberal theories of national preference formation, see national governments securing and maintaining power by forming coalitions of support among interest groups, particularly economic interest groups that have clear material preferences that can translate into coherent foreign economic policy preferences. The set of interests outlined at the domestic level drives governments towards seeking cooperation with other states. Thus, Level I produces a demand for cooperation (Moravcsik 1998).

Despite the complexity of domestic preference formation, LI considers nation-states as unitary actors based on the aggregation of interests in the policy formation process. Moreover, it assumes that the preferences formed by bargaining and interaction between a wide range of actors at the national level eventually generate a consistent set of interests (Moravcsik and Schimmelfennig 2009). Interest groups articulate preferences that are likely to be stable over time, and governments aggregate them to secure their support and stay in office.

Once national preferences are defined, the game moves on to the international negotiating table (Level II), which aims to satisfy the demand for cooperation with the supply of integration. Here, intergovernmental theories of inter-state relations help understand how national governments seek alliances and use power to strike deals that reflect their domestic demands (Moravcsik 1993). Within LI, negotiations are defined as a process of collective choice through which conflicting interests are reconciled. States are considered rational actors and thus are expected to pursue the course of action that maximizes their gains or satisfies preset requirements (Moravcsik 1993; Moravcsik and Schimmelfennig 2009). Although solutions aligned with national preferences are to Member States the best possible outcome, states are willing to compromise: second and third best options that are often more acceptable than walking away (Moravcsik 1993). This has important implications for implementation: all Member States are sufficiently satisfied with the results to generate and perpetuate a stable equilibrium. What Member States can't stand, they don't establish.

LI sees relative power as having crucial impacts on the outcome of international negotiations. Relative power is shaped by asymmetrical interdependence, and Member States exploit it while bargaining in order to get the most advantages out of the deal (Moravcsik 1998). Those with the greatest ability to survive without an agreement possess a heightened capacity to walk away and are likely to have better bargaining positions than others and achieve outcomes closer to their optimal scenarios. Others, meanwhile, may require a deal more urgently. Those countries are expected to move down their list of preferences quickly to secure a deal. As long as there are positive-sum gains to be made in the agreement, one should be expected, even when the relative gains are uneven (Cini 2016). EU institutions and agreements solidify agreement on the terms of collective action by enhancing credible national commitments (Pollack 2002) and monitor compliance into the future. EU institutions can raise the cost of non-compliance for individual states, thereby deterring it. For the EU as a whole, the implicit threat of widespread non-compliance is the return of unbridled national competition, which Member States originally sought to suppress.

In this sense, LI treats defection as a relatively minor problem, given that concessions have already been made and institutionalized. This has implications for the study of economic nationalism in the EU: while we may assume that governments will do the utmost to protect and promote their 'own' companies, we should expect them to do so within the recognized bounds of EU law and institutions. It also allows us to distinguish between sanctioned and illegal behavior, between expected and unexpected. Liberal economic nationalism (LEN) is fully compatible with liberal intergovernmentalist expectations, while economic nationalism without liberal guardrails is not. LI expects states to restrain economic nationalism that pursues mercantilist politics to the detriment of international commitments, due to the losses and opportunity costs that would follow from defection. These losses would extend into the future as the country would remain outside trade-enhancing institutions, and the state's reputation for breaking commitments would impede the agreement of new arrangements when it wished.

While there is a multitude of research on how domestic preferences coupled with power politics have shaped the development of Banking Union (Howarth and Quaglia 2016), the Italian case in particular raises questions about the possibility of defection or renegotiation of European rules by a large Member State. These are found in the fields of bank supervision, capital adequacy standards, state aid and bank resolution. In other words, the Italian case puts the LI assumption of stable equilibria into question at the implementation stage.

We suggest further in line with intergovernmentalist thinking that size matters. Being the Eurozone's third-largest economy, Italy, as a member of the G7, is likely to have considerable leverage when requesting flexibility on state aid and Banking Union rules that affect the ownership of banks and the role of the state in shaping it in comparison to countries with a smaller portion of the EU's GDP, much less than small states like Greece or Cyprus. What is interesting here is that while we think of access to financial resources as a critical power resource when designing institutions that benefit Germany, the sheer size of an economy and the implications of policy failure can also be a source of bargaining power when it comes to implementation, which benefits Italy. This appears to be most useful in bargaining with European institutions, particularly the European Commission and the Single Resolution Board, rather than the ECB. But the concessions that Italy wins with the Commission and Single Resolution Board (SRB) must also pass muster in Council, meaning that Italy's size is considered there as well when deciding on the flexibility of European rules. Given this, we look next to a discussion within the intergovernmentalist literature that theorizes how the EU deals with national sensitivities on EU policy that generate instability.

New intergovernmentalism

New intergovernmentalism takes aim at two of LI's main assumptions. The first is that negotiations result in stable equilibria, and the second is that EU institutions are strong enough to ensure credible commitments on the part of the Member States (Bickerton et al. 2014). Bickerton, Hodson and Puetter develop six hypotheses that they argue explain an integration paradox, that is the occurrence of integration that empowers national governments rather than supranational institutions.

The first hypothesis concerns the wide use of *deliberative and consensual decision-making* in day-to-day EU-level politics. Although deliberative and consensual decision-making has traditionally been seen at the EU level as a tool used by supranational institutions to pave the way to supranationalism, it is elevated to a routine and defining procedure for EU governance and policy-making within the most intergovernmental European institutions such as the European Council, the Council of Ministers and the Eurogroup (Bickerton et al. 2015: 29–30). It is through inter-state deliberative and consensual decision-making that the European Union achieved further integration in the last 25 years, including in key economic areas such as the Economic and Monetary Union (Puetter 2012). This fact cannot be explained by existing theories of integration and is therefore identified as the first theoretical gap that new intergovernmentalism aspires to fill in.

The second hypothesis is that *supranational institutions since 1992 have been reluctant to extend their powers.* While neo-functionalist analyses expect supranational institutions to actively seek further integration and institutional responsibilities, and liberal intergovernmentalism foresees strong EU bodies where there is political agreement to bestow them, new intergovernmentalism sees the Commission in particular pursuing projects that do not require further supranationalism, such as enlargement under the Prodi Commission, or institutional reform under the Santer administration (Bickerton et al. 2015: 31). This cautious attitude is thought to reflect a decrease in permissive consensus and the complexity of preference formation at the supranational level (Hodson 2015). Rather than pursuing supranationalism, new intergovernmentalism expects EU institutions to engage in strategic behavior that leads to fewer proposals for supranational powers.

The third hypothesis is that the *EU pursues integration without supranationalism* in many cases (Bickerton et al. 2014). Rather than being assigned to traditional supranational institutions, new tasks are delegated to so-called *de novo* bodies. De novo institutions have considerable autonomy and discretion in filling in the details of European public policy, as well as control over their own resources. Their governance structure guarantees room for national competent authorities to dominate the decision-making and defend national interests, which leads to considerable deliberation and mutual accommodation. The European Central Bank, the European Banking Authority and the Single Resolution Board are held forth as examples (Bickerton et al. 2015: 3, 264). While the ECB can better be thought of as a strong institution in its own right, the latter two certainly fit the definition of a de novo institution.

The fourth hypothesis expects that *domestic political problems become inputs of the integration process.* Rather than assuming the domination of business interests that favor integration, new intergovernmentalism contends that Euroscepticism and concerns around representation and legitimacy of EU institutions degrade the permissive consensus around EU integration and incorporate the post-functional politics of dissent and identity that underlie constraining dissent on EU policy-makers (Hodson and Puetter 2019; Hooghe and Marks 2019; Börzel and Risse 2009; Webber 2019). The decline of structured, organized interest associations and political party affiliation makes interest aggregation and articulation more difficult, resulting in a dysfunctional working of representative democracy (Bickerton et al. 2015: 33–34).

The fifth, related hypothesis is that *societal changes outlined above undermine national willingness to support new supranational powers.* Disorganized domestic politics blur the distinction between high politics, which are matters of crucial importance for nation-states, and low politics that Member States are willing to compromise on, with fewer agreements on binding EU powers and rules as a result. This uncertainty for national governments is also suggested as an explanation for the rarity of ultimatums and withdrawal threats in EU politics (Bickerton et al. 2015: 34). However, to the extent that banking becomes high politics rather than normal economic policy, it is precisely then that defiance of EU rules might be most likely.

The sixth hypothesis is that *the EU is in a state of disequilibrium* as a result of the previously mentioned phenomena. The EU is thought to lack a coherent strategy or direction, unable to fully square intergovernmental cooperation with domestic preferences. This disequilibrium is the reflection of changing and potentially unstable EU Member States, dysfunctional democratic processes, concerns around EU representation and legitimacy and a rise in populism. It is not seen as a phase, but as a lasting feature at the core of the integration process, which needs to be addressed with a new, creative approach that takes the reasons for domestic pushback against supranational powers into account (Bickerton et al.

2015: 36–39). Indeed, this disequilibrium is a point that others have taken up and attributed to the strong impact of domestic politics on national executives, who may then find it difficult to agree to and abide by new institutions and law (Hix 2018; Donnelly 2021). As we argue below, we find the most promising avenue of inquiry to be a robust analysis of domestic institutions and interests in the tradition of sociological institutionalism, as a subset of historical institutionalism.

Overall, new intergovernmentalism captures elements of instability and national involvement in policy implementation that liberal intergovernmentalism tends to overlook. But their findings can be found in liberal intergovernmental analyses of Banking Union as well. Howarth and Quaglia (2015) confirm that the hypotheses expecting de novo institutions and weak ambition to build up supranational powers are confirmed in the process of Banking Union.

NI's premise that EU institutions have weak supranational ambitions is reflected in some but not all of the Commission and the Parliament's behavior during the post-2008 crisis period. The empirical record suggests that supranational institutions are not hardwired to pursue an ever-closer union but can act strategically if the situation in the Council requires it, promoting stronger or weaker institutions as political circumstances permit. Out of the two pillars of Banking Union established, the SSM, which functions through the ECB and the national banking supervisors, bears the hallmarks of a strong EU institution. It is by far more powerful and independent than the SRM, which functions through the *de novo* body SRB and the national resolution authorities (NRAs). Considering the remarkable set of powers that a supranational institution such as the ECB has received through the establishment of the SSM, and the general importance that resolution has for what happens when the supervisor does its job aggressively, we can conclude that neither LI nor NI generate clear expectations on how EU institutions and legal obligations for Member States develop. It seems to be relevant, however, that in the case of resolution, which potentially involves the closing of a bank and is therefore laden with more political and economic consequences, a de novo institution was chosen.

As seen above, the symmetry between the premises of new intergovernmentalism and the development of Banking Union is mixed. Like Schimmelfennig (2015b), we concur that new intergovernmentalism provides useful insights into the post-Maastricht integration process (intergovernmental negotiations reflecting the domestic politics of the Member States generated institutions that were sometimes quite strong and supranational despite high stakes and politicization) but that these need to be combined with theories of domestic politics to explain outcomes. Unlike a classic liberal intergovernmentalist focus on domestic interest group coalitions driving national government preferences, however, those theoretical tools should unpack the blurring of domestic and intergovernmental politics, and the political difficulty of making adjustments to domestic laws, institutions and practices. At the same time, we share intergovernmentalism's treatment of preferences as one-half of the equation. The supply of EU institutions and law and of delegation remains subject to intergovernmental negotiations and asymmetries in power that can help explain why some institutions are strong and others de novo, and we contend, why some are able to fulfill their regulatory functions while others have more difficulty, at least with regard to some countries. It is here that we can benefit from a corresponding framework for understanding how domestic politics fit into the European framework. Part of that domestic political concerns reasons that national governments are expected to have to comply with or defy European obligations.

LEN has been singled out so far as possibly being an important element in shaping Banking Union, not only at the design stage but in implementation (Donnelly 2018). Nevertheless, LI considers national decision-making to be shaped by preferences which are put forward by interest groups and aggregated by national governments, which then negotiate, based on such preferences, at the international level. With its assumption that institutions develop their own cultures, which might entail sets of ideas similar to LEN, sociological institutionalism can therefore help fill this gap and provide a modification to LI that is closer to the empirical record. The next section will therefore focus on new institutionalism in its different forms and will linger on historical and sociological institutionalism.

However, critics of LI have underlined its inability to explain events from the historical perspective, and for the integration process as a whole (Pierson 1998). Rather, LI serves as a theory of intergovernmental bargaining (Rosamond 2016; Cini 2016). This limit is underlined by Moravcsik (1998)'s definition of integration as a series of choices made by national leaders.

A solution to overcome LI's focus on snapshot moments is to integrate it with historical institutionalism (Schimmelfennig 2015a; Verdun 2015). Historical institutionalism understands political processes as historical phenomena and stresses how previous events shape current choices (Pierson 1998). Historical institutionalism makes use of the concept of path dependence, which neo-functionalist authors (e.g. Niemann and Ioannou 2015) use as a theoretical basis to explain the spillover effect. Within this book, historical institutionalism will not be associated with LI, but with neo-functionalism, with which it has more common features. The potential complementarity of these two theories is however noted and will be discussed in the conclusions. One manner of binding these insights together is presented in the failing forward framework. While both intergovernmentalists and neofunctionalists recognize the power of previous decisions and institutions, Jones, Kelemen and Meunier's (2016) failing forward framework fuses institutions and intergovernmental negotiations into an endogenous cycle of intergovernmental bargaining over EU institutions that then have baked-in weaknesses (institutions are poorly designed to meet the needs of countries that have weak negotiating hands in Council), which leads to future crises and intergovernmental bargaining for new solutions. Howarth and Quaglia (2021) use this model to explain the underdeveloped nature of EU institutions and resources in Banking Union, while Donnelly (2021) focuses on the extraordinary influence of German preferences on these outcomes. In this study, looking at implementation after institutions are created, we look at the potential of states to protect and promote their own domestic arrangements, even when EU law appears to provide little room for this. What we suggest here is that even countries with relatively weak bargaining positions react to institutional rules that do not necessarily fit them well in different ways and exert voice to EU institutions as well as their peers in the Council. A country like Spain can choose to undergo painful adjustment to comply, or a country like Italy can challenge the Commission and the Single Resolution Board for adjustment. We nevertheless are of the view that the larger the country's economy, the greater this voice is likely to be heard in EU institutions responsible for monitoring, decision-making and enforcement, as they consider the financial and political effects of escalating pressure on national banks, supervisors and governments.

New institutionalism

New institutionalism refers to a body of literature that concentrates on the impact that institutions have on political and social behavior, as well as societal efforts to create and reshape the institutional landscape. It criticizes traditional institutionalism for its excessive focus on formalized institutions and for missing out on those crucial interactions between groups that are at the core of political processes (Rosamond 2016). By contrast, new institutionalism approaches propose a broader definition of institution, one that includes all those continuous social interactions that form the 'compliance procedures and standard operating practices' within politics (Hall and Taylor 1996). Within new institutionalism, Hall and Taylor (1996) distinguish three types of institutionalism: rational choice institutionalism, historical institutionalism and sociological institutionalism. We focus below on a combination of historical and sociological institutionalism as key parts of a framework for understanding and explaining the behavior of public and private actors within the EU's Banking Union.

Rational choice institutionalism

Rational choice institutionalism, which lies at the heart of both neo-functional and liberal intergovernmental theory, holds that individuals, groups and states behave rationally and strategically. Within this framework, institutions are considered an important element in understanding political dynamics, as they act as intervening (mediating) variables. Institutions are expected to seek policy outcomes that are consistent with their goals (preferences). Rational choice institutionalism makes use of principal-agent theory and is particularly fitting in EU studies to explain why Member States empower institutions such as the Commission and the European Court of Justice (see Pollack 2002). Rational choice institutionalism has been criticized for focusing mainly on formalized institutions and ignoring informal processes, which are fundamental in explaining policy outcomes. Furthermore, rational choice institutionalism tends to take preferences as given, rather than considering how external pressures can modify interests and preference formation (Rosamond 2016).

In its assumptions of rational state behavior, rational choice institutionalism is used rather heavily in LI approaches to EU institutional development (Rosamond 2016). As a result, rational choice institutionalism shares LI's assumptions that Member States delegate tasks to European institutions as long as it is strategically fruitful, on the basis of rational calculation, and with the purpose of maximizing gains. On this basis alone, Member States should have already priced in the costs and advantages of the agreement to a particular negotiating outcome before it is established, leading to acceptance and credible commitment. In addition, rational choice institutionalism understands the dynamics between actors in the European arena under the lens of principal-agent theory, where Member States (the principal) empower European institutions (the agents) to carry out tasks, while questions of non-implementation do exist and are approached with tools of rational institutionalism through the idea of institutional fit (implementation is poor when European and national institutions are at odds with one another and make it costly: Knill and Lehmkuhl 2002; Börzel 2002).

Historical institutionalism

Historical institutionalism, on the other hand, distances itself from LI and aims to provide a historical perspective on the European integration process. Historical institutionalism (HI) understands political processes as historical phenomena and therefore stresses the importance of temporality and previous events on given political events and institutions. In addition to that, HI pays particular attention to institutions, and to how political processes are embedded in them (Pierson 1998). As a result, historical institutionalism focuses on the long-term effect of institutional choices (Rosamond 2016).

Due to the importance it gives to historical processes and phenomena, historical institutionalism is tightly related to the theory of path dependence and increasing returns. As already defined in the section about neo-functionalism, path dependence concerns the difficulty of changing direction once certain institutional choices are made, whereas increasing returns represent the advantages of continuing on the same path, which arise from a set of institutional adaptations to the selected direction. As a result, it becomes increasingly costly for institutions to undertake choices that were available at the beginning (Pierson 2000).

Path dependence affects institutions in two ways. Firstly, institutions are designed in a specific time and set of circumstances, and for specific purposes. In order to comply with the given purposes, institutions develop agendas and preferences. Institutions might need to interact with other agencies, potentially giving way to a path-dependent dynamics. Secondly, institutions may outlive their creators. In time, institutions may take on tasks they were not originally intended to face, but when they do so they have available the limited set of tools the original institutional design offers them. As a consequence, path dependence constrains and limits policy choice (Rosamond 2016).

Historical institutionalism expects Member States' decision-making to be heavily affected and limited by previous choices. In fact, despite Member States' initial motivation to create institutions with the purpose of maximizing their power (as assumed by LI), path dependence and increasing returns eventually influence the integration process and governmental actions, to the point where the costs of 'non-Europe' are so high that they are not easily considered viable (Pierson 1998). As a result, Member States are considered locked into a process that they initiated but have no longer control of (Schimmelfennig 2015a, 2016; Verdun 2015).

Supranational institutions, on the other hand, are created by Member States to fulfill preset purposes. However, institutional goals might change over time, due to the institution's will to survive, or due to agendas that institutions develop along the way. As a result, institutions develop their own goals, which might differ from the original ones they were created for (Rosamond 2016). Therefore, supranational institutions have their own goals, and a certain degree of autonomy to pursue them. All in all, historical institutionalist expectations are closer to neo-functionalism than to LI, although it distances itself from the notions of ever-closer union that are pervasive in neo-functionalism (Pierson 1998).

Since its formulation, historical institutionalism set out to address and 'challenge' the lack of historical understanding of the integration process within LI (Pierson 1998). However, the point has been made, even among authors embracing an LI perspective, that historical institutionalism and LI can in fact complement each other in providing a thorough account of post-crisis European integration (Schimmelfennig 2015a). Verdun (2015) more specifically applies historical institutionalism to post-2008 changes within the Euro-area financial domain. The author concludes by confirming the historical institutionalist assumption that past institutional choices affect present choices. In this case, they affect the way new institutions are established: new institutions tend to carry over and reinforce the principles and starting points of those that already exist. An example of this can also be found within Banking Union, which replicates EMU policy fundamentals of creating strong limits and supervision of economic activity, limiting Member State capacity to serve as a lender of last resort, and limiting collective responsibility and capacity to provide that function instead. In addition, the choice to establish a combination of strong, centralized supervision for E-SIBs, coupled with more decentralized supervision for other banks and with a weak Single Resolution Board and a decentralized SRM, also reflects this institutional isomorphism between EMU and Banking Union.

Historical institutionalism and LI certainly disagree both on the amount of freedom of choice that Member States retain, on the role and autonomy of supranational institutions and on the impact that existing EU institutions have on both Member States and EU bodies in designing solutions to pressing problems. At the same time, they both overlook the potential importance of domestic, Member

State institutions that can shed light on why European agreements might be difficult for national governments to comply with, and which might consequently form a source of economic nationalism. We consider this in the next section in the context of sociological institutionalism.

Sociological institutionalism

The third and last type of institutionalism is sociological institutionalism (SI). Sociological institutionalism is based on a constructivist understanding of society. This means that sociological institutionalism understands interests as the result of social interactions between actors that have been crystallized into norms of appropriate behavior and public policy, and embedded in institutions. Therefore, sociological institutionalist scholars focus on the role of persuasion and communication within institutions, and on the study of institutional culture (Rosamond 2016).

The first branch of SI, concerning the role of persuasion and communication within institutions, includes empirical studies on so-called 'norm entrepreneurs'. Norm entrepreneurs are individuals and institutions that are able to mold their personal beliefs into shared understandings through processes of socialization (Checkel 2001: 31). This dynamic is most likely to be found where local institutions and the people who lead them are open to adapting to their broader environment. This may happen through norms propagated by supranational institutions but also by the activity of transnational institutions, in which horizontal policy learning and norm adoption based on best practices is expected. While the first method directs attention to strong European institutions like the Court of Justice of the EU, the second argues for greater attention to the Council Committees responsible for discussing national public policy and regulation where the EU's powers are relatively weak. Knill and Lenschow (2005) point to a voluntary process of mutual discussion or problems, comparison of solutions and openness leading to more comprehensive policy adjustment than institutional diversity would otherwise lead us to expect (Börzel 2002).

The second branch of studies, on the other hand, which we focus more on at the national level, focuses on institutional culture. It is concerned with the structure of frames of reference, norms and 'cognitive filters' within particular institutions and their impact on the behavior of political actors. Here, sociological institutionalism holds that institutions heavily influence individuals and go as far as to shape their most basic preferences and their very identity (Hall and Taylor 1996: 948). In so doing, they shape actors' understandings of who they are, what their preferences are and what the preferences of other actors might be (Rosamond 2016). While not necessarily denying change, this more structural approach to norms, institutions and their impact on state and other actors' behavior stresses national, even local, diversity and resistance to change.

There are different ways one might conceive of institutional culture in terms of content. Here, we are primarily concerned with the institutional cultures of banking and bank supervisory and resolution policy. This includes whether and to what extent the institutions in which banking, bank supervision and bank resolution are embedded are infused with norms that are compatible with, or in conflict with the demands of Banking Union, and in particular, the Single Resolution Mechanism. A liberal view of the state, in which regulators and politicians view bank failure or foreign takeover with equanimity, is certainly compatible with the SRM but not found in Spain or Italy. The SRM only truly forbids economic nationalism in the mercantilist sense of the word, in which the state protects and promotes national banks without regard to international commitments and expectations. The SRM does not forbid state aid, but it does place conditions and limits on it. This is compatible with a view of the state that seeks to ensure continuity of business while respecting collective rules of fair play and level playing fields between national governments.

While we primarily think in terms of the scripts that national authorities use to orient themselves and make strategic choices, we include the norms that sub-national levels of government cultivate, possibly in conflict with those at the national level. This proves relevant in the comparison of Italy and Spain since many of the regional, alternative banks under study are intertwined with local councils that may have more specifically particular interests than the national government. The question is then: what impact do these norms have on economic nationalism, banking nationalism in particular? We outline three different possibilities and their nuances in the following sections.

Institutional culture and economic nationalism

Within sociological institutionalism, the study of institutional culture offers a theoretical basis to understand economic nationalism. Although economic nationalism manifests itself through decision-making and policies, it is primarily a set of ideas. Due to the fact that economic nationalism is a set of ideas, and therefore one of the possible frames of references through which actors understand reality and shape their preferences (Rosamond 2016; Wiener 2006), it can be understood to be part of, or driven by, a country's institutional culture. As seen above, institutions develop ideational narratives, which are widely pervasive and influence their members and shape their preferences.

Liberal economic nationalism is one of the possible attributes of national economic cultures, and, just like economic nationalism without the liberal qualifier, it can best be seen as part of a state's ideational toolkit (Pickel 2003). A key difference between the two is that economic nationalism traditionally equates with mercantilism shaped only by the power of government in the international system, while liberal economic nationalism is mediated by international institutions that govern trade and investment, and which are seen as part of the international infrastructure in which companies and states operate. A mercantilist frame entails a role for the state in protecting and promoting the position of the national economy within the international system in terms of market share, and in terms of ownership. Rules, if they exist, are meant to be broken if they are recognized at all. Liberal economic nationalism sees the state as an actor interested not only in protecting and promoting national businesses but respecting its own commitments as it does so.

Core literature within sociological institutionalism with relevance to economic nationalism is the variety of capitalism literature, which has an offshoot known as the varieties of financial capitalism. From its starting point comparing national economic systems financed through either banks or financial markets (Story and Walter 1997), it has evolved to study how financial markets have become more pervasive alongside banks in traditional bank-financed countries (Hardie and Howarth 2013). But differences do persist and are thought to motivate liberal economic nationalism, as national governments seek to protect and promote their own financial systems within the institutions and practices of global exchange.

As with other institutionalisms, there are trimmed-down versions that explain national inertia as the consequence of rational behavior within a given set of institutional rules governing finance within a national economy. This includes whether the state is expected to intervene or not to protect banks (Hall 1986; Moschella 2011), which it usually is in some way. Change is slow and incremental, if it happens at all, since economic, social and even political institutions are thought to be mutually reinforcing—they depend on one another to function in a way that provides for industry, employment, consumption and so on. This is one explanation we test for. We are also interested here in the more norm and value-laden understandings of varieties of capitalism in which these institutions not only exist but are established and maintained by laws and practices imbued with norms—generally accepted practices and legal rules that speak to logics of appropriateness rather than logics of consequence (Colomiris and Haber 2015) that James and Quaglia (2022) apply in their analysis of epistemic differences between regulators internationally. These are expected to be even harder to reconcile with European commitments to the extent that they collide and lead to economic nationalism, either in intent or in practice. These collisions are covered in the literature on compliance with EU law based on transaction costs of change (Börzel 2002), logics of appropriateness (Schmidt 2000) and the question of how politically salient an issue is (Versluis 2007). Alongside economic nationalism that collides with EU obligations outright but is difficult to find in practice, we can conceive of either liberal economic nationalism, which protects and promotes banks within the limits of EU law, exploiting loopholes, or functional economic nationalism (FEN), in which government's failure to comply with external commitments leads it to attempt a renegotiation rather than adjusting domestically. The differences between these are unpacked further in the next section.

Linking (liberal) intergovernmentalism and sociological institutionalism

Liberal intergovernmentalism and sociological institutionalism are not traditionally associated. In fact, the very premises of these two approaches create a gap between them: LI is based on the same rational choice perspective that sociological institutionalism, with its constructivist approach, criticizes. However, some scholars have called for an integration of sociological insights into integration theory, including intergovernmentalism (Saurugger and Mérand 2010; Donnelly 2011), while others have argued in favor of moving beyond rational choice and towards a more constructivist approach (Risse-Kappen 1996). We adopt the first of these approaches to bring insights into economic nationalism from nationally institutionalized ideas.

In so doing, we contend that sociological institutionalism does not contradict LI's assumption that Member States aggregate preferences domestically and negotiate them internationally with strategic purposes, but it adds a normative layer within which these actors frame their interests. Institutional culture is understood to be a set of scripts giving identity to the actors, giving meaning to the policy area and to the actors' places, interests and relationships within it. These are mutually constituted and institutionalized between banks, communities and state institutions. They are capable of evolution and even radical change but prone to inertia that flows from institutional and actor complementarity. Institutions possess institutional culture, which shapes their view of the world and their strategies for dealing with interest groups' preferences.

Several authors have theorized the existence of liberal economic nationalism within EU Member States (Deeg 2012; Clift and Woll 2012), but Donnelly and Asimakopoulos (2020) theorize a connection between banking systems, economic nationalism and intergovernmentalism that we wish to build on here, in which institutions, interests and ideas are bound together with material impacts on bank resolution. We also seek to go beyond that contribution in comparative political economy to make connections between domestic socio-economic institutions that make up the domestic political economy, and the preferences of the state itself as not only a mediator of societal interests.

Institutions and marketization: pulling in different directions?

Donnelly and Asimakopolous (2020) draw on Hardie and Howarth's (2013) framework for investigating varieties of financial capitalism, which focuses on the transformation of banking across countries from more garden-variety banking with risks concentrated in loan repayment rates and the saving rate (as a source of deposits, and therefore lendable capital), to more heavily marketized banks that raise their capital on financial markets—stock, bond and derivative markets. Hardie and Howarth argue that banks can become unstable not only from long periods of economic stagnation (leading to poor repayment of loans), and from a combination of poor risk management and corporate governance (leading to poor lending decisions), but also from tapping financial markets as a source of leverage and risk management. While the additional influx of capital can strengthen the bank's balance sheets for a time, they eventually expose the bank to downturns in financial markets, making them more unstable than otherwise would have been the case. Financial markets dry up and instruments decline in value, forcing banks to either reduce their assets in kind or acquire new capital at a time when it is least willing to invest. Where Hardie and Howarth argue that this can be a rationale for states to seek assistance from governments as lenders of last resort, Donnelly and Asimakopoulos argue that if the investors are widely spread throughout the voting community, governments are likely to be coerced into acting in ways that are effectively nationalist, choosing local politics over European obligations. Such a situation would arise when banks tap depositors as major creditors in the institution, who would be damaged by a closure of the bank (leading to expectations of a bailout), and whose protection would scare off other investors, particularly foreign ones. Governments supervising such banks find it difficult to save or resolve them and stay in compliance with rules and expectations that provide for economic openness, understood as cross-border ownership patterns. This is a phenomenon we call functional economic nationalism.

State strength, liberal and functional economic nationalism

We distinguish here between three types of economic nationalism that are distinct styles of public policy alongside liberalism, as different patterns of domestic influence on foreign economic policy, entailing different perceptions of the state, its capabilities, and its strategy. *Economic nationalism* equates with mercantilism in the traditional realist sense, using the power of the state to protect and promote national companies regardless of international demands and commitments (Gourevitch 1986). *Liberal economic nationalism* uses the state to protect and promote companies within the confines of agreed commitments and rules. Those rules are agreed upon and supported at the international level to ensure a level playing field across national jurisdictions as they open their national economies to trade in goods and services. Thus there are rules and institutions to establish these limits, monitor compliance and allow national governments to retaliate against defection at the global level, at the World Trade Organization (Narlikar 2005; Mitchell 2008), and at the EU level. *Functional economic nationalism*, meanwhile, is characterized by a weak state confronted with domestic institutions, both public and private, that it can poorly protect and promote within existing international commitments. It acts in nationalist ways more by default than by design. The key difference between liberal and functional economic nationalism lies in the capacity of the state to reform societal institutions to pursue gains within international commitments. This is considered relatively high in LEN and low in FEN.

State strength in the sense of regulatory capacity has well-established literature. Quaglia and Maes (2004) posit that state strength varies in important ways across states. In their comparison of France and Italy, this state strength is rooted in the coherence of state institutions that allows for central control. Whereas France has a 'monolithic' state with coherent links between state agencies, Italy has an 'archipelago' state with weaker links between institutions that make state power stronger to consolidate and execute. We adopt, along these lines, state strength as a variable that consists of both infrastructural power and the willingness to act, in the sense of state culture (Hall 1986). Where the power of the state to intervene in the economy and society is strong, we should see a greater willingness to abide by EU obligations than in countries that have weak states. This is compatible with liberal economic nationalism—countries are not expected to break the rules they are supposed to live within (Harmes 2011). Where the state can be characterized as weak, with poor capacity to intervene and reshape the economy, and the socio-economic institutional base is ripe for economic nationalism, we should expect defection and attempts to break EU law, with or without the permission of EU authorities.

Liberal economic nationalism is characterized by state actions that protect and promote national businesses within the bounds of international agreements. This implies a sufficient degree of state autonomy to impose changes on domestic businesses to ensure compliance while hewing to local institutions governing business arrangements as much as possible. States are not expected to be passive. On the contrary, they can be expected to exploit official rules and loopholes, they may lobby for rules a priori that provide this room and they can test gray areas in the rules in court, but the state's behavior should be characterized by working within the rules.

The coincidence of sufficient state autonomy from business to protect and promote business but respect international commitments infers that there exist situations where the state lacks the capacity to do so. The reasons for this may lie with the state itself, but they may also lie with the problems they confront, in the sense that domestic institutions, values and demands are in conflict with international obligations. Within the EU, these are situations where banks cannot be recapitalized and/or restructured or resolved under the SSM and the SRM without inflicting widespread damage on domestic constituents. Banks are naturally interconnected with their environments, but some are more so, making them *too interconnected to fail* for local and national politicians, regardless of size. We theorize that where there are strong, broadly based conflicts between domestic socio-economic institutions and the legal requirements of complying with EU institutions and rules, the capacity of national governments to devise compliant adjustment strategies will drop (Börzel 2002), and their propensity to resist implementation will rise (Donnelly and Asimakopoulos 2020). If weak state capacity is added to the equation (second variable, below), this situation is likely to generate *functional economic nationalism (FEN)*. Functional economic nationalism is not principled in its rejection of foreign ownership and its unwillingness to follow EU rules on state aid and resolutions. In practical terms, however, it will feel compelled not only to not implement its obligations but to lobby for special treatment, particularly from the EU. Economically, it remains too inward looking and interconnected with voters to be of any meaningful interest to outside investors.

As a third variable, we build in external pressure for reform that national governments have invited into the country's banking system. Effectively this is the *agency of the European Stability Mechanism (ESM) and its demands on the national government in exchange for financial assistance.* Where external pressure is accepted (ESM conditionality) and instrumentalized by the national government (European body as a useful scapegoat, laying down conditions that the national government wants to adopt), we expect the capacity of the national government to intervene in the banking system decisively to grow (Lombardi and Woods 2008; Woods 2014). Conversely, where there is a lack of external pressure on the national government in question because the ESM has not been invited, we expect government's capacity to address weaknesses in the national financial systems to be weaker. In cases like these the national government takes on the responsibility for adjustment to financial access pressure without resorting to ESM, as is periodically the case in Italy (Magone 2016; Balbona and Begega 2015).

Overall, we expect the discussion of integration and institutional theory to reinforce Proposition 1 in the chapter above. EU structures in Banking Union not only provide room for economic nationalism in its different forms but should lead to different strategies based on persistent biases in state actors responsible for implementation. Beyond institutional culture and preferences, however, we expect the extent and direction of bank marketization to create incentives for national authorities to choose a corresponding strategy.

Marketization, internationalization and the strong state strategy

The strategies above are independent of the actual pressure exerted by financial markets and concerns about access to investment. We expect exposure to market investment to raise the incentives for states to engage in either liberal or functional economic nationalism under stress, and exposure to international sources of investment to increase the incentives to pursue a liberal economic nationalist strategy. We expect therefore that *the greater the reliance on international investment for the national banking system, the stronger and earlier the government will be incited to pursue a strong interventionist, but open and liberal strategy that meets the needs of financial markets.* Conversely, where the system is largely domestic, we expect the impulse to be slower. The difference in the severity of need, and in prior policy decisions to open up the national financial system to outside investment, can make the difference between liberal economic nationalism, where problems can be handled without breaking international and EU commitments, and functional economic nationalism, which is too busy with its internal problems to deal with them easily.

All of this requires us to raise the issue of how we conceive of the relationship between institutional culture (for the central bank, national bank supervisors, finance ministries and prime ministers) and situational factors such as domestic or international marketization in explaining state behavior. We see these as mutually influencing, even reinforcing each other over time, and as therefore capable of meaningful change. But in crisis situations where the need to act is urgent, we do not expect radical change. Bank systems which are highly exposed to international investment frequently coincide with national governments that permit and promote this feature as part of a national economic strategy that incorporates an ideational affinity for ensuring international investor confidence and high banking standards where this is required. Conversely, bank systems that are highly exposed to domestic marketization frequently coincide with national governments that embrace the protection and promotion of an entire ecosystem of domestic stakeholders whose power only rises as marketization rises. This even means turning on European institutions and commitments where required to make a choice.

The discussion thus far allows us to posit two further propositions and attendant hypotheses as they relate to the case studies undertaken in this book.

Proposition 3: LEN and FEN are tied to varieties of financial capitalism, whereby a weak or strong state is of key importance, but also whether any significant marketization is domestic or international in orientation. International marketization (as well as state strength) increases LEN incentives, while local interconnectedness (as well as weak state strength) increases FEN incentives.

Proposition 4: European institutions provide external reinforcement to these national trends. Member States can forum-shop to a significant degree depending on their desire to reinforce a LEN or FEN strategy.

If we follow through on the outcome of these propositions, we come to the following situational hypotheses that apply to the comparative cases of Italy and Spain:

H1: states comply strategically within Bank Recovery and Resolution Directive (BRRD)/SRM/Directorate General (DG) Comp (LEN)

- States solve problems for EU authorities in advance, allowing national solutions.
- State aid as temporary, patient capital, avoiding distortions of market competition.
- Where state strength to resolve banks is relatively high, and the market imperative to keep international investors satisfied is high, government agencies will implement resolutions quickly and thoroughly. If European support is needed, those agencies will approach the institution with the strongest adherence to resolution law.

H2: states negotiate exemptions to BRRD/SRM/DG Comp (FEN)

- States fail to solve problems for EU authorities, renegotiate terms (special treatment).
- State aid as necessary to save local depositors and stakeholders.
- Where state strength to resolve banks is relatively weak, and the market imperative to keep domestic investors satisfied is high, government

agencies will drag their feet on implementing resolutions in accordance with the BRRD.

Beyond these two strategies, there are two further conceivable outcomes that are useful for checking state behavior:

H3: states comply fully with the BRRD and SRM institutions (liberalism/neo-functionalism)

- States accept bank closures or changes of ownership to secure investment.

H4: states reject compliance with BRRD/SRM/DG Comp (Mercantilist EN)

- States use state aid liberally to prop up insolvent banks.
- National (or regional) ownership guarantees.

When examining state attitudes towards supporting banks, we therefore see fairly clear differences that make it possible to distinguish which of the hypotheses is supported. Liberalism should be confirmed where the state is primarily interested in ensuring the integrity of the banking system as a whole rather than the continuity of a particular bank or the interests of its creditors. Targeted state aid is unexpected. Liberal economic nationalism should be confirmed where the state exploits all legal room to act to ensure the continuity of nationally owned banking systems, including the application of any relevant resolution mechanisms and rules regarding state aid. Functional economic nationalism should be confirmed where the state prioritizes the protection of local stakeholders (bank clients) over adherence to EU bank resolution standards. This can be seen in justifying attempts to renegotiate terms by protecting them. Finally, mercantilist economic nationalism should be confirmed where the state protects and promotes national ownership and deploys state aid where required, regardless of EU rules.

Overall, we envisage a decision-making model regarding how to respond to bank insolvencies in which a stress moment requires a decision from the state over the use of state aid. In such situations, institutional culture, reinforced by the material challenges faced, is key in determining the response. Where functional economic nationalism prevails, state aid will be used generously to ensure national ownership and negotiation with accommodating EU institutions undertaken to generate room for this. Where liberalism prevails, private investment to save banks will be preferred over state aid, even if it is of foreign origin. Where liberal economic nationalism prevails, state aid will be used strategically to restructure banks and promote national solutions as much as possible within international (EU) commitments. Where functional economic nationalism prevails, attempts to avoid restrictions on state aid and bank continuity will be preferred over compliance, in this case with the BRRD.

Methods and further plan of the book

In order to explain the original research question, which is whether and potentially how the Italian and Spanish governments acted in ways that kept distressed banks' ownership national, we need to investigate a multilayered set of European, Italian, Spanish and private actors; matters of national preference and institutional culture; regulatory structures and initiatives, policy implementation and monitoring; and interactions between European, national and even municipal and regional actors. The complexity of this task calls for a comparative case study approach that incorporates actor behavior and statements of intent (Newton Suter 2012; Sturman 1997; Stake 1995; Hays 2004: 218) and supports understanding of the nuanced complexity of European and national policy-making dynamics and explanation of patterns of economic policy and nationalism in a particular environment or context (Starman 2013). We strive first to describe events in a structured, focused comparative case study (George and Bennett 2005; Yin 2003) that leverages process tracing and attention to sequence analysis to demonstrate the goodness of fit with competing theories and hypotheses outlined above (Jacobs 2014; George and Bennet 2005; Collier 2011; Trampusch and Palier 2016; Schimmelfennig 2014) and make causal-process observations (CPOs) (Collier, Brady, and Seawright 2010) on what motivates state, bank and EU institutional behavior. This necessarily requires not only a description of variables (Mahoney 2010) but a clear link.

The case studies take into account the need for construct validity and reliability through multiple sources, cross checking (Bennett and Checkel 2014) and sequencing (Riege 2003) of alternative decision-making models. Internal validity concerns about causal relations are handled by using process tracing to test and falsify specific causal mechanisms (Mahoney 2004), using pattern matching (Trochim 2000), including whether the causal mechanism in question passes hoop, smoking gun or double decisive tests (Collier 2011). In doing so, we strive for external validity, which refers to the extent to which the results of the study can be generalized (Dooley 2009) through multiple observations within the cases (Geddes 2003) without sacrificing internal validity, which process tracing provides (Schimmelfennig 2014). As Clift and Woll (2012) note in their study of banking nationalism, however, we should not exclude the possibility that the results do not decisively support one conclusion over another.

In order to help the data analysis, observations will be categorized under one of the three outcomes enlisted above, or, as might happen, somewhere in between the three. Once categorized, the CPOs will be exposed to four tests and classified into four groups depending on which one of the tests they pass. Such tests are known as straw in the wind, hoop, smoking gun and double decisive tests (Van Evera 1997). These tests revolve around the concept of necessary and sufficient conditions to determine causality. Each of the four results represents a different level of certainty and can be used to confirm, disconfirm, strengthen or weaken hypotheses.

Firstly, hoop tests set necessary but not sufficient conditions for causality and are useful in that they can convincingly eliminate hypotheses. They present one or more pieces of evidence that contradict a given hypothesis and thus disconfirm it. They nevertheless are not sufficient to corroborate a rival one. A smoking gun test, on the other hand, represents sufficient but not necessary conditions for causality and can convincingly confirm hypotheses but cannot disprove one (Bennett 2010).

However, if for any reason the evidence is not sufficient to convincingly confirm or disconfirm hypotheses, hoop and smoking gun tests become straw in the wind tests (Mahoney 2012). In fact, the conditions of a straw in the wind tests are neither necessary nor sufficient to prove causality and therefore can strengthen or weaken hypotheses but do not represent decisive proof (Van Evera 1997: 32).

Finally, CPOs that pass the fourth and last test, the double decisive test, are both necessary and sufficient in assessing causality (Collier 2011). Unfortunately, though this type of test rarely occurs in social science (Bennett 2010).

The scope of the data collection has been limited in terms of time to a period starting with the onset of the Global Financial Crisis of 2008, when economic problems for banks started to build, leading to the use of state aid, followed by demands from Italian, Spanish and European authorities for the banks to raise capital, until 2022, when Monte dei Paschi di Siena in Italy was due to repay temporary state aid received to keep the bank afloat. This temporal limitation protects the data collection from the risk of falling into the problem of infinite regress. Data has been drawn from newspaper articles; journal articles; EU, think tanks and non-governmental organizations' reports; EU, Italian and Spanish government documents and legal texts, central bank documents, and press and journal articles regarding banks. Within this pool, the data has been selected while keeping in mind its dual purpose to describe the incidents and to detect causality (causal-process observations or CPOs).

References

Balbona, D.L., & Begega, S.G. (2015). Austerity and welfare reform in South-Western Europe: A farewell to corporatism in Italy, Spain and Portugal?. *European Journal of Social Security*, *17*(2), 271–291.

Bennett, A. (2010). Process Tracing and Causal Inference. In H.E. Brady & David Collier (Eds.), *Rethinking Social Inquiry: Diverse Tools, Shared Standards* (2nd ed., pp. 207–219). Lanham: Rowman and Littlefield.

Bennett, A., & Checkel, J.T. (2014). Process Tracing: From Philosophical Roots to Best Practices. In A. Bennett & J.T. Checkel (Eds.), *Process Tracing in the Social Sciences: From Metaphor to Analytic Tool* (pp. 3–37). Cambridge: Cambridge University Press.

Bickerton, C.J., Hodson, D., & Puetter, U. (2014). The new intergovernmentalism: European integration in the post-Maastricht era. *Journal of Common Market Studies*, 53(4), 703–722. doi:10.1111/jcms.12212

Bickerton, C.J., Hodson, D., & Puetter, U. (2015). *The New Intergovernmentalism: States and Supranational Actors in the Post-Maastricht Era* (pp. 263–285). Oxford: Oxford University Press.

Börzel, T.A. (2002). Member state responses to Europeanization. *JCMS: Journal of Common Market Studies, 40*(2), 193–214.

Börzel, T.A., & Risse, T. (2009). Revisiting the nature of the beast–politicization, European identity, and postfunctionalism: A comment on Hooghe and Marks. *British Journal of Political Science, 39*(1), 217–220.

Checkel, J.T. (2001). A Constructivist Research Programme in EU Studies. *European Union Politics, 2*(2), 219–249. doi:10.1177/1465116501002002004

Cini, M. (2016). Intergovernmentalism. In M. Cini, & N. Pérez-Solórzano Borragán (Eds.), *European Union Politics* (pp. 86–103). Oxford: University Press.

Clift, B., & Woll, C. (2012). Economic patriotism: Reinventing control over open markets. *Journal of European Public Policy, 19*(3), 307–323. doi:10.1080/13501763.2011.638117

Collier, D. (2011). Understanding Process Tracing. *PS: Political Science & Politics, 44*(4), 823–830. doi:10.1017/S1049096511001429

Collier, D., Brady, H.E., & Seawright, J. (2010). Sources of Leverage in Causal Inference: Toward an Alternative View of Methodology. In H.E. Brady & David Collier (Eds.), *Rethinking Social Inquiry: Diverse Tools, Shared Standards* (2nd ed., pp. 161–199). Lanham, MD: Rowman and Littlefield.

Calomiris, C. W., & Haber, S. H. (2015). *Fragile by design: The political origins of banking crises and scarce credit.* Princeton University Press.

Deeg, R. (2012). Liberal Economic Nationalism and Europeanization: The Rise of Spanish and Italian Banks. Paper presented at the Annual Meeting of the American Political Science Association, New Orleans, Aug. 30–Sept. 2, 2012.

Donnelly, S. (2011). The public interest and the economy in Europe in the wake of the financial crisis. *European Political Science, 10*(3), 384–392.

Donnelly, S. (2018). Liberal economic nationalism, financial stability, and Commission leniency in Banking Union. *Journal of Economic Policy Reform*, 21(2), 159–173.

Donnelly, S. (2021). Failing outward: power politics, regime complexity, and failing forward under deadlock. *Journal of European Public Policy*, 28(10), 1573–1591.

Donnelly, S., & Asimakopoulos, I.G. (2020). Bending and Breaking the Single Resolution Mechanism: The Case of Italy. *JCMS: Journal of Common Market Studies, 58*(4), 856–871.

Dooley, D. (2009). *Social Research Methods.* Upper Saddle River, NJ: Prentice Hall.

Epstein, R.A., & Rhodes, M. (2016). The political dynamics behind Europe's new banking union. *West European Politics, 39*(3), 415–437.

Geddes, B. (2003). *Paradigms and Sand Castles: Theory Building and Research Design in Comparative Politics.* University of Michigan Press.

George, A.L., & Bennett, A. (2005). *Case Studies and Theory Development in the Social Sciences.* Cambridge, MA: The MIT Press.

Gourevitch, P. (1986). *Politics in hard times: Comparative responses to international economic crises.* Cornell University Press.

Haas, E.B. (1958). *The Uniting Europe: Political, Social and Economic Forces, 1950–1957.* Stanford: Stanford University Press.

Hall, P.A. (1986). *Governing the Economy: The Politics of State Intervention in Britain and France.* Oxford: Oxford University Press.

Hall, P.A., & Taylor, R.C.R. (1996). Political science and the three institutionalisms. *Political Studies, 44*(5), 936–957. doi:10.1111/j.1467-9248.1996.tb00343.x

Hardie, I., & Howarth, D. (Eds.). (2013). *Market-based Banking and the International Financial Crisis.* Oxford: Oxford University Press.

Hardie, I., Howarth, D., Maxfield, S., & Verdun, A. (2013). Banks and the false dichotomy in the comparative political economy of finance. *World Politics, 65*(4), 691–728.

Harmes, A. (2011). The rise of neoliberal nationalism. *Review of International Political Economy, 19*(1), 59–86. doi: 10.1080/09692290.2010.507132

Hays, P.A. (2004). Case study research. In K. deMarrais & S.D. Lappan (Eds.), *Foundations for Research: Methods of Inquiry in Education and the Social Sciences* (pp. 217–234). Mahwah, NJ: Lawrence Erlbaum Associates.

Hix, S. (2018). When optimism fails: Liberal intergovernmentalism and citizen representation. *JCMS: Journal of Common Market Studies, 56*(7), 1595–1613.

Hodson, D. (2015). De Novo bodies and the new intergovernmentalism. The case of the European central bank. In C.J. Bickerton, D. Hodson, & U. Puetter (Eds.), *The New Intergovernmentalism: States and Supranational Actors in the Post-Maastricht Era* (pp. 263–285). Oxford, UK: Oxford University Press.

Hodson, D., & Puetter, U. (2019). The European Union in disequilibrium: New intergovernmentalism, postfunctionalism and integration theory in the post-Maastricht period. *Journal of European Public Policy, 26*(8), 1153–1171.

Hoffman, S. (1966). Obstinate or obsolete? The fate of the nation-state and the case of Western Europe. Dedalus, *95*(3), 862–915.

Hooghe, L., & Marks, G. (2019). Grand theories of European integration in the twenty-first century. *Journal of European Public Policy 26*(8), 1113–1133.

Howarth, D., & Quaglia, L. (2016). *The Political Economy of the European Union*. Oxford, England: Oxford University Press.

Howarth, D., & Quaglia, L. (2015). The New Intergovernmentalism in Financial Regulation and European Banking Union. In C. J. Bricketon, D. Hodson, & U. Puetter (Eds.), *The New Intergovernmentalism: States and Supranational Actors in the Post-Maastricht Era* (pp. 263–285). Oxford, England: Oxford University Press.

Howarth, D., & Quaglia, L. (2021). Failing forward in Economic and Monetary Union: explaining weak Eurozone financial support mechanisms. *Journal of European Public Policy, 28*(10), 1555–1572.

Jacobs, A.M. (2014). In Andrew Bennett and Jeffrey T. Checkel, (eds.), *Process Tracing in the Social Sciences: From Metaphor to Analytic Tool*. Cambridge, MA: Cambridge University Press.

James, S., & Quaglia, L. (2022). Epistemic contestation and interagency conflict: The challenge of regulating investment funds. *Regulation & Governance, X.*, https://doi.org/10.1111/rego.12457.

Jensen, C.S. (2016). Neo-functionalism. In M. Cini, & N. Pérez-Solórzano Borragán (Eds.), *European Union Politics* (pp. 86–103). Oxford: University Press.

Jones, E. (2015). Getting the story right: How you should choose between different interpretations of the European crisis (and why you should care). *Journal of European Integration, 37*(7), 817–832.

Jones, E., Kelemen, R. D., & Meunier, S. (2016). Failing forward? The Euro crisis and the incomplete nature of European integration. *Comparative Political Studies*, 49(7), 1010–1034.

Keohane, R.O. (1984). *After Hegemony: Cooperation and Discord in the World Political Economy*. Princeton: Princeton University Press.

Keohane, R.O., & Hoffman, S. (1991). *The New European Community: Decision Making and Institutional Change*. Boulder: Westview.

Knill, C., & Lehmkuhl, D. (2002). The national impact of European Union regulatory policy: Three Europeanization mechanisms. *European Journal of Political Research, 41*(2), 255–280.

Knill, C., & Lenschow, A. (2005). Compliance, competition and communication: Different approaches of European governance and their impact on national institutions. *JCMS: Journal of Common Market Studies, 43*(3), 583–606.

Lombardi, D., & Woods, N. (2008). The politics of influence: An analysis of IMF surveillance. *Review of International Political Economy, 15*(5), 711–739.

Magone, J.M. (2016). The politics of Troika avoidance: The case of Spain. In Magone, J.M., Laffan, B., and Schweiger, C., eds. *Core-periphery Relations in the European Union.* London: Routledge: 233–243.

Mahoney, J. (2004). Comparative-historical methodology. *Annual Review of Sociology, 30*(2004), 81–101.

Mahoney, J. (2010). After KKV: The new methodology of qualitative research. *World Politics*, 62(1), 120–47.

Mahoney, J. (2012). The logic of process tracing tests in the social sciences. *Sociological Methods & Research, 41*(4), 570–597. doi:10.1177/0049124112437709

Milward, A., Brenner, G. and Romero, F. (1992). *The European Rescue of the Nation State* (2nd ed.) London: Routledge.

Mitchell, A.D. (2008). *Legal Principles in WTO Disputes.* Cambridge University Press.

Moravcsik, A. (1993). Preferences and power in the European community: A liberal intergovernmentalist approach. *Journal of Common Market Studies, 31*(4), 473–524. doi:10.1111/j.1468-5965.1993.tb00477.x

Moravcsik, A. (1998). *The Choice for Europe: Social Purpose and State Power from Messina to Maastricht.* Ithaca: Cornell University Press.

Moravcsik, A. (1999). A new statecraft? Supranational entrepreneurs and international cooperation. *International Organization, 53*(2), 267–306. doi:10.1162/002081899550887

Moravcsik, A. (2018). Preferences, power and institutions in 21st-century Europe. *JCMS: Journal of Common Market Studies, 56*(7), 1648–1674.

Moravcsik, A., & Schimmelfennig, F. (2009). Liberal intergovernmentalism. In Wiener, A., & Diez, T. (Eds.), *European Integration Theory* (pp. 67–87). Oxford, UK: Oxford University Press.

Moschella, M. (2011). Different varieties of capitalism? British and Italian recapitalization policies in response to the sub-prime crisis. *Comparative European Politics, 9*(1), 76–99.

Narlikar, A. (2005). *The World Trade Organization: A very short introduction.* Oxford University Press.

Nielsen, B., & Smeets, S. (2018). The role of the EU institutions in establishing the banking union. Collaborative leadership in the EMU reform process. *Journal of European Public Policy, 25*(9), 1233–1256.

Newton Suter, W. (2012). *Introduction to Educational Research: A Critical Thinking Approach* (2nd ed.). Thousand Oaks, CA: Sage.

Niemann, A., & Ioannou, D. (2015). European economic integration in times of crisis: A case of neofunctionalism?. *Journal of European Public Policy*, 22(2), 196–218. doi: 10.1080/13501763.2014.994021

Pickel, A. (2003). Explaining, and explaining with, economic nationalism. *Nations and Nationalism, 9* (1), 105–127. doi:10.1111/1469-8219.00077

Pierson, P. (1998). The path to European integration: A historical institutionalist analysis. In W. Sandholtz, & A. Stone Sweet (Eds), *European Integration and Supranational Governance* (pp. 27–59). Oxford: Oxford University Press.

Pierson, P. (2000). Increasing returns, path dependence, and the study of politics. *American Political Science Review 94*(2), 251–267. doi:10.2307/2586011

Pollack, M.A. (2002). *The Engines of Integration: Delegation, Agencies and Agenda-setting in the EU.* Oxford: Oxford University Press.

Puetter, U. (2012). Europe's deliberative intergovernmentalism: The role of the Council and European Council in EU economic governance. *Journal of European Public Policy*, 19(2), 161–178. doi:10.1080/13501763.2011.609743

Putnam, R.D. (1988). Diplomacy and domestic politics: The logic of two-level games. *International Organization*, 42(3), 427–460. doi:10.1017/S0020818300027697

Quaglia, L., & Maes, I. (2004). France and Italy's policies on European monetary integration: A comparison of 'strong' and 'weak' states. *Comparative European Politics*, *2*(1), 51–72.

Rajoy, M. (2013). Discurso del presidente del Gobierno en la inauguración de la reunión del Grupo de Reflexión sobre el futuro de la Unión Europea Palma de Mallorca. July 19, Madrid.

Riege, A. M. (2003). Validity and reliability tests in case study research: a literature review with "hands-on" applications for each research phase". *Qualitative Market Research: An International Journal*, *6*(2), 75–86. doi:10.1108/13522750310470055

Risse-Kappen, T. (1996). Exploring the nature of the beast: International relations theory and comparative policy analysis meet the european union. *Journal of Common Market Studies*, *34*(1), 53–80. doi:10.1111/j.1468-5965.1996.tb00560.x

Rosamond, B. (2016). Theorizing the European union after integration theory. In M. Cini, & N. Pérez-Solórzano Borragán (Eds.), *European Union Politics* (pp. 86–103). Oxford: University Press.

Sadeh, T. (2019). How did the euro area survive the crisis?. *West European Politics*, *42*(1), 201–226.

Saurugger, S, & Mérand, F. (2010). Does European integration theory need sociology? *Comparative European Politics* *8*, 1–18. doi:10.1057/cep.2010.1

Schimmelfennig, F. (2014). Efficient process tracing: Analyzing the causal mechanisms of European integration. In A. Bennett & J.T. Checkel (Eds.), *Process Tracing in the Social Sciences: From Metaphor to Analytic Tool* (pp. 98–125). Cambridge: Cambridge University Press.

Schimmelfennig, F. (2015a). Liberal intergovernmentalism and the euro area crisis. *Journal of European Public Policy*, 22(2), 177–195.

Schimmelfennig, F. (2015b). What's new in 'new intergovernmentalism'? A critique of Bickerton, Hodson and Puetter. *Journal of Common Market Studies*, *5*(4), 723–730. doi: 10.1111/jcms.12234

Schimmelfennig, F. (2016). A differentiated leap forward: Spillover, path-dependency, and graded membership in European banking regulation. *West European Politics*, *39*(3), 483–502.

Schmidt, V.A. (2000). Democracy and discourse in an integrating Europe and a globalising world. *European Law Journal*, *6*(3), 277–300.

Schmitter, P.C. (2005). Ernst B. Haas and the legacy of neofunctionalism. *Journal of European Public Policy*, *12*(2), 255–272. doi:10.1080/13501760500043951

Stake, R.E. (1995). *The Art of Case Study Research: Perspective in Practice*. London: Sage.

Starman, A. B. (2013). The case study as a type of qualitative research. *Journal of Contemporary Educational Studies/Sodobna Pedagogika*, 64(1).

Story, J., & Walter, I. (1997). *Political economy of financial integration in Europe: The battle of the systems*. Manchester University Press.

Sturman, A. (1997). Case study methods. In J.P. Keeves (ed.), *Educational Research, Methodology and Measurement: An International Handbook* (2nd ed., pp. 61–66). Oxford: Pergamon.

Sweet, A. S., & Sandholtz, W. (1997). European integration and supranational governance, *Journal of European public policy*, 4(3), 297–317.

Trampusch, C., & Palier, B. (2016). Between X and Y: How process tracing contributes to opening the black box of causality, *New Political Economy*, 21(5), 437–454. doi: 10.1080/13563467.2015.1134465

Trochim, W. (2000). *The Research Methods Knowledge Base* (2nd ed.). Cincinnati, OH: Atomic Dog.

Turkina, E., & Postnikov, E. (2012). Cross-border Inter-firm Networks in the European Union's Eastern Neighbourhood: Integration via Organizational Learning, *JCMS: Journal of Common Market Studies*, 50(4), 632–652.

Van Evera, S. (1997). *Guide to Methods for Students of Political Science*. Ithaca: Cornell University Press.

Verdun, A. (2015). A historical institutionalist explanation of the EU's responses to the euro area financial crisis. *Journal of European Public Policy*, *22*(2), 219–237.

Versluis, E. (2007). Even rules, uneven practices: Opening the 'black box' of EU law in action. *West European Politics*, *30*(1), 50–67.

Webber, D. (2019). Trends in European political (dis) integration. An analysis of postfunctionalist and other explanations. *Journal of European Public Policy*, *26*(8), 1134–1152.

Wiener, A. (2006). Constructivism and sociological institutionalism. In *Palgrave Advances in European Union Studies*. London: Palgrave Macmillan, pp.35–55.

Wittrock, P. (2011). Merkels Euro-Fighter rings um seen Vermächtnis. *Der Spiegel*, 10 June https://www.spiegel.de/politik/deutschland/schaeuble-und-die-griechen-hilfe-merkels-euro-fighter-ringt-um-sein-vermaechtnis-a-767883.html.

Woods, N. (2014). *The Globalizers: The IMF, the World Bank, and their borrowers*. Ithaca: Cornell University Press.

Yin, R.K. (2003). *Case study research: Design and methods* (3rd ed.). Thousand Oaks, CA: Sage.

Zimmermann, H. (2016). The euro trilemma, or: How the Eurozone fell into a neofunctionalist legitimacy trap. *Journal of European Integration*, *38*(4), 425–439.

5

BANKING NATIONALISM IN SPAIN

In this chapter we chart the activity of interest groups, state institutions and government on liberalism, nationalism and functional (involuntary) nationalism, with a view to testing the hypotheses in Chapter 2 regarding the impact of banking institutions on government behavior. We assume that interest group pressure for bailouts is constant but that differences across countries may exist depending on the degree to which corporate outsiders and international investors are welcome, both in principle and in practice, and on the assertiveness of the state vis-a-vis the banking sector. We also assume that the willingness to accept European legal restrictions on state aid in particular, and changes to patterns of ownership (that have protectionist impacts) as well, may vary.

As we shall see, Spanish savings banks in particular operated and were financed in ways that made them financially vulnerable early on at the onset of the Eurozone crisis. There were more foreign stakeholders invested in the banks, and there was a more pronounced real estate bubble financed by banks that burst after 2008, undermining the solvency of many banks. This contrasts strongly with banks in Italy, which have predominantly domestic stakeholders and investors, and a more conservative banking culture with traditionally less exposure to foreign investors and financial engineering, which insulated them from pressure to attract international investment in 2009.

By 2009, the Spanish financial downturn had sent banks reeling. Repayment of loans for housing and real estate development stagnated or declined. This stronger fragility motivated the Spanish state's decision to act earlier and more intrusively than in Italy to restructure banking. The Spanish government intervened with a resolution authority, a resolution fund, state aid to finance it while this was still possible, and new regulations were designed to rein in the country's regional savings and loan institutions to prevent the kinds of lending mistakes that had (partly) gotten them into difficulty.

DOI: 10.4324/9781003334583-5

As in Italy, the ability of the state to resolve the banks and have them reduce their non-performing loans (NPLs) encountered resistance from local stakeholders, including city councils and local savings banks. In contrast to Italy, the government was able to borrow money from the EU's European Stability Mechanism (ESM) in 2012 tied to promises to break those links between local councils and banks. International investors were enticed back again after this work had been done. Since then, the Spanish government was able to take an earlier, more proactive approach to restructuring, resolution and state aid as it deals with insolvent banks in conformity with EU law. Liberal economic nationalism can be said to exist in the sense that government and banks act in ways that effectively keep ownership national, but in ways that remain open to outside investment and respect EU legal obligations both in practice and in design.

The rest of this chapter is structured as follows. The next section provides an analysis of the banking sector situation preceding the onset of the Great Financial Crisis, of the initial restructuring challenges and of the early intervention measures undertaken by the Spanish state in the period between 2008 and 2010. The following section provides an analysis of the situation between the first set of reforms already covered and the next wave of reforms that took place through 2012, up to and including the involvement of the European Stability Mechanism for the first time. The next section then deals with the situation after 2012, including new tests for Spanish banking regulators, agencies and the finance ministry. This section provides for an understanding of how restructuring and resolution work differently in Spain, and how that leads Spanish authorities to make the Single Resolution Mechanism (SRM) appear to work well without requiring leniency and flexibility from the Single Resolution Board (SRB) and the Commission's Directorate General (DG) Competition, as is frequently the case in Italy. The final section concludes.

Bank Restructuring before 2012

Early restructuring, 2008–2010

Successive Spanish governments before 2008 had a remarkably consistent approach to bank regulation and reform, which was to privatize, liberalize, deregulate and consolidate the Spanish banking sector. Cognizant of their stronger banking competitors in the European Economic Community at the time of Spain's accession, governments used the seven-year transition period after joining the European Economic Community for the full application of single market rules to encourage banking modernization: the transformation of the country's larger banks from mid-sized, state-owned enterprises to marketized, commercial, global and European players with cost structures that could compete with established banks elsewhere. Santander and Banco Bilbao Vizcaya Argentaria (BBVA) absorbed Spanish competitors by 1994, shifted from family blockholdings to dispersed shareholding by international and domestic investors and then invested outward from 1995 onward, emerging from this ongoing process as internationally diversified conglomerates. These two banks could therefore rely on sources of capital and customers that were more diversified and therefore resilient than those found elsewhere in the Spanish market (Deeg 2012; Royo 2013).

After starting with commercial banks, the Spanish government extended the drive to modernize banks to smaller savings and loan institutions (*cajas* and *bancos populares*) as well. As savings and loan institutions, they would not be able to exploit the type of radical cost-cutting and stock market listing strategy that their larger commercial counterparts engaged in. But they could be freed up to expand their business dramatically, which they did. The starting point for the weakness of Spanish savings and loans in 2008 is characterized by their deregulation, expansion and eventual overextension. Traditionally not-for-profit institutions were responsible for and confined to specific geographic areas, and they were encouraged to liberalize from 1988 onward: moving beyond their home regions, making riskier investments (very high mortgages that both drove and followed a boom in housing prices: Quaglia and Royo 2015) and, finally, borrowing more on wholesale markets to fund the increased lending. A good portion of this wholesale borrowing took place internationally, which amplified the potential fragility of the banking system under stress (Deeg 2012). This effectively shows the liberalization and marketization that Hardie and Howarth (2013) identify as sources of bank fragility.

This also meant that the kinds of challenges Spanish alternative banks faced were different than those of their Italian counterparts. Both were heavily invested in loans to finance local businesses and public works, but the housing bubble in Spain took on much larger proportions than in Italy, with alternative banks making the loans that they held on the books. And since these assets were made possible by enhancing savings (deposits) with leverage, they were immediately vulnerable to the country's housing bubble bursting and investors' reluctance to roll over existing debt (Royo 2013). In other words, the need to solve the problem became quickly acute for the banks and the Spanish state.

Despite this internationalization, expansion and increased exposure to international financial markets to fund themselves, these banks continued to have strong ties to local city and regional councils. These councils in turn acquired vested interests in the growth capacity of the cajas, and close ties to local government, largely in the form of board members and close mutual reliance of public sector decision-makers and the cajas. Half of the banks' boards were appointed by them until a legal change in 2010 reduced that number to 40% (Royo 2013). Corporate governance, both in structure and strategy, therefore remained static, so that the new risks that cajas undertook were neither managed nor regulated sufficiently (Deeg and Donnelly 2016).

When the credit crunch hit Spanish banks, including cajas, in 2008, the Spanish state was preoccupied first with the overall macroeconomic situation and public finances, which had been deteriorating all year, rather than focusing on banks per se. There was a sense that after the previous crisis in 2001, new buffer capital requirements would give them breathing space. Spanish banks meanwhile suffered damage to both the assets and the liabilities on their balance sheets and began using European Central Bank (ECB) repo mechanisms throughout 2008 and 2009 as a primary source of cash, which was then put into buying Spanish government bonds. This was not so much a strategy for recovery as for stopping the rapid drop in banks' exposures to risk. In Spain, banks did this even more strongly than in Italy, holding 67% of government bonds, compared to 45% in Italy by 2012. In addition, Spanish banks turned to their own depositors as in Italy, with some of the same vulnerabilities, though in smaller magnitude. This can be seen in the parallel issuance of 14 billion euros of '*preferentes*' (subordinated debt to retired households) (Santos 2018: 12).

This search for improving balance sheets was driven not only by banks themselves but by the Bank of Spain, through stress test exercises conducted in 2009 and new capital requirements that would put pressure on banks to raise capital (Deeg and Donnelly 2016), and by the Spanish government, which was organizing the institutions for restructuring banks and the banking sector overall. Quaglia and Royo (2015) attribute the sense of urgency in the Spanish government as one informed by bank weaknesses that in turn made it difficult for the public sector to borrow. They show that this imperative for the state to tackle bank problems quickly to solve sovereign lending constraints was far more acute than in Italy. One particular pressure point noted by Santos was a reliance on foreign investment: the large exposure of French and German banks to various sorts of debt in cajas (Santos 2018: 21) as part of the overall foreign indebtedness of the banking system. Repayments were in jeopardy as refinancing on wholesale markets became difficult with the global contraction of credit contracts in 2008/2009.

Institutional innovations can be seen in June 2009, when the Spanish government set up a special purpose vehicle to assist in the financial restructuring of banks, both commercial and cajas. Distress began in 2008 and elicited the government's response to establish funds for buying toxic assets/NPLs. This was the FAAF—the *Fondo para la Adquisición de Activos Financieros* (Fund for the Acquisition of Financial Assets). It was augmented by the *Fondo de Reestructuración Ordenada Bancaria* (FROB) (detailed below), which went further to provide recapitalization combined with restructuring efforts in 2009. But efforts to reform banks faltered on low willingness to bail in, to provide public recapitalization, and even to assess the magnitude of the banks' financial problems (Santos 2018: 8). The Bank of Spain itself stood back and let the FROB handle interventions early on (ibid.: 41).

The FROB, established on 28 June 2009, started with a capacity of 9 billion euros to help restructure banks and was then leveraged to a total capacity of 99 billion euros guaranteed by the government. Royo (2013) notes that the Bank of Spain then impressed on cajas that many of them would have to merge to survive the crisis, decreasing the number of cajas from 45 to less than a dozen and that the FROB would play an important role in the process of bringing the sector back to health. The intent domestically was also to sweeten the pot for large commercial banks with healthier balance sheets and income streams to agree to take over savings and loans' cajas, in the event that mergers proved insufficient to solve the problems those smaller institutions faced.

Outwardly, the government sought EU's approval of state financing and guarantees for the FROB. The Commission's permission was required to approve state aid terms, which would affect the size, interest rates and other terms attached to the loans as well as the prospects for future state aid. Those prospects in turn were related to the reliability of asset modeling for the Spanish real estate market, which also affected stress testing and capital requirements. Spanish authorities had been recording single-digit real estate price declines, while in practice, they had been much greater (Hugh 2010).

The terms of the Commission's approval underlined the administrative powers of the Bank of Spain and of the FROB vis-a-vis the banks. Banks would first have to present plans to the Bank of Spain, as the national banking supervisor, detailing how they would return to solvency. A plan for using the bad bank's funds in the process would then be forwarded to the FROB for assessment, which would then report to the EU's DG Competition for a review of whether the financial benefits would distort economic competition (providing unfair advantages to particular institutions) or otherwise be misused (for example, in providing dividends to shareholders or paying for bonuses to bank management) (European Commission 2010).

The FROB's effectiveness at cleaning up bank balance sheets initially depended on the willingness of bankers to recognize losses, which they were reluctant to do. Among the cajas, the case of Caja de Castilla-la Mancha showed resistance to recognizing losses in 2009. Auditors revealed more losses than the Bank of Spain had been able to detect (ibid.: 36–37). The government's next step was to introduce a 2010 Royal Decree focused on reforming the corporate governance of banks (reducing political ties), making it easier to raise capital and merge banks (Royo 2013). New rules were also introduced to establish a German-style institutional protection scheme, in which banks would pay into a common fund to insure each other but also supervise each other's lending practices, with a focus on maintaining solvency (Deeg and Donnelly 2016). This institutional protection system was the *Banco Financiero y de Ahorros* (BFA).

Early restructuring: regional cajas in 2010

A rapid set of caja consolidations took place in 2010 as problems continued. This was not something the cajas did willingly and which required the state to put pressure on local financial institutions. The result was the creation of Bankia into Spain's largest financial institution after the big commercial banks, alongside a number of small regional institutions that had not yet failed. Caja Castilla-La Mancha (CCM) had received government assistance already in 2009 before the rollout of a restructuring and aid system (FROB). CCM was sold off to Cajasur with guarantees backed by the government, then the caja deposit insurance *Fondo de Garantia de Depositos en Cajas de Ahorro* (FGDCA) in May 2010. Seven cajas (Bankia, Bancaja, Caja de Canarias, Caja de Avila, Caja de Laeitana, Caja de Segovia and Caja de Rioja) then agreed to create the BFA with the help of the FROB in June 2010. Bankia then constituted by far the largest of the cajas. The latter cajas survived another two years with strong ties to regional governments until corporate governance reforms separated the banks from regional government control and moved social service responsibilities to foundations (below). This state of affairs persisted until these cajas were folded later into Bankia.

The BFA was finally established in December 2010, starting operations in January 2011. It began working as a holding company for the cajas. Shortly thereafter it was transformed into a special purpose vehicle, a so-called bad bank which took over NPLs from the member institutions, and simultaneously received 4.5 billion euros in five-year loans from the FROB, the government's emergency restructuring and recapitalization fund. The BFA was to gradually sell off assets that had frozen and declined in value. Bankia then served as the good bank that took over the rest of the business and is supposed to raise further capital by 2012.

Bankia was to raise additional capital on (international) financial markets in 2011 to provide a private sector contribution to the resolution of the caja problem. An initial public offering (IPO) was announced in July 2011 for 55% of shares, with advertisements internationally, with FROB retaining the balance. However, investment banks found that international investors remained concerned about remaining and future NPLs, particularly since the assets of BFA consisted primarily of real estate loans that had dropped in value as a result of Spain's collapsed real estate bubble, as well as potential accounting problems at the bank. Bankia was forced to go to its own depositors when demand proved insufficient to raise enough capital. The search for international investors itself, however, was an indication that outright economic nationalism can be ruled out.

The next sector-wide step mandated by the government in 2011 was effectively a forced merger of commercials and several cajas, in which commercial banks effectively assumed the costs of saving their savings and loan counterparts by linking their deposit insurance systems (Deeg 2012). This bought time to sort out the problem of the cajas more sustainably, during which time the government maintained that further public cash injections were not required. Instead, the search started for international investors to complement the investment taken on by Santander and BBVA. A key stumbling block found by Santander and BBVA when approaching investors was that the latter seemed worried about the overall level of the mortgages on the books of the newly consolidated banks, given Spain's economic downturn, and the potential for high levels of future non-performing loans (Quaglia and Royo 2015).

As this situation dragged on, this insistence that the measures taken were sufficient gave way to a government request for EU's assistance from the European Financial Stability Facility (EFSF) that was activated in June 2012, in conjunction with the forced restructuring of the Spanish banking landscape.[1]

How well did it work? What did it resolve and leave unresolved?

The Spanish cases of bank *resolution* up until this point show that they start earlier than those in Italy, and well before Banking Union becomes an agenda item or negotiation starts with the Commission and Eurogroup over terms of state aid, mergers and ESM loans. A principal context for restructuring happening earlier in Spain was the decision of the Spanish government in June 2012 that its banking system was underfunded and that it required restructuring and recapitalization. Whereas the difficulties of the Italian government were acute and visible primarily in the public sector in 2011, the Spanish government took great care to emphasize that the assistance it sought from the ESM was intended to be spent on recapitalizing banks and that it would go hand in hand with government-mandated mergers and other forms of restructuring. In this sense, the Spanish government was ahead of the curve in adopting measures that would impose costs on banks.

The question, of course, is how these early interventions were motivated, and whether there were structural factors, especially characteristics present at the national level, that made the Spanish government's range of options different, and incited it to behave differently. Furthermore, if there were differences in 2012, were they and the actions that flowed from them sufficiently important to affect attitudes toward banks, state aid and national ownership over time?

This section suggests the following takeaways. Together they point to a variety of financial capitalism that is different than Italy's and that is more capable of adjusting to the pressures of Banking Union and the Bank Recovery and Resolution Directive (BRRD) in particular when they are negotiated and take hold later on between 2013 and 2016. The key differences were the power of state institutions, and the reliance of Spanish savings banks on wholesale finance rather than depositors as bondholders in the years leading up to 2012.

First, state intervention in banking activity was facilitated by the presence of stronger, more diversified Spanish commercial banks that could take over (or be compelled to take over) weaker institutions. The country's largest commercial banks were diversified across the Atlantic (particularly Santander) and Europe (particularly BBVA). This had less of an impact on their relative capitalization and income flow, in comparison to the magnitude of non-performing loans held by their Italian counterparts. They and their supervisors at the Banco de Espana were in a financially more robust position as a result to absorb smaller banks in distress. This in turn was made possible by a national government that looked at bank restructuring as part of a liberal economic nationalist agenda.

Second, the Spanish banks that had become insolvent were primarily savings and loan institutions that had been deregulated in the 1990s and gotten into trouble in ways that were out of line with their original mandates. They had expanded in terms of their geographical reach, the kinds of financial services offered (having been local public banks devoted to lending to households, local businesses and government), and in the context of the Spanish housing bubble, by the magnitude of the loans they had made in relation to the income of borrowers. The newness of these activities, coupled with the swift and evident unsustainability, made it easier for the government to justify their re-regulation as an appropriate move. This was part of a local variant of liberal economic nationalism. Deeg and Donnelly (2016) and Fioretos (2011) identify LEN in the practice of both Spain and Italy promoting national champions through bank mergers. While this domestic consolidation proved insufficient to save the banks on its own, Fioretos points out that the creation of a large savings and loan entity in Spain along the lines of the country's previous commercial consolidations helped overcome political resistance to reform by protecting the social missions of the cajas, and the continued importance of regional authorities. But until mid-2012, this had proved to be insufficient. Unlike the efforts revolving around large commercial banks, the impact of intimate political links between cajas and local or regional governments placed limits on reform and restructuring once the system came under stress. Regional and local governments remained intimately intertwined in the governance of cajas, and major reforms of the savings and loan sector would require further effort on the part of the national government to pry the cajas from the control of its regional counterparts. This is analyzed in the next section.

Third, the overall profile of bank-client relationships was ironically one in which Spaniards were more indebted than their Italian counterparts. Pumped up on credit (both consumers and banks through capital markets), there was little attempt by banks and savers to seek higher rates of return on their deposits on any grand scale by resorting to subordinated debt.

Fourth, and of critical importance in contrast to Italy, was the collective strength of the state, both through the Bank of Spain and through the Ministry of Finance and the administrative/bad bank/restructuring bodies it created (FROB and SAREB), to twist the arms of reluctant banks into mergers, NPL restructuring and finally corporate governance reform and a stripping down of the cajas' political and social policy responsibilities at an early date. This willingness to take the Spanish banking sector by the horns remained incomplete by mid-2012, at which point the Spanish government enlisted the leverage of the EU, through the ESM (below).

Second wave of restructuring: 2012

NPLs were rising very quickly in 2011–2012, and the economic recession was continuing. Recapitalization via normal means (raising capital) continued to be impeded by the not-for-profit nature of the cajas, and the strong regional political control over bank boards (Santos 2018). This extended to Bankia as well as the other remaining cajas, as seven cajas sat on Bankia's board.

As the previous section shows, by 2012, the job of restructuring large commercial banks had largely been completed (though two smaller commercial banks, Banesto and Banif, would be absorbed into Santander by year's end).

The first wave of restructurings and mergers in the savings and loan sector had taken place, but the latter sector was still beset by serious problems. The strategy of merging smaller savings and loans into a larger entity had not generated the hoped-for stabilization of the sector, and Bankia itself proved to be a major source of the difficulty. This led to a series of reforms over the course of the year that would break the control of regional authorities over the banks and place the central bank in charge of their affairs. The Bank of Spain would take over the supervision of banks that made up more than one-third of all banking assets in an autonomous community or have more than 10 billion euros in assets.

At each stage of these 2012 reforms, local politicians and regional autonomous communities prove to be fairly important considerations for national officials in determining whom to blame for the insolvency of banks, and what to do about it (Royo 2013). The interventions that cracked down on corporate governance issues were taken in conjunction with a government request to the ESM for 40/100 billion euros in assistance/line of credit to use in cleaning up the banks without causing further financial contagion. These in turn were taken together with obligations by the Spanish government to restructure the banks thoroughly, including the creation of a bad bank that would be independent of and work better than the BFA. The use of this assistance for recapitalization, coupled together with restructuring within and between banks takes place through the FROB fund, then the bad bank SAREB and the Bank of Spain as supervisor. The Spanish government therefore weaponized the Memorandum of Understanding (MoU) between itself and the ESM to push through these reforms. Spain further agreed to support the introduction of a European Banking Union, with rules and institutions governing supervision, resolution and bail-ins in exchange for loans from the ESM. These terms and measures to reduce risk are written into the MoU with the ESM.

ESM disbursements were made in December 2012 and January 2013, coupled with a Memorandum of Understanding focused on restructuring and recapitalizing the banks. This included cleaning up balance sheets, order reduction of bank exposures to real estate, reduced reliance on central bank liquidity and better risk and crisis management systems. The MoU also included a bail-in of subordinated debt (preferentes), giving the government and banks political cover (Santos 2018: 27).

To handle the stock of NPLs, SAREB (*Sociedad de Gestión de Activos Procedentes de la Reestructuración Bancaria*) was established in December 2012 as an asset management company with private and public capital (de la Torre Viscasillas 2013). It would act as a bad bank for the Spanish banking system and help implement the first use of bail-ins. Small saving banks (cajas) were nearly wiped out: of 45, only 2 remained independent. NPLs and bad assets (especially in real estate) were transferred to SAREB, and capital injections were made. The impact on the banking sector was largely positive—which enjoyed renewed access to capital markets. But the recovery process would be a long-term process. SAREB, as a bank with NPLs as assets, would continue to lose money as long as real estate prices remained lower than at the height of the country's bubble. One of the last steps in returning to the Spanish banking system was underway in 2021. Caixa agreed to a friendly takeover of Bankia in March, which was to be completed by year's end (Reuters 2021).

Leveraging ESM assistance: the 2012 reforms

In advance of the Spanish government's decision to ask the EU for financial assistance, evidence was mounting that there had been an insufficient restructuring of the alternative banking sector and that the supply of new investment capital was lower than needed if the banks were to survive. Bankia played a central role in these developments as one of the country's largest financial institutions. Bankia had attempted to raise capital by selling off the foreign investment arm of BFA (*Banco Financiero y de Ahorros*) for 1.8 billion euros in May 2011 and then on the stock market through an initial public offering (IPO). The IPO plus the sale increased Bankia's capital to just under 3.5 billion euros but ultimately failed to attract enough investment capital from international investment banks and financial institutions. Lingering concerns about NPLs outlined above remained. In the absence of an international market, Bankia eventually turned to domestic investors, selling financial instruments to the Spanish state and to their own customers. While we can rule out the existence of economic nationalism, given the attempt to secure foreign capital, a functional need for domestic capital can be confirmed.

In 2012, the pattern was repeated. An attempted capital increase failed in February, securing just under 4 billion euros in capital. Once again, Bankia found itself struggling against rumors that NPLs out of the mortgage sector were increasing, given the weak state of the economy, and that Bankia would have trouble paying investors back. For its part, Bankia was reporting a profit of 300 million euros, which it touted as evidence of the bank's health.

Concerns about Bankia's accounts proved to be justified when the Head of Bankia, former Spanish Finance Minister and International Monetary Fund (IMF) Head Rodrigo Rato, stood down on 9 May 2012, and evidence of accounting fraud started to come to light. A new head was appointed for Bankia—Jose Ignacio Goirigolzarri, the retired Head of BBVA, who then proceeded to audit the bank's books. Instead of a healthy profit margin in excess of 300 million euros, Bankia was shown to have a loss of more than 4.3 billion euros. Rato was later charged with accounting and reporting fraud in connection with the revelation but exonerated in 2020 of wrongdoing (Aguado and Pinedo 2020). Boirigolzarri requested a government bailout on 25 May. Over the course of the year, Bankia would participate in stress tests organized by the Bank of Spain and involving outside consultancy Oliver Wyman. The results were published on 28 September. It would come to light that Bankia alone had losses of just over 21 bn euros for 2012 (out of just over 59 billion euros system-wide), necessitating not only government intervention but Spanish government negotiations with the Eurogroup for financial assistance. In the meantime, domestic shareholders from the IPO and subordinated bondholders would lose their investments. Court action ensued in 2013.

On 10 May 2012, the reorganization of Bankia started in which Spanish government took control of the bank. The government converted preferential shares bought previously into voting shares, suspended share trading and a bailout of 19 billion euros was negotiated, which the European Commission later approved in November (Reuters 2012). Bankia and BFA were nationalized through FROB (Barrón 2012). This meant that the seven cajas which put money into the BFA lost their investments and the financial support derived from the BFA's loans. Beyond Bankia, Caja Madrid, Bancaja, Caja Insular de Canarias, Laietana, Avila, Segovia and La Rioja (plus Novacaixagalicia and Catalunya Caja, which had already been nationalized by the FROB) were also affected.

Foreshadowing attention in Spain to the corporate governance of cajas from 2012 onward, Boirigolzarri forced the resignation and replacement of the Bankia board, which had previously consisted of directors from the seven cajas that had been merged in 2010. This transformation was intended to professionalize Bankia's corporate governance and pave the way for a resolution of the bank by removing the local and social welfare functions of the cajas from Bankia's decision-making process. Those functions would henceforth be handled by foundations (El País 2012). The regional governments then set up a management board for the foundations. The governments and caja boards were not allowed to block the hiving off of the foundations, and if they did resist, the banks would be closed within five months (by the end of the year). The foundations do not get their budgets from the banks per se but are allowed to own property that generates income earmarked for social purposes. The rest of the money must be raised through donations. This reduces a significant potential source of functional economic nationalism: the social policy obligations of cajas to their local communities.

This separation of cajas from regional governments, and divesting them from obligations to serve social policy, was designed in response to two cases in particular where the conversion of cajas had failed. Caja de Ahorros del Mediterráneo had been besieged by depositors who had bought subordinated debt and been wiped out in the resolution, and in Catalunya Caixa, where the board had required a 75% vote to approve transformation and could not reach it.

Overall, the cajas were unable to repay the FROB's original 4.5 billion euros in financial assistance. The FROB converted this debt into shares, becoming Bankia's primary owner, and then added another 19 billion to totally own BFA and 45% of Bankia. This move had implications for other investors as well, including the bank's clients: preferential shares and subordinated debt were also bailed in and wiped out in 2012. The Spanish government asked for 37 billion euros from the ESM in June 2012, 13.5 of that was earmarked for Bankia in December. A much smaller amount was intended for smaller savings banks (below).

Meanwhile, stress tests were conducted in the summer of 2012 to determine how much money was needed for individual banks and collectively, the broader financial system, so that the government's final request to the Eurogroup for loans could be quantified. The government and Bank of Spain's decision to undertake the stress tests came in May, and the report was presented in September, just before the government tables its annual budget and prepares to finalize its request to the ESM for assistance. Outside consultancy Oliver Wyman was involved, the same company that assisted the ECB in its Asset Quality Review (AQR) reviews in 2014.

Preparing for what came next, the Spanish government issued a decree on 31 August 2012 that upgraded the powers of the FROB to allow it to work as a fully fledged resolution authority. It gained the power to order banks to transfer non-performing assets from their balance sheets if these posed a threat to the bank's viability, transferring them to a bad bank. SAREB was established in December 2012 to take on this role, as a temporary special purpose vehicle with a time horizon of 15 years. The intent was not only to wind down the assets in an orderly fashion but to incite private investors to put up capital to buy the assets, with the prospect of a 15% return on investment by the end of the exercise. In the time between 31 August and 31 December 2012, the Spanish government organized private investors for SAREB, for a total of 55% of the bad bank's capital, with another 45% provided by the state. Among the private investors were most of the remaining Spanish cajas (but not Bankia), and later Santander, ensuring a strong Spanish presence at SAREB. But foreign investors were also represented, including Deutsche Bank and Barclays Bank. SAREB also sold subordinated debt that was primarily bought by insurance companies. It was purchased by a similar portfolio of Spanish investors supplemented by foreign companies (Generali, Zurich and Axa). This establishment allowed Bankia, plus regional cajas Catalunya, Valencia and Novagalicia to transfer 40 billion euros of assets by year's end, and another 15 billion from Banca Mare Nostrum (BMN), Caja3, CEISS and Liberbank in January 2013.

The ECB weighed in on 14 December suggesting that SAREB improve its capacity to incite potential buyers to take on the NPLs. This could be done by turning SAREB into a bank, with the capacity to extend credit to buyers, or by making arrangements with servicer companies who would manage such arrangements on its behalf. The Spanish government elected for the latter of these two options, and these proposals were reflected in SAREB's business model. SAREB then concluded four contracts with investors with US private equity firms that were interested in being involved in the Spanish real estate sector. Texas Pacific Group (TPG), Apollo, Blackstone and Cerberus invested in Spanish platforms that specialized in winding down real estate assets and deriving value from this debt. The payoff for the firms was to be first in line to purchase. TPG invested in Servihabitat for Caixa Bank, Blackstone invested in the Catalunya/Caixa platform, Apollo invested in the Altamira platform for Santander and Cerberus into Haya Real Estate for Cajamar. SAREB awarded contracts to these four servicers in 2014, which got the process started. After these interventions, Caixa made a recovery (Buck 2015), consolidating and later expanding its position in the Spanish market (below).

On the other side of the equation, SAREB also made contracts with local governments to increase social housing in the wake of cajas no longer having legal responsibility for local social policy, and the far more limited resources of the foundations that were supposed to promote local social policy goals in their stead. This side of the equation was politically necessary because as the private investors bought up and repossessed real estate, they also evicted residents from where they were and often ended up in court to combat residents who would not move and were designated as squatters (Hale 2017).

These foreign investments have been sufficiently stable to be deemed a successful if long-term management of Spain's real estate portfolio that landed on hard times at the start of the Great Financial Crisis. Blackstone still manages its portfolio, from which it sells properties according to plan (Durán 2021). Cerberus managed a large portion of rentals through Haya (Sousa 2020). TPG still managed a portion but sold back more than 50% of its holdings to Caixa in 2018 (Diaz 2018). Meanwhile, Apollo sold Altamira to doBank, a subsidiary of the American-based Fortress Investment Group in 2018 (Expansión 2018). There has to date been no indication that new owners could not be found when an investor wanted to sell. On the contrary, the funds appear to have held their attraction, even during the Great Pandemic that started in 2020.

SAREB's creation provided important tools for the Spanish state and Spanish cajas, as well as the broader banking sector, to reorganize what was left of the savings and loans sector in ways that had not previously proven possible, and which turned out to have advantages when contrasted with the lack of such an instrument in Italy (discussed below). Before the creation of SAREB, it was difficult for Spanish savings banks to offload NPLs to institutional investors, which made it difficult to resolve the bank short of closing it down. SAREB helped change that, taking on nearly 100 billion of NPLs. Private equity groups, including foreign ones, were then keen to purchase these mortgages, although naturally at reduced rates. (Chassany, Hammond and Johnson 2013). With SAREB as a middle merchant between the cajas and investors, sales could be made and connections cultivated that might not have happened otherwise, given the reluctance of cajas to sell at a discount, their lack of international investment bank or private equity connections, and the new issue of detaching the cajas from their social policy obligations (above). The establishment of SAREB in 2013 also provided a means to meet acute pressure on the part of the European Banking Authority to reduce NPLs, raise capital and reduce forbearance. This was given further impetus through the selection of the ECB as the Single Supervisory Mechanism supervisor, and its independent conduct of the Asset Quality Review in 2014 (Masters 2013). This meant that more effort would have to be put into offloading NPLs.

In the context of Spain's willingness to act on making resolution and bad banking workable, the Eurogroup had already approved a 100 billion euro line of credit through the ESM for the Spanish government, but Spain needed to express how much it needed. It asked for 38 billion at the end of September 2012. This would help it manage the undercapitalization of banks, which was estimated at 59 billion euros (Tymkiw 2012). The capital injections would require restructuring and resolutions, which would need to be approved by DG Competition at the European Commission. This was still at a moment when the Commission's Banking Communications underlined the need for state aid to be available for as long as the Eurozone's economic difficulties persisted, but for an exit strategy to exist, and for DG Competitions' right to impose conditions on market dominance and national discrimination be respected (Doleys 2012).

All of these reviews were pre-BRRD. However, the use of state aid came with conditions that foresaw the BRRD. Banks had to shed branches and staff and bail in shareholders and creditors. The cost of restructuring the savings banks in Spain was thereby considerably cheaper, to the tune of 14 billion euros (Thompson 2012). Between November and December of 2012, state aid talks with the Commission allowed for Bankia, Catalunya Banco and NCG Banco to return to market. Banco de Valencia was sold to Caixa Bank (European Commission 2012b).

These initiatives came with a number of conditions: shareholders would be wiped out. Balance sheets were to be reduced by 60% and refocus on lending to households and small and medium-sized enterprises in their historical regions (post-merger). They were to stop financing real estate development and wholesale business. Non-performing real estate assets would be transferred to SAREB industrial stakes, and subsidiaries would have to be sold off. Bankia and Catalunya would have to divest trading/treasury portfolios for fixed income instruments, and Catalunya Banc would have to divest from venture capital funds, making them garden variety savings and loans again. Pay limits for management would be introduced. With this in the background, the FROB would be tasked with selling NCG Banco and Catalunya Banc within five years or provide an orderly resolution plan (Garrigues 2012; Toyer and Dowsett 2012).

A residual issue for Bankia was the corporate governance of the bank. As with many cajas, including the ones that preceded it, Bankia had strong links to local government, business associations and union representatives. While this constellation of actors on the board of the caja is not synonymous with poor governance and financial performance (see Sparkasse savings banks in Germany), it was synonymous with political direction based on lowest common denominators. These in turn inhibited reform during the time of contraction and encouraged expansive and debt-fueled behavior under conditions of deregulation. This strategy of leveraged lending, fueled by stakeholder governance and deregulation attracted criticism from Bankia's new CEO in 2012, who wished to see Bankia operate and behave as a private institution rather than a public concern (Garcia 2016).

After the reorganization, Bankia remained alive and able to access financial markets, but in fragile condition and under effective government ownership, with the FROB holding more than 60% of voting shares in 2019 according to the country's securities regulator CNMV (*Commissione Nacional del Mercado de Valores* 2020). A major task for Bankia's management between 2013 and 2015 was to replenish reserves. Bankia could eventually return to capital markets, albeit on terms that would make investors cautious and prevent an accelerated recovery. On 24 May 2013, Bankia underwent a bail-in of subordinated debt and an increase in capital through new preferential subscription rights. It then issued subordinated debt in 2014 to increase tier 2 capital at rates of 4% and was in a position to redeem the bonds early in May 2019 (Bankia 2014; Rosell 2018; Public Now 2019). In 2019, it issued another 750 million. All this time, the share price continued to be low, so low that government plans to sell the shares it held to recoup its 22 billion euro investment though the FROB could only have raised less than 5 billion on the stock market.

This situation changed not long afterward when Bankia was taken over by Caixa Bank. An announcement was made in December 2020 by the two banks that they would merge. But while a merger is friendly, it also involves the creation of a new entity in which both banks find themselves represented. Instead, there are two indications that this was indeed a takeover of Bankia by Caixa. The first is that Bankia's own announcement of the merger indicates that Bankia customers would have their accounts transferred to CaixaBank by the end of 2021 (Bankia Caixa 2021). Another is that according to the ECB's supervisory division, Caixa "absorbed" Bankia, i.e. took it over, rather than speak of a merger of two equals, as Bankia had previously done.

Other banks

Beyond Bankia, a number of smaller institutions were also restructured starting in December 2012 under terms and programs included in the MoU with the ESM, and with the approval of the European Commission (European Commission 2012b). Liberbank, Caja3, BMN and Banco CEISS restructured in December 2012, with 1.9 billion euros in aid approved by the Commission. The Commission's conditions were designed to ensure that the banks could return to viability without relying exclusively on the Spanish treasury and without damaging a level playing field for banks in the single market. The conditions included a reduction in the banks' balance sheets (between 30% and 40% for each within five years), the transfer of real estate-related assets to SAREB and the bail-in of shareholders and creditors, which was to reduce the cost to the state by an estimated 2 bn euros, and a ban on the banks deriving any competitive advantage from the aid and the restructuring (no advertising, no acquisitions of other banks). Intercaja would absorb Caja3. Like Bankia, the banks would focus on retail and SME lending in historical districts.

Liberbank

Liberbank was formed out of regional savings banks in north-west-northwest Spain in July 2011: Cajastur (Asturias) Caja Extremadura, and Caja Cantabria.

The bank was restructured in December 2012, using state aid in the form of contingent convertible securities (cocos) from the FROB (124 m), and with permission from the European Commission. Liberbank had to close some branches as well.

Ibercaja

Ibercaja was created in July 2011 out of east/northeast Spain, from Caja de Ahorros y Monte de Piedad de Zaragoza, Aragon y Rioja. Its role in taking over a group of three other cajas proved problematic, due to the audits of their financial situations. Nevertheless, the absorption took place gradually between 2012 and 2014, with state aid approved by EU authorities.

In May 2012, Ibercaja attempted to absorb Caja3 (which was an amalgamation of three further cajas: Caja de Badajoz, Caja Inmaculada and Caja Circulo) during the wave of mergers in Spain. A stress test of Caja3 revealed problems that would impact Ibercaja negatively. The boards agreed in November to proceed, and during the December deals between Spain and the European Commission, Caja3 was able to raise the sizable sum of 407 million euros in cocos (European Commission 2012a). Liberbank's control was confirmed by July 2013 and followed up with contingent convertible bonds (cocos) worth 163 million euros in 2016, with ECB approval. By 2018, the bank had no difficulties with capitalization (Sarries 2018).

Unicaja

Unicaja formed out of caja consolidation in central Spain, in the region of Castilla y Leon. Its formation proved to be a particularly tough case involving legal fights over creditor rights.

Unicaja attempted to absorb EspanaDuero (from Caja Espana Duero) (Banco CEISS) in 2012. First moves were made in 2011, but lack of agreement on terms (how much weight for each preceding bank). A threatened nationalization from the national government was the shotgun behind the door for the actors to agree to a merger.

Most of the problems revolved around CEISS debt, including contingent convertible bonds. The bondholders did not initially approve the takeover deal with a threshold of 75%, meaning that terms could be imposed on all under Spanish law. Holdouts resisted a bail-in and wanted a better payout than they would have had to accept. Meanwhile, CEISS managed to raise 604 million euros in ordinary shares sold to the FROB in an attempt to save the bank's independence. While this was accomplished in December 2012 in the context of Spain's negotiations with the European Commission, the same kinds of conditions would be imposed on CEISS. And ultimately, CEISS' independence did not continue.

In May 2013, the FROB and Bank of Spain approved a merger of the two entities, with Unicaja in control, set out terms on consequences, including a new CEISS leadership elected in June 2014, followed by acceptance of the deal. Cocos were converted to shares in 2014 after this change in leadership, leaving the bank with fewer liabilities to bondholders. Unicaja later paid back aid in August 2017 and acquired EspanaDuero in December of that year. Absorption was complete by March 2019 (Caja España Vida) after approval by the pension insurance fund (*Dirección General de Seguros y Fondos de Pensiones*). As a result of these mergers and takeovers, Unicaja became the only savings and loan institution in the region of Castilla y Leon.

Banco Popular

Banco Popular would later become a test case for the Single Resolution Mechanism as soon as the BRRD was passed in Council in 2014. Popular was situated in Madrid, and like other cajas it had expanded services throughout Europe in the 1990s. In 2008, at the start of the financial crisis, it absorbed subsidiaries Banco de Castilla, Banco de Credito Balear, Banco de Galicia, Banco de Vasconia, in 2009 Banco de Andalucia and in 2011–2012 Banco Pastor with the blessing of the Spanish government and the Bank of Spain. All of this took place without the government leveraging the terms of ESM assistance. Popular furthermore brought in foreign investors from 2013 onward: Varde Partners (2013) and Citibank (2014) from the United States; Bx+ from Mexico; and Dexia from France. Later on, Popular's aggressive move to consolidate ownership of local banking by leveraging foreign investment proved unsustainable, as we discuss in the next section.

Overall, the changes that took place from 2012 until Popular's insolvency in 2017 were characterized by five things: first, a competition among the banks themselves to absorb competitors within their geographic regions, by which the autonomous communities that control the regional government in Spain; second, persistent financial problems related to non-performing mortgages that had not been resolved, coupled with the strategy to compensate for weaknesses with contingent convertible bonds, creating a vested interest in avoiding resolution; third, a serious issue of corporate governance that stood in the way of resolving the cajas; fourth, the Spanish government's use of conditions for financial assistance to cut through the Gordian knot of bank resolution for the regional savings and loans. While the terms of resolution; and finally, while the reorganization of Spanish savings and loans institutions was largely an inward-looking affair, the banks themselves were willing to work with and seek out foreign investors. Ultimately, the national nature of the savings and loan side of the Spanish financial system, like the commercial side which was managed earlier, was due in large part to a combination of financial problems involving domestic investors that tempered the attractiveness of Spanish cajas to foreign investors until those problems were resolved, and the willingness of the Spanish state to encourage and then cudgel banks into merging with other Spanish entities, with the help of special purpose vehicles (the FROB, SAREB and the BFA) and terms and conditions negotiated with European entities: the Commission and the Eurogroup (the ESM). Jürgen Strauch at the ESM himself attributed Spanish success in restructuring small regionals to three things: strong government ownership of the problem; burden-sharing (meaning bail-ins); and SAREB's removal of impaired assets all before the Single Resolution Mechanism was agreed upon and entered into force. Given the experiences and centrality and timing of the Spanish cases outlined here, one can assert that these cases provided the blueprint for the terms and conditions that would be systematized later in the SRM as a quid pro quo for using the ESM as a bank restructuring mechanism.

The sequencing of events and recorded action speak against outright nationalism in the Spanish banking sector. Liberal economic nationalism can be reasonably claimed. Meanwhile, it is less the case in Spain than in Italy that there is functional economic nationalism driven by features of the financial system that tie the hands of politicians. Those features play a very significant role up to and including the end of 2012, but the government's actions in reaching out to the Eurogroup and in weaponizing the terms of the Memorandum of Understanding to cut through those hurdles to restructuring are a difference of enormous importance.

Banco Popular: Spanish state capacity and the SRM

As early as 2014, the FROB became part of the Single Resolution Mechanism as the executive resolution authority in Spain. The timing of the decision-making to establish the SRM was fortuitous for Spain: the BRRD was passed one week after problems became acute at Popular on 15 July 2014. Law 11/2015 implemented the BRRD for Spain. The Spanish system was therefore set up, able to accept and work with SRM (minimal adjustment required, as already done) in very short order, without the need for adjustment or confrontation with European authorities, unlike in Italy.

This raises the question of how important Spanish law was in terms of state strength, and how.

The upgrading of the FROB and its position within the new SRM was useful to the Spanish authorities since Banco Popular proved to be the main source of financial market's instability after the wave of resolutions that started in 2012. In 2014, Popular was already so deeply in trouble that the SRB and FROB had commissioned and received an external report in July 2014 on the bank and the impact of various resolution schemes—particularly a write-down and conversion of capital instruments for loss absorption. The report indicated that the bank was short by between 2 and 8.3 billion euros, depending on the future state of the economy. This meant that a booming economic recovery generating strong revenue for the bank would still leave it short 2 billion euros compared to its minimum capital requirements (FROB 2017).

The FROB report, stemming from mandatory valuation, showed over 2 billion euros in tier 1 capital, 500 m euros in tier 2 capital and less than 50 million euros in subordinated debt. This was not enough to compensate for the bank's shortfalls. To help remedy the situation, the FROB took two kinds of measures that amounted to a bail-in of the bank's creditors. The first of these measures was to raise capital internally, by converting contingent convertible bonds from debt instruments to shares. This ensured that instead of owing regular interest payments and the initial capital loaned, Popular would only owe shareholders dividends once the bank was profitable again and owe no additional capital. The second was to write off debt instruments entirely. Existing investors would hurt, but a future investor prepared to take over the bank would find the cost greatly reduced, without debt obligations.

The FROB determined that 1.346 billion euros of tier 1 capital would be converted to shares, while the rest of the tier 1 category would be valued at zero (rendering the bonds a total loss for the remainder above 1.3). Similarly, 684 million euros of tier 2 capital was converted to shares, and the rest was valued at zero (FROB 2017). This financial engineering resulted not only in a reduction of the bank's liabilities through the bail-in but also an increase in the bank's capital. This was provided by the conversion of contingent convertible bonds into shares (worth 1.346 billion euros), which showed up on the bank's balance sheet as capital. The same applied to 684 billion euros of tier 2 capital. While this did not guarantee recovery, it gave the bank a second lease on life and did so without any state aid. From this point, the bank would have to ensure that it dealt with any potential NPLs to ensure the quality of its assets in the future and that its revenue was sufficient to restore its long-term financial viability.

Three years later, Popular was not in better shape. The bank periodically sold various assets and divisions (Aguado and Berwick 2017), including property-backed NPLs (Berwick 2017) to raise cash until the ECB declared that the bank was Failing or Likely to Fail (FOLTF) on 7 June 2017. At the European level, the Single Resolution Board then ascertained in Decision SRB/EES/2017/8 that the FROB would be responsible for the resolution plan for Popular, using Spanish regulations in the context of the BRRD. This meant that shareholders and creditors (holders of tier 1 and tier 2 capital instruments) were to be bailed in the first equivalent to the bank's negative value, plus the price of transferring business, but not lose more than in an ordinary insolvency proceeding.[2] However, the prior valuation reports that normally would apply under Spanish company law were not required. Instead, the FROB would obtain an ex post valuation to ensure that shareholders and creditors were not worse off than under insolvency. This would ensure the resolution was handled quickly (Buck and Brunsden 2017).

The case study of Popular's transfer provides an interesting insight into how Spain's preparation beforehand both at home and in connection with European authorities helped it win same-day approval from the SRB and the European Commission. The resolution was remarkably quick, given the potential in the Single Resolution Mechanism for delays (Donnelly and Asimakopoulos 2020). The Single Resolution Board took the decision to resolve the bank immediately after receiving ECB's FOLTF verdict based on a recommendation provided by the FROB as the Spanish resolution authority. Banco Santander would assume all of Popular's shares and capital for 1 euro. Santander, meanwhile, would have to invest 7 billion euros to compensate for holes in the balance sheet (MercoPress 2017). The government/FROB would not have to subsidize the sale. The SRB and FROB agreed that the sale was in the public interest as it protected depositors, investors and financial stability in Spain and Portugal and cost no public money. The Commission approved the sale within a few hours (European Commission 2017).

In the context of this resolution decision, the FROB Board of Governors drafted conditions for the final sale of Banco Popular. According to the FROB, only Santander fulfilled the requirements for a suitable takeover candidate (providing continuity of service, best price for the bank to be acquired and no conflict of interest). No mention of nationality was present. However, it is hard to discern how well known it was in the investment community that Popular was up for sale, on what terms and whether there were actually any other contenders. If there were, what were the exclusion criteria? What would constitute a conflict of interest? In effective terms, it does not appear that there was any outright nationalism regarding the sale in the mercantilist sense, though effectively, we see Spanish authorities interacting almost exclusively with a Spanish bank as the main contender. Foreign investors were involved, but primarily as customers for NPLs that Santander then proceeded to sell onward as it effectively resolved what was left of the bank itself.

Overall, the sale of Popular is consistent with room for Spanish authorities to act with the purpose of taking charge of a large bank resolution, and securing continued Spanish dominance in the banking market in the process, while the SRB and Commission approved the plans of their Spanish counterparts, given the financial stability considerations involved. Continuity of business would be ensured, and a legacy problem of the country's earlier banking crisis could finally be laid to rest (Donnelly and Asimakopoulos 2020). What is more telling than the speed of the sale is the effect on the Spanish banking market. At the time of sale, Banco Popular had 13.8% market share in deposits, while Santander had 11, so Santander suddenly had 25% of the retail and commercial deposit market, thereby consolidating ownership in Spanish (commercial) hands (Banco Santander 2017b).

As resolutions go, which sometimes involve separation and sale of assets and bridging banks at the point of resolution, the transfer was also as simple as it could be. Contingent convertible bondholders were wiped out, but Santander took on the work of selling Popular's assets to recoup the 7 billion euro cost rather than negotiating complex arrangements as was done with Intesa's takeover of the Veneto and Vicenza banks in Italy the same year (see Chapter 6). Santander sold 51% of Popular's real estate holdings to Blackstone in 2017 for 5 billion euros, and subsidiaries outside of Spain were sold off to competitors in those countries (Portugal, Chile and the United States) (Blackstone 2017). The flip side of this relatively simple resolution was that there would be an ex post evaluation in 2018 to ensure that terms and conditions were met and to confirm that the terms of the initial agreement had been fulfilled.

Critique came from investors, who argued that the resolution came in too late and at too high a cost to bondholders, given signs that Popular was in trouble before the ECB's declaration, and people were taking out their deposits (Mullin 2017). This critique led to adjudication at the Central Resolution Tribunal (Junta Unica Resolucion: JUR), which also received the positions of the FROB and the SRB in September 2018 supporting the move. It finally rejected the bondholders' claims in March 2020 (Guarascio 2020). After losing their case at the tribunal, a consortium of national and international investors sued at the European Court of Justice and the EU General Court and lost their cases in May and June 2022, respectively. However, these claims took a different direction. Instead of arguing that the resolution should have taken place earlier, the investors based their case on the claims that the bank should not have been declared FOLTF, that it was impossible for an evaluator to fully know the financial affairs of the bank, particularly in such a short time frame, and that the bail-in constituted an unreasonable confiscation of property. However the Court of Justice of the EU ruled that losses incurred in a bail-in were legal under the BRRD, while the General Court ruled that it was reasonable for the resolution to take place quickly, and for the evaluation of the bank to have some uncertainties, given the speed of the review, without preventing it from being 'fair, prudent and realistic' (Aguado 2022).

These outcomes were hugely important for demonstrating the Spanish state's capacity to organize an orderly transfer of business (as one means of organizing a resolution) and therefore signal credibility to various stakeholders: depositors, the investment community and European authorities, with the Single Resolution Board as the most direct point of contact. In addition, it is striking that the outcome effectively replicated a strategy of liberal economic nationalism, ensuring consolidation of the Spanish banking sector, the continued dominance of Spanish ownership of the sector, the continued confidence of Spanish finance for international investors and the continuity of financial services for households and businesses. These outcomes contrast strongly with some of the Italian outcomes discussed in the chapter above.

Liberal economic nationalism in Spain

We begin our conclusions with a review of how well the findings of the Spanish case fit the respective rubrics of liberalism, liberal economic nationalism, economic nationalism and functional economic nationalism. As with the Italian cases, we can subject our analysis to three kinds of tests to determine how compelling the findings are. Straw in the wind tests provide circumstantial evidence without conclusive proof. Hoop tests accumulate more evidence that reinforces conclusions about patterns of behavior. Smoking gun tests seek proof of causality in the decision-making process.

Straw in the wind tests are the only level at which we find some indication for economic liberalism, by which we mean that banks and bank supervisors are open to international investment and ownership of Spanish banks, as long as the solvency of the bank is provided for or guaranteed. The attempt to attract international investors in the case of Bankia under Goirigolzarri's leadership in 2012 is the one moment where we can see such intent. We could also stretch the definition of support for liberalism by directing attention to any significant involvement of foreign capital. This is certainly the case in the involvement of foreign hedge funds investing in cajas, but it is mediated by the state institution SAREB, which has considerable state control over what does and does not happen to the cajas, their financial management, and any political and social obligations that they used to have before the 2012 reforms. A liberal search for investment is embedded in a state body that manages it, in other words. On the other side of the liberal-nationalist spectrum, there are no empirical grounds suggesting the existence of outright economic nationalism designed to keep ownership national for its own sake, regardless of the consequences. EU constraints on state aid were respected, and international investors sought where appropriate (largely for Bankia in a direct fashion, and indirectly through SAREB for the other cajas).

In contrast, we find that straw in the wind tests for liberal economic nationalism and functional economic nationalism generate some supporting evidence. There is a combination of seeking investment from all quarters, foreign and domestic, but also significant caja entanglements in economic, social, political and government obligations that make external investment riskier, more complicated and therefore less clearly profitable than that is typical of functional economic nationalism. There is also clear intervention from the state in Spanish banking. Does it constitute liberal economic nationalism?

The *hoop tests* suggest a pattern of liberal economic nationalism at the national level that designs and deploys state institutions over the course of the 2010s to restructure regional savings banks, keeping them solvent, but keeping international investors involved, and its European partners (Commission and the Eurogroup) happy. This means pushing back actors and practices at the local level that would otherwise generate functional economic nationalism, as seen in Italy. But this strategy encounters delays and reluctance from various vested interests that take time, effort and eventually external assistance to overcome. Before 2013, we see that the Spanish government acts aggressively to take on the issue of reforming cajas and popular banks with a significant degree of success but that it reaches limits that coincide with two kinds of consequences: imposing costs on bank customers who had bought the subordinated debt, much like Italian bank customers had done, and on local government councils and social partners that rely on the cajas to fund a wide range of community and social goals. This contrasts with the period from 2013 onward, in which resolutions involving bail-ins and takeovers take place, in part using EU-sanctioned government assistance (through FROB), and in part using private capital, much of it foreign (SAREB), but which ultimately shifts ownership to either a large commercial bank or amalgamates it into an enormous caja-like entity, both of which remain Spanish-owned.

The *smoking gun tests* reinforce this pattern of liberal economic nationalism grinding away at the opposition that could otherwise develop into functional economic nationalism. It also reinforces the conclusion that the heightened prevalence of foreign investment in Spain added impetus to the drive to reorganize, recapitalize and resolve banks rather than letting their problems slide. Critical for demonstrating intent in the smoking gun test is the Memorandum of Understanding between the Spanish government and the ESM which mandated sweeping corporate governance reforms of the Spanish cajas that cut them off from their erstwhile patrons and non-bank responsibilities. Until this point, local political resistance appears to have been decisive in limiting bank reform, which is consistent with functional economic nationalism. Although the government and the Bank of Spain present the bank resolution implications of that MoU as something that they regrettably must do, the behavior of the government suggests otherwise. From this point onward, the government acts swiftly and decisively to change the laws governing the banks and to effectively force mergers, which lead to continued Spanish ownership of the cajas, while simultaneously attracting government-managed private capital from abroad and keeping within the expectations of the Commission and ESM. This test is repeated in an even more striking fashion by the resolution of Banco Popular, which the government and Bank of Spain orchestrated to keep ownership national, but within the terms of the new SRM.

The exposure of Spanish banks to faster, sharper and deeper losses with greater prior involvement of foreign investors in 2008 accelerated the imperative for the Spanish government to react aggressively to restore the solvency of the banking sector. The Spanish state—both the Bank of Spain and the Spanish Ministry of Finance—found that the large commercial banks were in fairly resilient shape compared to their smaller, regional savings and loan counterparts, so much of the state's attention was devoted to cleaning up the latter sector. That happened in two stages, with reforms in 2009–2010 and another main round in 2012. The first of these reforms in 2009–2010 established state institutions and initial funding for resolving (relatively small) insolvent banks. But it was only partially successful in cleaning up the banking system. The 2012 reforms took further moves to impose restructuring, often over the objections of regional governments that had protected some of the cajas in the previous round. The national government was not able to handle this political task alone until it agreed to a Memorandum of Understanding with the ESM and the European Commission to take out loans for recapitalization and then to impose further restructuring on both banks and their client regional councils that could not be achieved before. The result is a much more consolidated banking sector anchored with large commercial banks and a smaller number of regional savings institutions incorporated into that structure.

This outcome, and the means by which it is accomplished, does not reflect the expectations of outright mercantilist economic nationalism in the sense of protectionism against foreign ownership. There is no sense that foreigners are to be kept at bay, nor is there any sort of rejection of using the ESM and conforming to its wishes, or the regular requirement to abide by decisions of the European Commission's Competition DG. Indeed, the Spanish government embraced requirements from these institutions to strengthen its vertical control over Spanish banks. The government's behavior does reflect a classic form of liberal economic nationalism in which large commercial banks were reinforced as global players (and thereby indirectly as national champions that the government could turn to), with an even greater share of the domestic banking market after absorbing failed savings and loans. This could have been a one-off, but in 2019, Spain demonstrated that a model of national commercial banks acting as (national) acquirers of last resort for failed banks was a workable model, even for the Single Resolution Board and the European Commission working with a fully functional Single Resolution Mechanism. This allows for banking continuity without appealing to European authorities for flexibility in EU laws and arrangements. This factor helps understand why Spain has the room to engage in liberal economic nationalism: because EU rules and institutions accommodate it, particularly if it makes banking solvency problems go away. This general tendency is reflected as well in Italy, where the Commission has accommodated state intervention, albeit with less resilient effects.

Notes

1 On cajas: Aceña (2014), Girón, Meireles and Reyes (2019). On Spain and ESM overview, see Strauch et al. (2016).
2 Articles 38 and 39 of Law 11/2015, reflecting articles 37.2, 59 and 60 of the BRRD (2014/59/EU).

References

Aceña, P.M. (2014). The Savings Banks crises in Spain: When and How?. *Documentos de trabajo de la Asociación Española de Historia Económica, 14*, 4.

Aguado, J. (2022). EU Court rejects claims over Banco Popular rescue deal. Reuters, 1 June. https://www.reuters.com/business/eu-court-rejects-complaints-over-banco-popular-rescue-deal-2022-06-01/

Aguado, J. & Berwick, A. (2017). Spain's Banco Popular to sell off assets to boost depleted capital. Reuters, 5 May. https://www.reuters.com/article/us-banco-popular-results-idUSKBN1810PN

Aguado, J. & Pinedo, E. (2020). Ex-IMF head Rato acquitted over Bankia IPO, prompts legal change calls. 29 September. https://uk.reuters.com/article/us-spain-court-bankia-rato/ex-imf-chief-rato-acquitted-in-trial-over-bankias-ipo-idUKKBN26K183

Banco Santander (2017a). Banco Santander informs of the acquisition of 100% of the share capital of Banco Popular Español, S.A. Banco Santander website: www.santander.com/csgs/Satellite/CFWCSancomQP01/en_GB/Corporate/Shareholders-and-Investors/Corporate-Governance/Banco-Popular-Acquisition.html

Banco Santander (2017b). Santander acquires Popular, becoming the leading bank in Spain. https://www.santander.com/content/dam/santander-com/en/documentos/historico-notas-de-prensa/2017/06/NP-2017-06-07-Santander%20acquires%20Popular,%20becoming%20the%20leading%20bank%20in%20Spain%20-en.pdf

Bankia (2014). Bankia issues 1 billion euros of subordinated debt and strengthens its solvency issues. 13 May. https://www.bankia.com/en/communication/news/bankia-issues-1-billion-euros-of-10-year-subordinated-debt-and-strengthens-its-solvency-ratios.html

Bankia Caixa (2021). Information on the CaixaBank-Bankia merger. Accessed 1 July 2021. https://www.bankia.es/en/retail-banking/caixabank-bankia-integration

Barrón, I. de (2012). El Estado nacionaliza el grupo de Bankia. *El País*, 9 May. https://elpais.com/economia/2012/05/09/actualidad/1336559567_240280.html

Berwick, A. (2017). Banco Popular sells 620 million euros in loans to Blackstone, Apollo. Reuters, 12 January. https://www.reuters.com/article/us-banco-popular-assets-idUSKBN14W1VC

Blackstone (2017). Banco Popular agrees to sell majority stake in real estate asset portfolio to Blackstone. 8 August. https://www.blackstone.com/news/press/banco-popular-agrees-to-sell-majority-stake-in-its-real-estate-asset-portfolio-to-blackstone/

Buck T (2015). La Caixa: Spain's quiet powerhouse. *Financial Times*, 9 April. https://www.ft.com/content/4b3340f6-d63d-11e4-b3e7-00144feab7de

Buck, T., & Brunsden, J. (2017). Emergency funds failed to save Banco Popular from death spiral. *Financial Times*, 8 June. https://www.ft.com/content/6f32eca2-4c62-11e7-a3f4-c742b9791d43

Chassany, A.-S. Hammond, E. & Johnson, M. (2013). Private equity groups compete for Spanish banks' property units. *Financial Times*, 24 July. https://www.ft.com/content/0ea1c48c-f444-11e2-8459-00144feabdc0

de la Torre Viscasillas, J. (2013). Spanish bad bank. *International Financial Law Review*. https://www.iflr.com/article/b1lt39pv0s1t30/spanish-bad-bank

Deeg, R. (2012). Liberal economic nationalism and Europeanization: The rise of Spanish and Italian banks. Paper presented at the Annual Meeting of the American Political Science Association, New Orleans, Aug. 30–Sept. 2, 2012.

Deeg, R., & Donnelly, S. (2016). Banking union and the future of alternative banks: Revival, stagnation or decline?. *West European Politics*, *39*(3), 585–604.

Diaz, J. (2018). CaixaBank recompra el 51% de Servihabitat al fondo TPG por 176 millones. Expansión. 8 June. https://www.expansion.com/empresas/banca/2018/06/08/5b1aa8a1268e3e7f068b460b.html

Doleys, T. (2012). Managing state aid in a time of crisis: Commission crisis communications and the financial sector bailout. *Journal of European Integration*, *34*(6), 549–565.

Donnelly, S., & Asimakopoulos, I.G. (2020). Bending and breaking the single resolution mechanism: The case of Italy. *Journal of Common Market Studies*, *58*(4), 856–871.

Durán, Y. (2021). Caixa, Blackstone y Sareb: así son los líderes del emergente negocio del alquiler en España Brainsre. *News*. 2 February. https://brainsre.news/asi-son-los-lideres-del-emergente-negocio-del-alquiler-en-espana/

El País (2012). Las cajas se convierten a la carrera en fundaciones tras una vida centenaria. 25 November. https://elpais.com/economia/2012/11/25/agencias/1353847869_181651.html

European Commission (2010). State Aid: Commission approves recapitalisation scheme for credit institutions. 28 January. IP/10/70. https://ec.europa.eu/commission/presscorner/detail/en/IP_10_70

European Commission (2012a). State Aid: Commission approves restructuring plans of Spanish banks Liberbank, Caja3, Banco Mare Nostrum and Banco CEISS. 20 December. https://ec.europa.eu/commission/presscorner/detail/en/IP_12_1432

European Commission (2012b). State aid: Commission approves restructuring plans of Spanish banks BFA/Bankia, NCG Banco, Catalunya Banc and Banco de Valencia. Press release IP/12/1277. 28 November. https://ec.europa.eu/commission/presscorner/detail/en/IP_12_1277

European Commission (2017). *European Commission Approves Resolution of Banco Popular.* Brussels, 7 June. IP/17/1556.

Expansión (2018). Apollo vende Altamira a doBank (Fortress). 13 December. https://www.expansion.com/empresas/inmobiliario/2018/12/31/5c2a2c72e5fdea624c8b4605.html

Fioretos, O. (2011). *Creative Reconstructions: Multilateralism and European Varieties of Capitalism After 1950.* Ithaca: Cornell University Press.

FROB (2017). Resolution of the FROB Governing Committee adopting the measures required to implement the Decision of the Single Resolution Board in its Extended Executive Session of 7 June 2017 concerning the adoption of the resolution scheme in respect of Banco Popular Español, S.A., addressed to FROB, in accordance with Article 29 of Regulation (EU) 806/2014 of the European Parliament and of the Council of 15 July 2014 establishing uniform rules and a uniform procedure for the resolution of credit institutions and certain investment firms in the framework of a Single Resolution Mechanism and a Single Resolution Fund and amending Regulation (EU) No 1093/2010. Madrid, 7 June. https://www.frob.es/en/Lists/Contenidos/Attachments/419/ProyectodeAcuerdoreducido_EN_v1.pdf

Garcia, B. (2016). "Goirigolzarri a Podemos: "No conozco ninguna banca publica que haya funcionado"". Libre Mercado,16 June. https://www.libremercado.com/2016-06-16/goirigolzarri-a-podemos-no-conozco-ninguna-banca-publica-que-haya-funcionado-1276576458/

Garrigues (2012) EC approves Spanish banks restrucruring plans. 28 November. Retrieved 27 October 2020. https://www.garrigues.com/en_GB/new/ec-approves-spanish-banks-restructuring-plans.

Girón, A., Meireles, M., & Reyes, A. (2019). Concentración bancaria y reorganización financiera: España y Portugal en la post-crisis. *Revista de Economía institucional, 21*(40), 185–205. http://www.scielo.org.co/scielo.php?script=sci_arttext&pid=S0124-59962019000100185 .

Guarascio, F. (2020). No compensation for Banco Popular's creditors, EU regulator says. *Reuters*, 18 March. https://www.reuters.com/article/eu-banks-srb-bancopopular/no-compensation-for-banco-populars-creditors-eu-regulator-says-idUSB5N27Y01U

Hale, T. (2017). Spanish bad debt comes good for US private equity. *Financial Times*, 1 May. https://www.ft.com/content/657504de-28d1-11e7-bc4b-5528796fe35c

Hardie, I., & Howarth, D. (Eds.). (2013). *Market-based Banking and the International Financial Crisis.* Oxford: Oxford University Press.

Hugh, E. (2010). Spain gets "FROB'bed off by the EU Commission. *Seeking Alpha*, 21 January. https://seekingalpha.com/article/183698-spain-gets-frobbed-off-by-the-eu-commission

Masters, B. (2013). European banks warned to expect tougher scrutiny. *Financial Times*, 17 May. https://www.ft.com/content/ebefe93e-be3b-11e2-bb35-00144feab7de

misc (2017). Santander rescues Banco Popular, which was "failing or likely to fail". 8 June. https://en.mercopress.com/2017/06/08/santander-rescues-banco-popular-which-was-failing-or-likely-to-fail

Mullin, K. (2017). What sank Popular? Supervisory negligence. *International Financial Review*, 16 June. https://www.ifre.com/story/1460097/what-sank-popular-supervisory-negligence-1nbxbpmwgs

Quaglia, L., & Royo, S. (2015). Banks and the political economy of the sovereign debt crisis in Italy and Spain. *Review of International Political Economy*, *22*(3), 485–507.

Reuters (2012). EU approves Spain bank restructuring, opens door to aid. 28 November. https://www.cnbc.com/id/49990732

Reuters (2021). Spanish regulator approves Bankia-CaixaBank merger with conditions. 23 March. https://www.reuters.com/article/us-caixabank-m-a-watchdog-approval-idUSKBN2BF2I0

Rosell, J. (2018). El Gobierno amplia hasta finales de 2021 la venta de Bankia. *Merca2*, 21 December, https://www.merca2.es/gobierno-venta-bankia-2021/

Royo, S. (2013). How did the Spanish financial system survive the first stage of the global crisis?. *Governance*, *26*(4), 631–656.

Santos, T. (2018). *El Diluvio: The Spanish Banking Crisis, 2008–2012*. Columbia University, Department of Finance, working paper.

Sarries, N. (2018). El BCE dará a conocer los requerimientos de capital de Liberbank en los próximos días. *Expansión*. 18 May. https://www.expansion.com/empresas/banca/2018/05/18/5afdd2cc268e3e546e8b4645.html

Sousa, V. (2020). Cerberus considers freezing the sale of Haya real estate. *Iberian Property*. 16 July. https://www.iberian.property/editorial/cerberus-considers-freezing-^$. the-sale-of-haya-real-estate/

Strauch, R., Rojas, J., O'Connor, F., Casalinho, C., de Ramón-Laca Clausen, P., & Kalozois, P. (2016). *Accessing Sovereign Markets: The Recent Experiences of Ireland, Portugal, Spain, and Cyprus* (No. 2).

Thompson, M. (2012). Bankia shares plunge as bailout looms. *CNN Business*, 27 December. https://money.cnn.com/2012/12/27/news/economy/spain-bankia-shares/index.html

Toyer, J. & Dowsett, S. (2012). Long-suffering Bankia shareholders set for more losses. *Reuters*, 27 December. https://www.reuters.com/article/us-bankia-idUSBRE8BQ0F320121227

Tymkiw, C. (2012). Most Spanish banks pass stress tests. *CNN Business*, 28 September, https://money.cnn.com/2012/09/28/investing/spain-bank-stress-test/?iid=EL

6

BANKING NATIONALISM IN ITALY

The Italian cases explored below are structured to deal first with the case of Monte dei Paschi di Siena, as a large, systemically important bank under the direct supervision of the European Central Bank (ECB) after 2014, and then a series of smaller, regional alternative banks, listed in chronological order, to control for the evolution of bank, creditor, government and central bank activity over time. There are two reasons for this structure. The first is that problems with Monte dei Paschi di Siena (MPS) came to a head earlier, and were never entirely resolved at the time of writing. The second is that MPS is a much larger bank than the others, with more obvious implications for financial stability and therefore more demanding expectations within the ECB's Single Supervisory Mechanism (SSM) and the Single Resolution Mechanism (SRM).

As we test for the hypotheses revolving around mercantilist, liberal and functional economic nationalist behavior, we wish to keep an open mind about developments over time. As we demonstrate, however, while we detect no mercantilist economic nationalism in principle, there is an observable tendency for the state to condone and protect connections between regional banks and local communities, even where this contradicts the country's obligations under the SRM. While the Bank of Italy as bank supervisor recognized problems with the capital adequacy of some banks as early as 2010, it was harder for a broader spectrum of state authorities (above all the Finance Ministry and the Financial Markets Authority) to force the harder work of compelling banks to restructure, raise capital and, critically, open up their corporate governance to make the banks more attractive to outside investors. Instead of heading down this path, the banks under review in Italy retained connections to local councils and prominent family shareholders, who then looked to their own depositors as investors, who in turn would accept their continued control of the banks. When this failed to solve the banks' financial problems, state authorities extended their protection

DOI: 10.4324/9781003334583-6

to local retail investors in the banks, who were simultaneously the banks' own depositors. This could only be accomplished by negotiating extraordinary permission from the European Commission. Likewise, Italian inaction in cleaning up these banks led the SRM also to hand the problem back to Italian authorities, by setting aside the bail-in terms of the Bank Recovery and Resolution Directive (BRRD) and retaining Italian insolvency procedures, which softened the blow of restructuring for stakeholders in Italian banks. This means that the process of cleaning up banks becomes much slower, legally contested and underfunded.

The reference point for ordering these cases is the moment at which the banks became insolvent and government interference became necessary in one way or another in order to supply financial stability. As with Spain, the problems started more or less simultaneously by 2009. But the test of how various actors were motivated and behaved is most fruitfully focused on the moment when intervention becomes necessary. At that point, one can look back in time to understand how the bank got into this position, testing the hypothesis on liberalization and instability.

The context of the Italian banking sector

For a long time, Italian banks were often thought of as a public good, and therefore were treated as such. This may be due to the fact that, in 1991, Italian state-owned banks counted around 80% of all deposits and gave out 90% of all loans (Marrelli and Stroffolini 1998), so much so that a court decision even considered banking as 'objectively having some of the characteristics of a public service' (Ciocca 2005).

Nevertheless, during the 1990s and the early 2000s, the Italian banking sector went through a series of important reforms, leading to the privatization of state-owned banks and the transformation of savings banks into commercial entities (Gazzetta Ufficiale 1990). This resulted in a series of mergers that eventually led Intesa Sanpaolo and Unicredit to become the two most important banks, covering together 47% of the Italian market (Schoenmaker and Véron 2016; Deeg 2012). Up to and including 2005, the Bank of Italy held a protective hand over the banking sector, blocking takeovers of Italian banks. This was in line with Italy's history of state intervention and support of national champions. Examples of governmental support to private firms can be found in the subsidies granted to the Fiat Group (Germano 2012), and in the use of the golden rule share within Telecom Italia (Ansa Italy 2017).

When the global financial crisis eventually hit the Italian banking system in 2011, Italy's two largest banks, UniCredit and Intesa, which held at the time €228 billion of Italian sovereign debt, lost almost 30% of their market value. In the same period, the amount of non-performing loans owned by banks throughout Italy increased dramatically, adding to a slow increase in non-performing loans dating back to 2008. The ECB's Comprehensive Assessment of 2014 took on a stricter definition of the non-performing loan (NPL) than that used by the Bank of Italy and the European Banking Authority, with the purpose of fighting forbearance. The test saw four Italian banks fail (Howarth and Quaglia 2016; Transparency International EU 2017). This in turn had consequences for the Italian state, which relied on Italian banks for its own public finances. Italy's two largest banks, UniCredit and Intesa Sanpaolo, supported Italy by buying significant portions of its debt in the aftermath of the financial crisis, in exchange for the government's previous support to the banks (Deeg 2012).

It is in this period that the Italian banking crisis began its most acute phase. MPS required assistance as a large, systemically important bank, and a series of regional banks all were forced into resolution within a short space of time. While the state initially had some success in getting large commercial banks to fund for a state-coordinated restructuring, the demand for funds outstripped supply, leaving too little for either MPS or any following regionals. At the end of 2015, right before the entrance into force of the BRRD bail-in rule, four small regional banks: Banca delle Marche, Cassa di Risparmio di Ferrara, Banca Popolare dell'Etruria e del Lazio and Cassa di Risparmio della Provincia di Chieti were resolved. The Italian Resolution Authority made use of a combination of tools to resolve these four local Italian banks, such as asset separation, bridge bank and burden-sharing. On top of that, the Italian Resolution Fund provided financial resources. In total, the Italian Resolution Authority bailed out these small banks by €3.7 billion, a remarkable amount of cash if compared to the €870 million which was bailed in. In order to supply the banks with such a large capital, the Resolution Fund needed to borrow considerable sums from the three largest Italian banks (Bodellini 2017). Throughout these resolutions, a recurring theme was the inertia exerted on these banks to retain their loan portfolios and to resist writing down loans as non-performing. This made the banks neither solvent nor resolvable, meaning that private investors, domestic or international, could not be found to inject new capital into the banks.

Monte dei Paschi di Siena

Established in 1472, Monte dei Paschi di Siena (MPS) is the oldest operating bank in the world and Italy's third biggest bank. It is also a domestically oriented bank, supporting lending for a considerable portion of the Italian economy, and in turn, depending on the performance of the Italian economy for its profitability and solvency. At the same time, given the lack of alternatives, and given a certain degree of forbearance by the Bank of Italy and the Ministry of Finance, MPS has exercised a certain degree of patience towards delinquent debtors. At the time of writing in 2022, MPS had still not been re-privatized after its nationalization in 2017, it continued to have problems keeping enough capital on hand to deal with a deteriorating balance sheet, and a takeover by commercial bank UniCredit that the government had been trying to orchestrate and incentivize had not borne fruit (Sirletti, Albanese and Migliaccio 2021).

Between 2009 and 2017, MPS had to raise capital for a total of 16 billion euros (Transparency International EU 2017), in a journey that eventually brought it to a precautionary recapitalization in July 2017. Although it considers the roots of the problems to have a more ancient origin, in its 2013 Financial System Stability Assessment the International Monetary Fund (IMF) identifies the beginning of MPS troubles in a series of transactions that took place between 2008 and 2009. In particular, the report mentions the purchase of AntonVeneta bank and a set of repo transactions as the main cause that triggered MPS' illiquidity (International Monetary Fund 2013). It is in this same period that, in order to raise capital in the aftermath of such events, MPS convinced thousands of retail investors to convert their savings into bonds for a total of 2b euros (Fior 2016b).

In 2009, MPS, among other credit institutions, made use of the Tremonti bonds, a form of subordinated and hybrid bonds named after the then-Minister of Economy and Finances Giulio Tremonti. The bonds were available from February to December 2009 and had the purpose of strengthening banks' so-called 'Core Tier 1' capital and, as a consequence, of stimulating banks to issue credit for businesses and households. The Core Tier 1 is an indicator of stability of a bank's capital, generally used by regulators to assess a bank's health (Il Sole 24 Ore n.d.).

Due to MPS' continued instability, the Bank of Italy exercised an increasingly intrusive supervision of the bank through measures such as intensified onsite inspections, close monitoring of the bank's liquidity and a ban on bonuses and dividends. Despite having no legal power to remove individual board members or managers, in 2012 the Bank of Italy exercised moral suasion to have the Chairman, the CEO and a number of board members of MPS removed (International Monetary Fund 2013).

In the same year, MPS failed the stress test and recapitalization exercise organized by the European Banking Authority. In an effort to further support the credit institution, the Italian government made available the so-called Monti bonds, adding them to the pre-existing Tremonti bonds and bringing the recapitalization to a total of €4.1 billion (International Monetary Fund 2013). Unlike the Tremonti bonds, issued in order to help a pool of Italian banks, Monti bonds represented an ad hoc measure aiming to rescue MPS. The Ministry of Economy and Finance bought bonds for a total of €3.92 billion. The bonds were paid back in two phases: the greatest portion, €3b, was repaid on 1st July 2014, whereas the rest of the debt was extinguished in July 2015. Nevertheless, part of the interests on the bonds was converted into shares, making the Italian state a stakeholder of 4% of MPS (Il Sole 24 Ore n.d.).

In 2014 and 2015, there were two further recapitalization attempts. On 27 June 2014, Monte de Paschi started a recapitalization campaign in the form of a capital increase with subscription rights, with the purpose of raising €5 billion. MPS managed to raise 99.85% of the offer and used part of this capital to pay back €3.5 billion of the €4.1 billion in state aid received by the Italian government through the Tremonti and Monti bonds (Peruzzi 2014). One year later, MPS decided to raise capital for the second time through a recapitalization of €3 billion. As of June 13th, 99.6% of the desired sum was subscribed by investors. Thanks to the capital raised, MPS was able to pay back the residual €1 billion of Monti bonds, in advance as compared to the 2017 deadline (Il Fatto Quotidiano 2015b).

In 2016, MPS was subject to a number of negative shocks. Despite collecting capital through two successful recapitalizations, the most acute phase of the MPS crisis began in the first two months of 2016, when its share price fell by 61% (Transparency International EU 2017), reflecting investor's uncertainty that MPS' financial problems had been put to rest. Thus, MPS headed off to the 2016 European Banking Authority (EBA) stress test with weak capacity to raise new capital if required. In addition, Prime Minister Renzi and Minister of Finance Padoan had publicly expressed their concern from the beginning of the year that the entry into force of the BRRD and the bail-in rule would undermine financial stability rather than mitigating it (Brunsden and Barker 2016; Politi and Brundsen 2016).

Furthermore, investors' confidence in MPS' financial credibility was further eroded by concerns about political instability for the country as a whole, with consequences for both the strength of the state and the country's political stance towards the EU. Italy's financial situation was coupled with the Renzi government's bid to change the country's constitution to decrease the powers of the Senate and increase the powers of the Prime Minister in directing and passing legislation. That bid had been approved by both houses of parliament, but required an additional constitutional referendum (to be held in December 2016) to be approved. Not only was the constitution at stake, but Renzi's government as well (the Prime Minister had announced he would resign in the case of a negative outcome) (Sky TG24 2016; Makortoff 2016). Renzi's polling in early 2016 was weak, while that of Italian parties Lega and the 5 Star Movement, who lined up on the no side of the referendum, was relatively strong.

State responses: the Atlas fund and lobbying for ECB and SRM exemptions

Preparing for a potential need to raise capital again, and not just for MPS but for Italian banks in general, the government required Italian banks to contribute to a newly established *Atlas fund*. The Atlas fund was established in April 2016 with the tasks of using up to 70% of its capital for recapitalizing insolvent banks, acting as the 'shareholder of last resort' and using up to 30% of its capital purchasing junior tranches of securitized Italian non-performing loans (Schoenmaker and Véron 2016; Il Sole 24 Ore 2016a; Il Post 2016). The private rescue fund was created with contributions from the majority of Italian banks and disposed of an initial capital of €4.25 billion (Transparency International EU 2017; Schoenmaker and Véron 2016).

The UK's decision to leave the EU in its June 2016 Brexit referendum further put MPS along with other Italian banks listed on the stock market under pressure. Milan's stock market plummeted from +3.71 on June 23rd to −12.48% on June 24th, with banks' shares suffering heavily (Di Cristofaro and Maurino 2016; Piana 2016; The Financial Times 2016). At this point, while unconfirmed rumors spread in the press around a €40 billion rescue plan being prepared behind the scenes (Evans-Pritchard 2016; Chicca 2016; Feltri 2016), the Italian government publicly took a stance against the BRRD rule, both in Italy and abroad. On 26 June 2016, Francesco Boccia, the President of the Committee on Budgets, stated that suspending the bail-in rule was 'not a heresy' (Boccia 2016; Feltri 2016). On the same day, the Secretary of the Council of Ministers Claudio De Vincenti released an interview on Sky where he stated that the government was ready to protect depositors and engage in 'interventions aiming to support bank's liquidity and solvency' (Bartoloni 2016; Feltri 2016).

The next day, on 27 June 2016, Renzi met German Chancellor Merkel and French President Hollande at the Brexit Summit in Berlin. When asked about the Italian position on troubled banks in the aftermath of Brexit, Renzi pointed to a desire to learn from the vigorous intervention by other EU Member States. He regretted the lack of systemic interventions by previous Italian governments and urged the need for 'caution, common sense and balance' in applying the BRRD, given the failure of those previous governments to take strong and timely action. The government, he added, would do whatever is necessary within the current legislative framework to address the issue (Palazzo Chigi 2016; Karnitschnig 2016; Evans-Pritchard 2016).

Through these declarations, Renzi seemed to be connecting the stock market shock caused by the Brexit vote to the kind of 'exceptional occurrence' during which state aid is permitted, according to Article 107.2(b) of the TFEU (Il Fatto Quotidiano 2016c; Chicca 2016). Such declarations triggered a set of reactions from the Commission, the ECB and the German government. Comments from the Commission arrived during the Brexit Summit, on 28 June 2016, when Juncker stated that the Commission would do anything to prevent a bank run in Italy (Rettman 2016; Il Fatto Quotidiano 2016c). On that occasion, Renzi met Commission President Juncker and Vice-President Dombrovskis (Guarascio 2016b). Dombrovskis stated that the Commission was monitoring the situation, and keeping close contact with Italian authorities concerning possible steps (Balestreri 2016; Il Sole 24 Ore 2016b). Meanwhile, on the same day Renzi visited the Party of European Socialists' headquarters in Brussels, from where he reassured Italian depositors, stating that their savings will be protected (Balestreri 2016; Il Sole 24 Ore 2016c).

The ECB, on the other hand, commented from the forum in Sintra, where ECB executive board member Benoît Cœuré insisted on the importance of respecting the bail-in rule, stating that the failure to comply with it would result in the end of Banking Union as we know it (Il Fatto Quotidiano 2016c; La Repubblica 2016a). As far as the German response is concerned, on 29th June

2016 Merkel answered Renz's requests by asking that the BRRD be respected. Rules, the Chancellor stated, 'cannot be changed every two years' (Sanderson 2016a; Guarascio 2016a; Il Fatto Quotidiano 2016c).

Cœuré's statement challenged both the Italian government and central bank. A day prior on 27 June, the Bank of Italy had sided with the government in calling for a complete overhaul of the bail-in rules. At the ECB Forum on central banking in Sintra, Bank of Italy Governor Visco stated that the central bank would use 'every available tool to support the banking system', underlining the importance of preventing a shock as strong as Brexit from creating contagion (Chicca 2016; Il Fatto Quotidiano 2016a). Going further, Visco condemned the bail-in rule as in conflict with the Italian constitution, claiming it infringed Article 47, which 'encourages and protects' savings (Merler 2016b). Nevertheless, as Merler noted, such an argument was 'naive and misplaced', since it 'neglects the fundamental difference between savings and investment', as investment by definition entails a risk factor (Merler 2016a). In other words, the Bank of Italy claimed that subordinated bonds could not be reduced in value, treating them like deposits rather than the financial instruments they are.

On July 4th MPS confirmed receiving a letter from the ECB, just a few weeks before the official publication of the stress test results. The letter confirmed the ECB's insistence on restructuring and contained a set of requirements to be met. MPS was required to:

a) Sell on the market a minimum of €9.7 billion of NPLs by turning them into shares.
b) Develop a three-year plan, to be ready by 3rd October 2016, with the objective of reducing the ratio of non-performing to performing loans (the NPL ratio) to 20% (Gruppo MPS 2016a; Greco 2016; Il Fatto Quotidiano 2016b).

When the stress test results were released on 29th July 2016, MPS turned out to be the worst performer among the 51 scrutinized banks, with a Cet1 ratio of 12.2% under normal circumstances, and of −2.44% under adverse conditions (Gruppo MPS 2016b; Festa 2016a; Il Fatto Quotidiano 2016c; Mesnard, Margerit and Magnus 2017). This meant that more NPLs had to be sold off or written off and that more capital needed to be raised.

Developing a plan in response to the ECB letter required concerted efforts by MPS, the Italian government and European authorities. In July 2016, negotiations continued and intensified. MPS' CEO Fabrizio Viola indicated he was working intensively with Italian and European authorities, with the goal of reaching a 'structural and ultimate solution' to the bank's problem with NPLs in a short amount of time (Ferrando 2016a; Sala 2016). Italian authorities, meanwhile, were working to arrange an increase of the Atlas fund's resources, after using most of it already to intervene in two regional banks (Vicenza and Veneto, discussed below). This prior intervention had left the fund with a capacity of

€1.7 billion. On July 4th, a meeting of the Atlas fund took place. Quaestio sgr, the company administering the fund, was given the task of raising an additional €1 billion euros (Sanderson 2016b; Massaro 2016b).

On 11 July, Italian Minister of Finance visited Brussels, from where he again reassured depositors, stating that their savings will be safeguarded (TG Com 24 2016; Romano 2016; Sala 2016). However, Eurogroup President Jeroen Dijsselbloem insisted on the necessity to abide by the bail-in rule, since Italy's banking crisis was not acute (CNBC 2016a; Williams 2016).

The Commission's position on the topic demanded that Italy respect the BRRD rules but showed more flexibility than Dijsselbloem. During a press conference on 14th July 2016, European Commissioner for Competition Vestager reminded the audience that the Commission had been willing to adapt the application of the BRRD to avoid hurting retail investors since the beginning of the month. The European Commission was thus in favor of finding room within the rules that would benefit Italian banking, but not in favor of breaking those rules (Romano 2016; Sanderson and Barker 2016; Sanderson 2016b; Sensini 2016).

On 29 July, MPS presented a plan which aimed to sell €10.2 billion of NPLs and raise €5 billion in new capital from the market. The NPLs were to be sold at 33% of their value in order to make them attractive to investors (Festa 2016a; Righi 2016) and were divided into three tranches:

1. One senior tranche of around €6 billion, to be bought by J.P. Morgan with a bridging loan of a year, at the end of which the Gacs government guarantee scheme would intervene.
2. A mezzanine tranche of around €1.7 billion to be absorbed by the Atlas fund.
3. Another €1.6 billion tranche, to be offered to the current investors, who could decide to subscribe if they wished (La Repubblica 2016b; Leardini 2016; Graziani 2016a).

The ECB approved the plan, showing flexibility, especially in regard to the plans to raise money on capital markets. In fact, it decided to ignore that the sale of NPLs would have required MPS to raise a further €2 billion on top of the 5 billion plan, bringing the total cost of recapitalization to €7 billion. In accepting MPS' plan, the ECB required it to be completed in its entirety (La Repubblica 2016b; Leardini 2016; Festa 2016b; Fior 2016a). Italian Minister of Finance Padoan expressed satisfaction with the plan presented by MPS (Leardini 2016; La Repubblica 2016b; Righi 2016).

It is interesting to observe how right after the approval of the rescue plan for MPS, PM Renzi continued his campaign against the bail-in rule. In an interview on August 2nd, the Prime Minister told CNBC he believed that the bail-in rule was a mistake, in that it would curb investors and citizens' confidence, but that he would nevertheless respect the law (Trovati 2016; CNBC 2016b).

Once the plan had been presented and accepted, MPS had two tasks left to accomplish: it needed its board to approve a three-year plan for the reduction of NPLs and to find investors willing to contribute to the third recapitalization of the bank in three years. The first task was completed on October 25th, when MPS published the bank's three-year plan for the reduction of NPLs (Gruppo MPS 2016c).

Finding investors proved more difficult to accomplish, particularly because it could not be achieved without dealing with the NPL problem. In order to facilitate the search for investors, PM Renzi decided to offer to JP Morgan, together with Mediobanca, the position of joint global coordinator and bookrunner for MPS. The two banks had already been collaborating for a year: it is the duo which came up with the idea to create the Guarantee on Securitization of Bank Non-performing Loans (Gaacs). PM Renzi took the decision to hire JP Morgan after meeting JP Morgan Chase's Chairman, CEO and President Jamie Dimon on July 6th (Pons 2016; Reuters 2016a; Meletti 2016).

Under the guidance of JP Morgan and Mediobanca, MPS engaged in three parallel efforts: the first two, namely the quest for investors and the conversions of subordinated bonds into shares, aimed to raise the required capital by the end of the year, whereas the third was an effort to prop up the Atlas fund, in order to make sure it could participate in the purchase of NPLs.

The *quest for investors* started off with considerable momentum. At the beginning of August, JP Morgan and Mediobanca released a statement listing a number of banks participating in a pre-underwriting concerning the increase of capital. The institutions involved were Banco Santander, Citigroup, Credite Suisse Securities (Europe) Limited, Deutsche Bank, Goldman Sachs International and Merrill Lynch International and Banco Bilbao Vizcaya Argentaria, Commerzbank, Ing, Jefferies and Société Géneral (Pons 2016; Reuters 2016a; Barbaglia and Davies 2016).

Nevertheless, a pre-underwriting is not a binding contract. Therefore, in an effort to find a secure anchor investor, MPS' new CEO Marco Morelli engaged in a promotional tour of MPS shares in London, Paris, New York, Doha and Singapore that lasted between October 24th and November 10th (Ferrando 2016b; Festa 2016c). On September 20th, Morelli replaced Viola as the new CEO (Gruppo MPS n.d.). Finance Minister Padoan speaking as both the Italian state and MPS' main shareholder had asked Viola to resign on September 7th on the suggestion of JP Morgan (Pons 2016; Meletti 2016; Graziani 2016b; Paolucci 2016; Il Fatto Quotidiano 2016d).

It is important to underline that MPS seemed, in this instance, to be open towards foreign investors and open to a reduction of NPL book values. In fact, Morelli's tour took place outside the national territory. The highlights of his journey included: the meeting with Axa, the shareholder of 3.17% of MPS shares, which took place in Paris; meetings with American funds such as Blackrock, Quantum Fund and Paulson in New York; and with Qia, the sovereign wealth fund of Qatar. Qia seemed to be interested in buying a €1 billion share of MPS

(Massaro 2016c; Festa 2016c). A problem was investor skepticism about the extent of MPS' troubles and the feasibility of a complex restructuring plan. This included the conversion of subordinate bonds into shares, and the provision of a bridge loan from the Atlas fund to provide more room for an orderly reorganization of the bank's finances.

Once again on 15th November 2016, MPS proposed a voluntary *capital restructuring to reduce NPLs* and raise the bank's capital ratio, in which bondholders would accept the conversion of the bank's subordinated bonds into shares (Fior 2016c; Kirchgaessner 2016; Rai News 2016). The total offer amounted to €4,288,791,663 (Gruppo MPS 2016d). Initially valid between November 28th and December 2nd, the offer was extended from December 16th to December 21st (Gruppo MPS 2016e). In contrast with MPS' search for foreign investors, MPS' attempt to raise capital from depositors focuses on national resources. This could be interpreted as an attempt to keep ownership national, and therefore economic nationalism.

An additional part of the scheme to save MPS also favored national investors. The contribution of the Atlas fund was a crucial part of MPS' plan to get rid of NPLs. More specifically, MPS' operations involved the newly founded *Atlas II*. Unlike its predecessor, Atlas II could only invest in NPLs. It was established on 8th August 2016 with a capital of €1.715 billion. The government's goal was to bring Atlas 2's capital up to €3 or 3.5 billion (Quaestio sgr 2016b; Ansa 2016; La Repubblica 2016c).

Plan failure, precautionary recapitalization and nationalization

MPS' efforts yielded some results but fell short of their target. The conversion of bonds into shares, for example, was partially successful, with MPS raising €2.44 billion of the €5 billion necessary to recapitalize the bank as of December 21st. Among the investors, Assicurazioni Generali contributed by converting bonds for a value of around €400 million (Il Corriere della Sera 2016). However, the total amount of share value purchased by retail investors was even more impressive, estimated at €1.06 billion (Ferrando 2016c).

Despite the efforts, MPS' plan fell apart due to the lack of an anchor investor, and the subsequent inability of the bank to raise the needed capital by the deadline. The withdrawal of investors was reportedly attributed to the negative result of the constitutional referendum on December 4th, and the subsequent resignation of PM Renzi. The sovereign fund of Qatar in particular blamed the uncertainty of the political environment as the cause of its withdrawal from a €1 billion euro investment. Another factor which reportedly played against the successful implementation of the plan was its complexity. Among the concerns was the need to arrange a €4.7 billion bridging loan, described by a banker as 'not a tidy process' (Provenzani 2016; Arnold and Sanderson 2016). Atlas would provide this loan but needed to collect enough private investment first to be able to do so.

Finally, after expressing serious concerns about the bridge loan in the absence of an anchor investor, the Atlas fund withdrew from participating in the purchase of NPLs (Za 2017; Go News 2016). As Atlas fund's manager Penati underlined on December 21st, the fund had agreed to intervene on the condition that a market solution be found by the end of the year (Reuters 2016c; Gruppo MPS 2016f). The withdrawal of the Atlas fund marked the ultimate failure of MPS' plan. As the ECB had underlined in July, for the plan to work it had to be fulfilled in its entirety.

Now that the market option had been excluded, the Italian government was left with two main options: it could either wind down the bank or bail it out. The first option does not appear to have been considered at all. Rather, the dilemma concerned the conditions under which the now imminent bail-out will take place. As already discussed, the standard procedure envisaged under the BRRD is to perform a bail-in of 8% of the value of the bank, before accessing any form of state aid, which can only be avoided in extraordinary circumstances in which the stability of the economy is jeopardized.

It is in this phase of the crisis that MPS, supported by the Italian government, made the decision to ask for a precautionary recapitalization.

As anticipated, on December 23rd, MPS triggered Article 32 (d) of the BRRD, requesting permission for a *precautionary recapitalization* (Gruppo MPS 2016g). On the same day, the Italian cabinet approved a €20 billion bail-out fund to recapitalize the bank, set to expire at the end of 2017. The fund was established through Decree-Law 237/2016, which new Prime Minister Gentiloni referred to as the 'Savings-Safeguarding Decree' (Decreto Salvarisparmio). In a press conference, Gentiloni stated that the decree's goals were 'the broadest possible coverage of savings, and the consolidation of our banking system' and that the measures had been approved by 'European authorities' (Vista Agenzia Televisiva Nazionale 2016; Treanor and Kirchgaessner 2016; La Repubblica 2016d). Intervening in the press conference, Finance Minister Padoan explained that the decree included a mechanism designed to protect 100% of retail investors' savings. In order to do this, retail investors would be asked to convert their bonds into shares and then into senior debt (La Repubblica 2016d; Treanor and Kirchgaessner 2016).

The ECB approved the precautionary recapitalization in two letters sent to the Italian Ministry of Economy and Finances on December 26th, in which it specified that MPS was solvent, thus eligible for a precautionary recapitalization; that MPS needed capital for around €8.8 billion; and that the bank's capacity had plummeted in the last few months. This latter fact justified the bank's increased need for capital (Il Fatto Quotidiano 2016e; Gruppo MPS 2016g; Transparency International EU 2017; Politi 2016).

The precautionary recapitalization effectively took place seven months later. On 1st July 2017, Commissioner Vestager and the Italian authorities agreed in principle on the restructuring plan of MPS (European Commission 2017b), and on 4th July 2017, the Commission officially approved the precautionary recapitalization. Within this framework, the Italian government was allowed to inject

€5.4 billion into MPS in exchange for shares bought at a discounted price. In the related press release, the Commission stated that MPS was solvent and had met the supervisory requirements, as assessed by the ECB in its supervisory capacity; that a burden-sharing had taken place within the bank for a total of €4.3 billion; that MPS had raised a further €0.5 billion by selling some activities; and finally, that the Italian government was allowed to use €1.5 billion to compensate junior bondholders which had been victims of mis-selling (European Commission 2017c).

Controversies remained. By approving the precautionary recapitalization, the ECB explicitly confirmed that MPS was solvent and implicitly stated that a bail-in of junior bondholders would pose a threat to the economy and needed therefore to be avoided. Both points remain fuzzy and appear to have originated from arbitrary decisions rather than clear indicators.

For one, the ECB determines a bank's solvency by evaluating stress test results (Gruppo MPS 2016g; Il Fatto Quotidiano 2016e). The EBA's 2016 stress test showed that MPS would be insolvent in the event of a hypothetical adverse scenario, but positive under the baseline scenario. The ECB thus decided to assess MPS as solvent based on a normal scenario. Nevertheless, in accepting MPS' request for precautionary recapitalization, the ECB stated that the bank's situation had deteriorated in the previous months, making the solvency of MPS even more borderline. The threat to financial stability and serious disturbance of the economy were also not clearly defined in the Italian government's plans. Doubt had been raised with regard to this point, especially since a bail-in had already taken place in Italy in late 2015, without causing any major disruptions (Merler 2016a). This decision might be explained by the intensive lobbying and negotiations the Italian government entertained with European institutions in 2016. The following dedicated section aims to cast light on the negotiations, both with the Commission and the European Central Bank.

EU-Italian negotiations on MPS

This section aims to provide an answer to sub-question 5:[1] 'How did the Italian government negotiate with the European Commission and the European Central Bank in order to enjoy higher tolerance towards state aid?' In answering this question, evidence is gathered for the two parallel negotiations, one between the Italian government and the EC, and the other between the Italian government and the ECB.

On the one hand, there is evidence that the negotiations between the European Commission and the Italian government took place at least since June 2016, when PM Renzi met Commission President Juncker and Commission Vice-President Dombrovskis in Brussels (De Francesco 2016; Guarascio 2016d). In the period between June and July 2016, sources repeatedly reported the Commission's frustration with the negotiations. The main reason for this frustration was the Italian government's refusal of the bail-in rule, and the claim that it would affect retail investors, despite the Commission's repeated reassurance about the possibility to reimburse junior bondholders (Guarascio 2016c, d; Romano 2016). In this regard, a member of the Commission close to the negotiations stated that Rome should 'stop pretending that there are no solutions other than setting the rules aside' (Sanderson and Barker 2016). The name of the Commissioner was unfortunately not reported. The Commission thus appears to have been rather open to accommodating the Italian government's requests, although it insisted, at least at the beginning, on Italy's compliance with the bail-in rule. Domestic political optics therefore seem to have played a stronger role in the Italian government's stance than the final outcome for its citizens.

On the other hand, information regarding negotiations with the ECB is much scarcer. The point has been made that the Commission's willingness to bend the rule resulted in the Italian government favoring the Commission over the ECB regarding information and consultation (Donnelly 2018). In support of this knowledge gap, Donnelly (2018) reports that the ECB was only notified of the Italian government's intention to promulgate a bail-out decree days *after* it had been effectively agreed upon with the Commission (European Central Bank 2017b). This stands in contrast to some hostility within the ECB itself. Jens Weidmann, President of Germany's Bundesbank and member of the ECB's governing council, invited the Italian government to consider closing the bank rather than bailing it out, given its precarious conditions, adding that 'the money cannot be used to cover losses that are already expected. All this must be carefully examined' (Davies 2016; Il Fatto Quotidiano 2016f). Although Weidmann was consistently in the minority at the ECB on a number of issues of critical importance to Italy, his statements indicate a more complicated and potentially less fruitful negotiation for the Italian government.

At the end of the day, the ECB's position on MPS demonstrated inconsistencies in the period between December 2016 and May/June 2017. In December 2016 it denied Italy a two-week extension to the market solution deadline (Sirletti, Speciale and Totaro 2016; Monaghan and Fletcher 2017). Then, it hastily deemed MPS solvent while stating it needed €3.8 billion more than expected (Gruppo MPS 2016g). It took months to settle disagreements and decisions, such as the precise amount of capital needed by MPS and the state of its finances, even after these questions had supposedly already been settled. Of further interest is that the ECB engaged in an exchange of letters with the Commission on the topic, coupled with visits to MPS to discern the actual state of things (Davi and Ferrando 2017; Sirletti, Groendahl and Totaro 2017).

The ECB's behavior is consistent with some combination of incomplete information, internal disagreement and political pressure as if it were trying to catch up with matters it had not been informed of and to accommodate someone else's demands. The ECB as Single Supervisor is responsible for making sound assessments of the solvency of a bank. But it is also responsible for the systemic stability of both the EU's financial system and that of individual member states. Without the full cooperation of other actors, this had to have been rendered difficult to manage in any other way. In other words, the ECB's behavior seems to point to the fact that a deal had been struck between the other actors regarding the precautionary recapitalization, that alternatives would threaten financial, economic and political chaos, and it had been left with the thankless job of proving MPS' solvency.

Results: functional economic nationalism and MPS

The MPS case can be broken into two phases: a brief liberal search for international investors and willingness to haircut NPLs, which is followed up by underlying problems that retrench themselves and scare investors away. These investors are both other Italian banks (through the Atlas fund), and then international investors, both in the underwriting process and the actual purchase of shares. This leads MPS, with government support, to turn to its own depositors to invest. Government then defends these depositor investors domestically, and at the European level, negotiating exceptions to state aid, to mis-selling reimbursement and to precautionary recapitalization, despite dubious claims to MPS' solvency. The Italian government attaches enormous importance to rejecting the idea of bail-ins on principle, even when MPS' investors get approval for compensation from the Commission.

The results point to the Italian government protecting and promoting a relatively newly found form of national ownership for distressed Italian banks that could not raise investment from neither international nor national financial markets. And finally, the state as the biggest shareholder until MPS can exit its troubles one day. This is certainly Italy protecting and promoting Italian banks, and with the effect of ensuring national ownership. But it is also more than doing so within the confines of the law, exploiting loopholes which we associate with liberal economic nationalism (LEN). It is trying to change the room to maneuver and challenge existing EU law, and EU institutions, holding them hostage to the prospect of financial systemic crisis, rather than trying to intervene to change the Italian variety of financial capitalism in accordance with those rules.

The empirical analysis above contains five hoop tests and one smoking gun test. The first of them concerns the Italian government's attempts to use precautionary recapitalization months before the market operation fails. This observation is in contradiction with the definition of no economic nationalism, liberal or otherwise. In fact, for the 'No LEN' hypothesis to be considered, the Italian government need not attempt to seek state aid unless all other options, and especially the quest for private investors, have been considered. 'No LEN' is thus eliminated.

The second and third hoop tests concern the attempt at raising capital through a market operation, and the tour aimed at attracting foreign investors. In what seems to be a sincere attempt, Prime Minister Renzi appointed JP Morgan and Mediobanca as joint global coordinators and bookrunners of MPS. There is no evidence of any attempt of the Italian government to prevent or hinder the involvement of the sovereign fund of Qatar or any other foreign anchor investors. This observation makes it hard to conclude that the Italian government had an economic nationalist or liberal economic nationalist approach throughout the crisis.

The fourth hoop test concerns the fact that the recapitalization plan included a conversion of junior bonds into shares. Given the fact that junior bonds were largely held by Italian households, this seems to point to the will to keep the banking ownership national. As seen in the third hoop test, however, the plan also entailed a search for foreign investors. With the purpose of being extra careful, this causal-process observation is not considered decisive: the conversion of bonds into shares might have been a backup plan in case foreign investors were willing to contribute but not cover the whole costs of recapitalization.

The fifth and last hoop test concerns 'functional economic nationalism'. This observation points to the Italian government's lobbying and the Commission's willingness to protect retail investors which had mis-sold MPS bonds. Several sources report that the Commission would have in fact been open to reimbursement of retail investors after the bail-in. Despite all this, the government insisted on using state aid. 'Functional economic nationalism' has as a necessary condition the fact that the precautionary recapitalization is used to protect retail investors which would otherwise be neglected. The fact that the Italian government was not content with the compensation of retail investors indicates a strong preference towards state aid beyond the contingencies of the case. The fifth hoop test indicated above has the potential to disconfirm functional economic nationalism, since it could be read as proof of the fact that protecting investors was not the main driver of the government. However, nine straw in the wind tests consistently point to the protection of investors as at least an important factor, with the Italian government opposing the bail-in several months before the precautionary recapitalization.

Additionally and most importantly, outcome two is supported by a smoking gun test. When approving the decree through which state aid is made available, the Italian government effectively formulates a way for retail investors to preserve their savings. Thus, it can be concluded that the purpose of the precautionary recapitalization is, at least in part, to reimburse retail investors.

If we apply tests for the degree of causation to the MPS case, we come to some fairly robust conclusions. Straw tests find evidence for more than one kind of motivation for state behavior: there are early indications consistent with liberalism (searching for foreign investors) or liberal economic nationalism (searching for takeover candidates from within the country, and twisting the arms of Italian banks to establish and fund Atlas), and later functional economic nationalism (lobbying EU institutions for special dispensation from the BRRD, from aspects of the SSM and from European competition law) to save the bank and its depositors when all else fails. Looking at hoop tests, liberalism is contradicted by the autumn of 2016, when the search for international investors has long faded into the background, and the Italian government has not only suggested state aid (Renzi, June) but started turning to the Commission. Functional economic nationalism becomes noticeable by December 2016. This includes the government's willingness to use state aid months before the market operation fails, and not as a last resort.

However, there is also a convincing smoking gun: strong refusal on the part of the Italian government to apply the bail-in provisions of the BRRD (statements by Renzi, Gentiloni and the Bank of Italy in late 2016) and its equally strong commitment by Finance Minister Padoan to stand by depositors, the willingness to provide large capital injections to rescue MPS; the dubious legality of the state aid decision regarding the precautionary capitalization, negotiating exceptions to the BRRD's bail-in rules and state aid restrictions with the Commission, and keeping the ECB out of the loop until a deal with the Commission was a fait accompli (circumvents the only truly strong Banking Union institution). In other words, the answer to the research question 'To what extent is the Italian government trying to keep the ownership national' for the first case study is: the Italian government is trying to keep the ownership national as long as it keeps the bank afloat, and it allows it to protect depositors and retail investors.

One more factor revealed from the analysis of MPS crisis is Italy's untamed will to keep the bank afloat. In fact, the Italian government opposed the resolution of MPS with the same fervor with which it opposed the bail-in. Over the course of four years, the bank went through two recapitalizations in two years for a total of around €8 billion and reported the poorest performance of all participants at the stress test the following year. Yet, the government never considered winding down the bank, even despite the fact that the bail-out cost billions of euros to a country with a sky-high sovereign debt.

What is surprising, it must be said, is the Commission's willingness to accommodate both of Italy's requests to keep the bank afloat without going through a bail-in. This all said, MPS certainly sets a precedent that casts a confusing light on the BRRD in only a few months after entering into force.

Regional banks

In this section we treat regional banks, for which the Italian government and central bank are more directly responsible. The resolution of these banks falls under the review of the Single Resolution Board (SRB), but the initiative remains with national authorities. We will see here that local connections are even more intense and powerful than for MPS and that the explanatory power of functional economic nationalism plays a correspondingly stronger role in the behavior of the Italian state. All of the banks here are Italian cooperative banks. They are ruled under the 'one shareholder one vote' principle. Banks of this kind are not part of the stock market, therefore the price of their shares is determined through other means, such as independent experts (Bank of Italy 2015). A 2015 law required these banks to update their status to limited companies in an effort to deal with chronic corporate governance problems that favored local businesses and councils, eventually to the detriment of local depositors. We deal in detail here with five banks: Etruria, Marche and Ferrera before the introduction of the BRRD, and Veneto and Vicenza banks after its introduction, to illustrate the mechanisms at work. To save space, we have not outlined two regional banks' collapse and closures which were made difficult by poor corporate governance: Charichieti and Bari.

Banca Etruria e del Lazio

According to Fitch, already in 2011 Banca Etruria held double the amount of NPLs compared to the Italian average (Pavesi 2015). This situation resulted from Banca Etruria's habit of granting generous loans to members of the banks, local mayors, politicians and companies without proper background checks, losing millions in doubtful ventures such as the construction of a luxury yacht that never came to fruition (Fontanelli 2019), all of which was further aggravated by the crisis and following the credit crunch.

In an effort to improve its capital, Banca Etruria took a series of more or less creative measures with the goal of strengthening its capital, including the issuing and conversion into shares of €109.9 million worth of subordinate bonds and a €100 million recapitalization (Senato della Repubblica e Camera dei Deputati 2017).

Eventually, a supervisory inspection brought the Ministry of Economy and Finance to first put the bank under extraordinary administration and then resolve it together with the other three regional banks in November 2015. The healthy assets of Banca Etruria were gathered into a good bank, which was purchased by Ubi Banca, under the name of Nuova Banca Etruria. The year 2012 marked the beginning of Bank of Italy's ever closer monitoring of the bank. In a letter sent on 24th July 2012 to Banca Etruria's President Fornasari, Bank of Italy's President Visco commented that despite the (few) corrective actions undertaken by the bank, the quality of credit had worsened rather than improved.

As a result, Visco urged interventions aiming to 'improve the structure and instruments controlling the different phases of the credit process, also with the purpose of eliminating the remarkable delays in the identification of problematic assets' (Sarzanini 2017a, *translated by the author*). Visco even suggested that the bank hire highly professional board members to be better equipped in facing the situation (Tonacci 2015b). In line with Visco's concerns, the Bank of Italy requested Etruria to write off an amount of non-performing loans four times higher than that of the previous year. As a result, Banca Etruria registered a total of €203 million losses throughout 2012 (Senato della Repubblica – Camera dei Deputati 2017).

At this point, the inspection turned from having a relatively narrow scope to a general investigation of its operations. Since March 2013, the investigation extended to all risk profiles and ended in a final assessment issued in September 2013, where the bank scored 5/6 on a scale of gravity (Senato della Repubblica

– Camera dei Deputati 2017; Tonacci 2015a). In its report, Bank of Italy underlined the bank's worrisome worsening of credit quality. The bank's capital still met legal requirements, but it needed strengthening (Bank of Italy 2016).

In the meantime, with the investigations still ongoing, Etruria's board kept fighting its fate, and in April 2013 the bank presented a plan to raise money with a *recapitalization* of €100 million, approved by both Consob and Bank of Italy, and in line with Bank of Italy's requests to strengthen its capital (Senato della Repubblica – Camera dei Deputati 2017). The recapitalization officially opened on 10th June 2013. Shares were sold for €0.6 each for a total of €100 million. President Fornasari commented that the successful operation was a further confirmation of the bank's popular recognition and crucial role in Central Italy, as well as of its sturdiness (Pavesi and Boda 2015).

In addition to the recapitalization, Etruria decided to pursue *domestic marketization* emit €110 million worth of subordinated bonds, split into €60 million offered between 3rd and 7th June 2013; and €50 million, to be emitted between 16th and 23th October of the same year (Senato della Repubblica – Camera dei Deputati 2017). In approving the emission of €110 million in subordinated debt, the Bank of Italy specified in a letter that they were 'suitable for institutional investors' (Capozzi 2015). Similarly underlying the risks implied in the very nature of the subordinated bonds, the Italian Companies and Exchange Commission (Consob) granted its approval (Senato della Repubblica – Camera dei Deputati 2017).

Despite these premises, however, the overwhelming majority of the bonds were not purchased by institutional investors, but rather by retail investors (Paolucci 2017). As it appears, institutional investors were all but interested in a product that was by definition targeted to them. This can be explained by the fact that the bank's precarious conditions had earned it an ever-worsening rating, so much so that Finch had lowered it to BB+ in February 2012, the worst rating among all Italian banks. As a result, selling bonds to institutional investors would have been too expensive after receiving such a poor rating: they would have asked for at least a 7% yield. On the contrary, Etruria offered a yield of only 3.5% on the *€60 bonds* emitted in June and of 5% on the €50 million emitted in October. Such a low yield is comparable to that of the Italian government's 10-year treasury bonds, which was 4.14% at the time (Nasdaq 2013) and has raised the hypothesis that Etruria's subordinated bonds were purposefully crafted to appear safe (Pavesi 2015; Paolucci 2017; La Repubblica 2011).

To be sure, they were sold as such. As witnesses' stories as well as emails made public during Arezzo's tribunal process testify, the bank's management pushed its employees to convince customers to invest in them, calling them on the phone and promising they could retrieve their investment anytime. A further indication of the bank's awareness of its action is the falsification of investors' profiles: the bank would, for instance, falsify the level of education of the 'investors' in order for them to be in line with Markets in Financial Instruments Directive (2004/39/EC) standards.

On top of that, in a letter sent to Consob on 30th November 2013, the Bank of Italy expressed its concerns about the mismatch between high risk and low yield in Etruria's bonds. A further letter from Visco to Banca Etruria, dated 3rd December 2013, underlined how the board's inadequacy and corporate governance failings had led it to engage in poor strategic planning resulting in a 'further, pronounced deterioration of the group's technical profile' and a 'progressive and irreversible decline' of the bank (Sarzanini 2017a). This letter and its concerns were not made public, however. The official statement released only ten days later did not express the same categorical views on Etruria's fate (Capozzi 2015). Despite these warnings, Consob did not investigate the bank's dealings (Paolucci 2017). On the contrary, Consob would later be accused of authorizing the sales of subordinated bonds to retail investors (Capozzi 2015). Overall, it appears that Etruria's approach to recapitalization was not improvised but was rather part of a strategy that was first mentioned in the bank's 2012 yearly report: *granularizzazione della raccolta.* This strategy, which can be translated as 'fragmentation of yields', expressly aimed to target retail investors rather than institutional ones (Pavesi 2015; Paolucci 2016b). Visco's 2013 letter had also urged Etruria to merge with a larger group, which would be able to provide it with the 'necessary professional and capital resources' (La Repubblica 2016; Sarzanini 2017b). In its 13th December public statement, Etruria announced it would follow the advice and pursue a merger with a prominent banking group (La Nazione 2013; Senato della Repubblica – Camera dei Deputati 2017).

In 2014, however, *Etruria's rejection of all outside investors*, even Italian ones, became apparent. On May 29th 2014, Banca Popolare di Vicenza offered to buy Banca Etruria for €217 million. The offer corresponded to €1 per share, that is 25.8% more than their official price on the stock market at the time (Fornovo 2014; La Repubblica 2014). The offer was quickly refused by Banca Etruria's board (Il Sole 24 Ore 2016; Bassan 2014). As we now know, Banca Popolare di Vicenza was itself in dramatic capital conditions; however, it remains unclear whether Etruria was aware of Vicenza's capital conditions at the time. In either case, in refusing the offer, Etruria did not mention capital concerns, but rather its commitment to defend its deeply rooted territorial presence and independence (Bank of Italy 2016). This would be the first and last offer of merger Etruria received.

The bank would enter extraordinary administration and resolution by the end of 2014; however, Banca Etruria's board took advantage of a relatively new national law on popolari (regional alternative) banks allowing them to transform into private companies and informed the Bank of Italy of its decision in August 2014 (Curridori 2015). The board had declared its willingness to transform into a limited company the previous summer, a statement which had been positively welcomed by the market at the time. In an interview, President Rosi had stated that the decision was taken with the purpose of opening the bank to international investment (Il Sole 24 Ore 2013). However, this plan never came to fruition. On 11th November 2014, Bank of Italy's task force returned to Banca Etruria for a new round of inspections that would mark the end of the bank as we knew it (Pavesi and Boda 2015).

The result of the final investigation was grim. The bank scored 6/6 on a scale of gravity: remarkable capital loss brought its capital below legal requirements, and Bank of Italy found several severe irregularities (Bank of Italy 2016). Among the irregularities, the bank's surety (debt guarantee) division was found to be completely ineffective in 91% of cases. Despite covering the crucial function of guaranteeing the ability of the bank's borrowers' to pay back the agreed sum, and taking responsibility to pay it back in case the borrower fails to do so, Etruria's surety division was remarkably understaffed. It counted only 19 employees, each of which was in charge of managing 550 cases, which severely impaired their ability to properly check the clients' financial status (Tonacci 2015b). Based on these results, Arezzo's tribunal opened a new investigation in order to inquire 'omission of communication of conflict of interests' concerning Etruria's former President Lorenzo Rosi and former board member Luciano Nataloni (Tonacci 2015b).

Under Bank of Italy's request, the Ministry of Economy and Finance officially put Banca Etruria under extraordinary administration with decree n. 45 of 10 February 2015 (Bank of Italy 2015). The following day, Bank of Italy's officials interrupted a board meeting which was supposed to approve the 2014 financial report and officially took over Banca Etruria. Banca Etruria's capital had been completely squandered (Pavesi and Boda 2015).

As emerged from President Visco's letter, the reasons for requiring extraordinary administration can be boiled down to Etruria's inability to contain the growth of NPLs, the amount of which had reached unsustainable levels (Sarzanini 2017a). On 13 February, Banca Etruria's shares on the stock market were suspended for an indefinite period (Senato della Repubblica – Camera dei Deputati 2017). With closure imminent, Etruria exacerbated corporate governance concerns by engaging in insider trading. On 17 November 2015, right before resolution, Credito Fondiario spa, formed by a number of Italian entrepreneurs (including the head of the Benetton Group), bankers, the Vatican bank's President and ECB executive board member Lorenzo Bini Smaghi, bought more than €300 million worth of Etruria's NPLs for only €49 million. The operation was authorized by Bank of Italy, right before Arezzo's tribunal declared the bank insolvent. This incident has been put under the scrutiny of Arezzo's tribunal, as the money could have been used to cover for the defrauded retail investors' losses (Malagutti 2016; Amendolara 2020).

The extent of Etruria's reliance on its own customers and their exposure to a bail-in culminated in late November 2015, when the retired investor Lui'ino D'Angelo committed suicide after losing his lifelong savings. The employee who made him sign the deal once again confirmed that the bank had required him and his colleagues to make retail investors purchase subordinated debt, and to convince them of their safety (Roncone 2015; Angeli 2015).

Overall, Etruria demonstrates serious problems with non-performing loans, corporate governance and strong connections to local households and businesses, and a penchant for turning to both its own depositors and prominent national investors to bridge its solvency problems. There is less evidence for outright economic nationalism than there is for preserving local connections through the bank that the Bank of Italy was unable to turn around until it had to close the bank.

Banca Marche

Unlike the other regional banks in this section, Banca Marche had been a publicly quoted bank since 1996, that is two years after its establishment through the merger of two regional banks. Between 2004 and 2007, Banca Marche pursued a geographic expansion throughout Central Italy, opening branches in the neighboring regions of Abruzzo, Lazio, Emilia-Romagna and Umbria. While this geographic expansion aimed to increase market shares and diversification, it also exposed the bank to less familiar territories and entrepreneurs, loosening the bank's signature tight relationship with the territory.

The period between 2004 and 2010 also saw a radical increase in both the amount of money loaned to clients and the clients' exposure to the bank, with 40,000 retail investors, most of whom were also depositors and clients at the bank, holding as much as 32% of the bank's shares. Banca Marche distinguished itself in the Italian scenario due to its refusal to stop lending money during the credit crunch. Unfortunately, rather than being well thought-out investments or small household loans, Banca Marche loaned hundreds of millions to very few clients, which produced a high rate of non-performing loans. The growing amount of non-performing loans, as well as an excessive exposure in the real estate sector, would result in a gradual weakening of the bank's capital (Commissione di Indagine Banca Marche 2016; Corriere Adriatico 2013b; Meletti 2013; Ferreri 2017).

As a result, the Bank of Italy began a series of investigations on the bank. Urged by the national supervisor, Banca Marche raised €180 million in 2012 and attempted to raise more capital in 2013. When the bank failed to find an institutional investor, and following the dire outcome of the 2013 investigations, the bank was put under extraordinary administration. Banca Marche was resolved in 2015, and its healthy assets were turned into the good bank Nuova Banca Marche, later rebranded as Banca Adriatica (Ansa 2017).

Between 2010 and 2011, the Bank of Italy performed three inspections on Banca Marche. Banca Marche's situation was deemed 'partially unfavorable', with a mark of 4 out of 6 on a scale of gravity. Together with a letter that enlisted the grim capital conditions of Banca Marche, Bank of Italy proceeded to sanction 17 members of the bank for a total of €280,000 due to procedural irregularities and they required the bank to recapitalize.

In 2011, Banca Marche sought to increase its capital by establishing the 12-year real estate fund Fondo Conero, which encompassed 135 investment properties (*immobili strumentali*), including around 128 banking institutes owned by the bank. The overall value of Fondo Conero was €243 million. This move initially had a positive effect on the bank in that it produced a capital gain of €86 million, boosting the bank's core tier 1 capital, which serves as the bank's most secure foundation (Commissione di Indagine Banca Marche 2016).

However, the establishment of the fund crucially increased the bank's exposure to the real estate sector, a choice that would have negative long-term effects. In fact, the end of 2012 meant Banca Marche's first negative balance of €518 million. The negative balance was particularly remarkable as it came right after a half-year balance which had reported a €42.7 million profit. The loss is to be attributed, for the most part, to the writing off of non-performing loans connected to these real estate investments (Banca Marche 2012; Cionna 2013a; Benedett 2013a). Doubling down on real estate investment rather than writing off non-performing loans therefore failed to solve the bank's problems.

Following the Bank of Italy's request to raise capital, Banca Marche was eventually able to raise €180 million in 2012 (Bank of Italy 2016). This capital was mainly raised from retail investors, who were unaware of the gravity of the Bank's capital. In fact, the letter sent by Banca Marche's President Ambrosini the day before the issuing of the bonds painted a much more positive picture than Bank of Italy's letter did and failed to mention the deteriorating quality of credit and the urgency of internal reforms present in the original letter (Cronache Maceratesi 2013). In this instance, the then-Director Bianconi only contributed €871,25 despite receiving an annual salary of €1.5 million (Il Resto del Carlino 2015).

The Bank of Italy began its final inspection of Banca Marche in November 2012, with the purpose of verifying the adequacy of provisions. Following the poor results of its first phase, the inspection was extended from March until September 2013. In an effort to enhance its capital, Fondo Conero sold some real estate between late 2012 and January 2013 (Patrassi 2013). But it was too little, too late. Despite the dire scenario, the bank's President was optimistic, based on a *strategy of domestic marketization*, in which depositors would fund the bank. On 16th March 2013, Mr Costa declared that Banca Marche would not need to be rescued because depositors would support it. In his words: 'our 40,000 members will understand the effort we ask of them' (Ferreri 2013a; Cionna 2013b).

However, the Bank of Italy disagreed on the further involvement of retail investors in the bank's rescue. In April 2013, the supervisor required Banca Marche to raise €300 million in shares by September, and an additional €100 million to be raised later. By doing so, the Bank of Italy strongly suggested raising this capital from an institutional investor, be it Italian or foreign (Gualtieri 2013a; Ferrando 2013).

Despite being unable to retrieve the needed capital from depositors, Banca Marche *refused to accept outside investors* without a fight, claiming a special relationship with the region. Throughout the bank's crisis, several commentaries and statements emphasized just how important the local character of investors was perceived to be by some of the actors involved. For instance, when interviewed about the possibility of selling the bank in 2012, Director of Banca Marche Luciano Goffi had answered that that was not an option and that, in any case, the bank had not received any proposal from foreign investors. The director also underlined the importance of '*radicamento*' as a strategy, that is the deep connection between the bank and the territory (Benedetti 2012). Similarly, the Governor of the Marche Region stated that it was important to defend the politico-industria 'Marchigianità' (that is, belonging and being close to the region of Marche) of Banca Marche. The Governor praises Banca Marche, which invested 30% more in the local economy than it yielded (Corriere Adriatico 2013a).

These two statements show, on the one hand, how aligned the mindset, goals and priorities of the local political elite and that of Banca Marche's board were, and, on the other hand, why Bank of Italy's insistence on finding an Italian or international institutional investor was such a hard pill to swallow for Banca Marche's board. In line with this, in May 2013, Banca Marche looked to persuade local entrepreneurs to invest in the bank in order to maintain the local nature of the capital, efforts that continued throughout the summer (Danieli 2013; Gualtieri 2013c; Ricci 2013). A group of Italian investors offered between 1 and 2 million euros each for a total of 200 million (Gualtieri 2013c). The President of Region Marche urged local entrepreneurs and investors to lend Banca Marche a helping hand in order to prevent it from being purchased by foreign institutes (Meletti 2013). In September, the same entrepreneurs announced their offer could cover all of the €300 million required (Il Sole 24 Ore 2013b). Overall, the pattern is more one of regionalism than nationalism. In their desperation to save the bank, both the bank's governors and local politicians were attempting to retrieve funds from the same businesses that were unable to repay their loans to support the bank.

By summer 2013, however, an insufficient volume of actual investment led to the last minute effort to seek investment from outside the region. Former Minister for Economic Planning Rainer Masera was elected as the new President of Banca Marche in an attempt to rescue the bank and reassure investors under difficult conditions (Buroni 2013). Masera worked on finding institutional investors, both at the local and international levels. French banks BNP Paribas and Crédit Agricole were possible investors, as well as Banca Intesa (Ferreri 2013b). In addition to the €300 million recapitalization required by Bank of Italy, in June 2013 Banca Marche issued €80 million worth of ten-year Upper Tier II subordinated bonds with an annual yield of 12.5%. The high yield points to just how desperate the situation was: without these €80 million by July 31, Banca Marche would not reach the minimum capital *coefficient* required by the supervisor. The main targets of these bonds were Cr Jesi, Cr Pesaro and Cr Macrata, institutions which owned in total 55% of Banca Marche's shares. Cr Jesi and Cr Pesaro subscribed to the initiative, gathering €20 million, whereas Cr Macerata refused to participate, and Banca Marche failed to gather the much needed €80 million before the deadline (Meletti 2013; Gualtieri 2013b; Benedetti 2013b).

The final results of Bank of Italy's investigation gave Banca Marche a score of 6/6 on the gravity index. Due to this and to Banca Marche's inability to find viable investors, the Ministry of Economics and Finance put the institute under temporary administration in August (Reuters 2013; Bernabei and Za 2015) and confirmed extraordinary administration in October (Commissione di Indagine Banca Marche 2016; Senato della Repubblica – Camera dei Deputati 2017). In addition to that, 18 members and former members of the bank received sanctions for a total of €4.2 million (Bank of Italy 2016). Once again, poor corporate governance and bank-council ties were core to the bank's problems.

Cassa di Risparmio di Ferrara

Between 2002 and 2008, Carife engaged in a territorial expansion, with the mission of growing while remaining a local bank (Santini 2004), and as the size of the bank grew so did the value of its shares, soaring from €17.5 in 2000 to €41.5 in 2008 (Murolo 2008). However, two unfruitful €140 million investments in the real estate sector and one just as unfortunate €86 million investment in Acqua Marcia filled Carife with non-performing loans and deteriorated the bank's capital, reaching a rate of non-performing loans higher than 20% (Mazzaro 2019; Senato della Repubblica – Camera dei Deputati 2017). This called the attention of the Bank of Italy, which in 2009 carried out an inspection on Carife. Despite a 150 million recapitalization, Carife never recovered. Bank of Italy performed a further investigation which resulted in extraordinary administration in May 2013, and the resolution in November 2015. In 2017 Carife was acquired by Banca Popolare dell'Emilia Romagna, one of the most profitable and internationalized Italian banks (Senato della Repubblica – Camera dei Deputati 2017; BPER 2017).

It took not more than two careless *real estate investments* in Milan to bring Carife to its knees. Through Vesagest Immobiliare, Carife invested in two big projects in the Milan area, namely Milano Santa Monica and MiLuce.[2] The two pieces of land were purchased for low prices and sold to Carife for highly inflated prices between 2006 and 2008: Santa Monica had been bought for €12 million in 2002 and sold to Carife per 117 million, whereas MiLuce had been bought for only 200 thousand euro and sold to Carife for €4.5 million three years later. These events triggered a judicial process for fraud perpetrated by members of Vesagest against Carife. Despite being initially found guilty, all the defendants were acquitted on appeal. The case nevertheless raised questions about corporate governance and local network ties.

Fraudulent or not, the carelessness of this investment cost Carife non-performing loans €160 million which, unfortunately for Carife, added up to a further €86 million NPLs coming from an investment in Acqua Marcia, for a total of over €240 million NPLs. Acqua Marcia had been a prestigious enterprise which went bankrupt in 2012 and which owed a total of €1 billion to Italian banks, including Veneto Banca (Elli and Pavesi 2013; Mazzaro 2019; Pavesi 2017).

In a letter dating June 2010, Bank of Italy urged Carife to strengthen and diversify its capital, simplify its structure and enhance background checks. Dissatisfied with Carife's reaction to its suggestions, in October 2010 Bank of Italy required the bank to raise €150 million, with the goal of guaranteeing a Tier I ratio of 8% (Senato della Repubblica – Camera dei Deputati 2017). The recapitalization was carried out during the summer and concluded in September 2011 (Senato della Repubblica – Camera dei Deputati 2017). Out of the total €150 million, an outstanding €115 million was purchased by private and retail investors. Once again, the massive involvement of retail investors in the purchase of subordinate debt would later result in thousands of households losing their savings, protests and lengthy judiciary procedures, and over two years of jail time for two top executives of Carife (Oppo 2019). Once again, retail investors were lured into buying the bank time until it ran out.

Unfortunately for Carife and its investors, the €150 million recapitalization did not suffice to cure the depth of Carife's troubles. In September 2012, a year after the successful completion of the recapitalization, Bank of Italy launched another inspection, which concluded in February 2013. This time, the assessment was a severe 6/6 on the scale of gravity. The Bank of Italy estimated that Carife's capital was in reality closer to €280 million than to the €599 million that was declared. The total capital ratio was 6.6%, well below the minimum of 8%. Bank of Italy implemented €1 million sanctions targeting 15 members of Carife (Senato della Repubblica – Camera dei Deputati 2017).

With such an unfavorable assessment, Carife had run out of time. The bank was put under extraordinary administration on 27th May 2013 (Barbagallo 2017). When the bank was resolved in November 2015, its assets were gathered into Nuova Cassa di Risparmio di Ferrara S.p.A. The good bank was purchased by and merged into BPER Bank in 2017 (La Repubblica 2017k).

Veneto e Vicenza

Veneto Banca (VB) and Banca Popolare di Vicenza (BpVi) were two locally important banks which shared a set of common features and followed a similar trajectory before being wound down under Italian insolvency law in 2017. Among their common features, it is important to mention that both VB and BpVi were, until 2016, cooperative banks. However, a decree issued in January 2015 by the Italian government required them to transition into joint-stock companies within 18 months (Gazzetta Ufficiale 2015; Il Fatto Quotidiano 2015a). In addition to that, the two banks went through a series of recapitalizations through operations that were later subject to European and national investigations (Galbiati 2016; Vanni 2017). Finally, due to their similar situations, VB and BpVi were paired up by both Italian and European regulators and policymakers from the beginning of their crises, and an attempt was made to save them through a merger (Corriere del Veneto 2016; Mandurino 2017c). Therefore, it is reasonable to treat the crises of VB and BpVi as one case study, and for the rest of this book the two banks will often be addressed together under the acronym 'V&V'.

Between 2010 and 2016, Banca Popolare di Vicenza's non-performing loans grew dramatically. The reason behind the bank's insolvency is two-fold. On the one hand, BpVi was tightly connected to local companies, and when the crisis hit the region and they were unable to pay their debts, the bank was affected. On the other hand, though, the bank was used to providing generous loans to habitual clients, family members and the bank's council members, independently of their ability to pay back the debt (Bilotta 2017b). In order to prop up its deteriorating capital, between 2013 and 2014 BpVi engaged in several recapitalizations, raising €1.3 billion and acquiring 116,000 new shareholders (Malagutti 2015a; Il Sole 24 Ore 2015; Banca Popolare di Vicenza 2015e).

In a similar fashion, the financial situation of Veneto Banca deteriorated amid a series of loans to companies lacking a solid financial situation (such as Alitalia, the Boscolo group, Acqua Marcia and Lotto Sport); as well as to politicians, including MP Verdini who in 2012 borrowed €7.6 million to temporarily cover the debt of his real estate and editorial companies; and to his family, including his wife, which used a loan to buy a villa in Sardinia. Veneto Banca lost €96 million in 2013, and €968 million in 2014 (Bilotta 2017b). Between 26th June and 28th July 2014, VB launched a recapitalization among its shareholders for almost €500 million (Davi 2014; Il Gazzettino 2014). The operation closed successfully, with shareholders subscribing to 95% of the offer (Il Mattino di Padova 2017).

The advent of *direct ECB supervision intensified V&V's known financial problems.* This also says something about the relative weakness of the Italian state prior to the ECB taking over responsibility. Due to their size in terms of assets, VB and BpVi passed under the ECB's direct supervision on 4th November 2014. The two banks had until then been supervised by the Bank of Italy (European Central Bank 2014b; Bank of Italy 2015; European Central Bank 2015). On 26th October 2014, the ECB and the EBA published the stress test results. The stress test revealed the poor performance of BpVi and VB, despite their efforts to raise capital (European Central Bank 2014a).

Right after taking over the bank's supervision, the ECB noticed irregularities in the way the recapitalizations have been carried out within Banca Popolare di Vicenza. Thus, between 26th February and 3rd July 2015, the ECB conducted an investigation on the bank. The results were published in a 103-page long report according to which the bank had engaged in several unlawful behaviors (Galbiati 2016; DBRS 2015).

Building on the ECB investigations, the tribunal to look into Vicenza started investigating BpVi on 22nd September 2015 (Vanni 2017), whereas the Italian Financial police issued a warrant for inspections in BpVi offices in Vicenza, Rome, Milan and Palermo. Chairman Zonin and former CEO Sorato were themselves under investigation. The charges against the bank included stock manipulation and impediment of supervisory functions. The bank's misconduct includes overestimating the price of its shares, granting loans to support share purchases, buying back its own shares without properly notifying the competent authority and spreading false information regarding the state of the bank (Carletti 2015; La Repubblica 2015; Vanni 2017).

Consob began an inspection on VB in January 2015. Rome's public prosecutor office searched the bank in February, eventually discharging CEO Consoli, who was arrested the following year under charges of impediment to supervisory functions and stock manipulation (Apponi 2017). The investigations brought to light the fact that the bank Veneto Banca would guarantee loans in exchange for bonds. This resulted in €1 billion of liabilities more than declared on the balance sheets (Bilotta 2017b).

Moreover, VB's 2014 recapitalization turned out to have been deeply rigged: in fact, VB had started selecting subscribers in March 2014, and before the official beginning of the recapitalization it had concluded 3,757 sales for a total value of €46 million. Thus, the recapitalization appeared not only to have been planned ahead of time but to have involved unaware shareholders, who had not even been provided with a copy of their purchase (Bilotta 2017a; Il Mattino di Padova 2017).

Despite the recapitalizations, at the end of 2015 VB and BpVi found themselves in need of more capital. In December 2015, given the increasingly serious situation, Veneto Region's President Luca Zaia sent a letter to PM Renzi, Minister Padoan, Bank of Italy's President Visco and ECB President Draghi. In the letter he stated that a strong governmental intervention was absolutely necessary in order to safeguard depositors and companies, arguing that a bail-in would actually result in higher costs for the state and Veneto's society (Corriere del Veneto 2015; RaiNews 2015; Il Gazzettino 2015). This situation was further underlined by the ECB's annual Supervision Review and Evaluation Process (SREP), at the end of which the ECB urged the two banks to present a plan to strengthen their capital by April 2016 (Todescan 2015; Banca Popolare di Vicenza 2015d; Gruppo Veneto Banca 2015).

In the meantime, the two banks were required to transition into joint-stock companies by June 2016. This transition proved challenging for the two credit institutions. This meant that for the first time the banks' share prices would be determined by the market, and this could result in further losses of capital and turn the situation from difficult to dramatic. On 5th March 2016, BpVi's Board of Directors approved the transformation of the institutions from a Credit Union (Cooperative Bank) into a joint-stock company (S.p.A.), in addition to raising capital and launching the bank into the stock exchange (Banca Popolare di Vicenza 2016). Veneto Banca, on the other hand, had approved the transition already on 19th December 2015. During the same meeting, the Board of Directors had also approved a capital increase of €1 billion (Bodellini 2017; Il Fatto Quotidiano 2015c).

UniCredit, the Atlas fund and V&V

Ironically, in order to raise capital by going public, BpVi first had to raise additional capital to be in good financial health. BpVi had a desperate need for capital by the start of 2016 (Zingales 2015; Malagutti 2015b). Under the request of the ECB, the bank had erased €1 billion from its balance sheet in early 2015 due to the heavy irregularities in the previous recapitalizations (Banca Popolare di Vicenza 2015a; Za and Aloisi 2015). In order to tackle the situation, on 21st September 2015 BpVi had announced UniCredit Group's pre-underwriting for a €1.5 billion recapitalization, to be carried out by April 2016 in the context of BpVi's debut on the stock market. UniCredit's operation would be supported by BNP Paribas, Deutsche Bank AG, London Branch, J.P. Morgan, and Mediobanca, acting together with UniCredit as joint global coordinators (La Repubblica 2015b; Banca Popolare di Vicenza 2015b).

However, in 2016, UniCredit's intention seemed to shift. In April, UniCredit's CEO Ghizzoni shared with the government his concerns about BpVi's €1.5 billion recapitalization. UniCredit was itself in a delicate situation (Legorano 2016), and being liable for BpVi's stock market offering would have exposed it to further problems if investors failed to buy. Given BpVi's urgent need of capital and the fact that the government was left with too little time to plan and negotiate a lawful intervention, PM Renzi, Minister Padoan and Bank of Italy's President Visco, together with Intesa, UniCredit, Ubi and Cdp and Acri, established the privately funded *Atlas* fund. The ECB approved the plan, requiring a minimum capital of €4 billion and asking that the section of the fund to be used in order to purchase NPLs wouldn't exceed 30% of the total resources (Greco 2017a).

On April 19th, Quaestio Capital management sgr, that is the company responsible for the establishment and management of the Atlas fund, signed a sub-underwriting deal with UniCredit and BpVi. By signing the agreement, the Atlas fund committed to replacing UniCredit in underwriting the bank's shares in case of failure of the market operation (Quaestio sgr 2016a; Ravallin 2016). This agreement proved fortuitous for UniCredit. When BpVi made its debut on Milan's stock exchange on May 2nd, it only managed to sell 7.66% of its shares, getting nowhere near the minimum 25% set by Piazza Affari. The main investor had been Mediobanca, alone among the joint global coordinators to intervene (Massaro 2016a; Veneto Economia 2016a). Thus, BpVi failed to enter the stock market, and the Atlas fund purchased 99% of BpVi's shares at €0.1 each, turning Atlas into BpVi's main shareholder. In doing so, the operation nullified the €6 billion recapitalization that BpVi's shareholders had performed in the previous years (Il Sole 24 Ore 2017c). Commenting on UniCredit's lack of action, now-former CEO Ghizzoni later explained that UniCredit's pre-underwriting was not binding and that BpVi's deteriorating conditions drove UniCredit's participation away (Gatti 2016).

In a similar fashion, Veneto Banca also needed to raise €1 billion in capital in order to comply with the requests of the ECB as a result of the SREP decision.

It also planned to do so by selling shares on the stock exchange. Thus, during the board meeting on 19th December 2015, the bank had decided to launch an offer of shares for shareholders up to a maximum of €1 billion in 2016 (Gruppo Veneto Banca 2015). In order to attract investors, VB reportedly engaged in around 250 meetings with potential investors. However, VB's prospects looked more and more dull as the months went by, and even more so after BpVi's failure to enter the stock market. Indeed when VB's attempt to enter the stock market at the end of May yielded poor results. In fact, only 3.43% of its capital was subscribed, and the price of VB shares stalled at €0.1 (Mandurino 2016; La Tribuna di Treviso 2016).

As a result, on the very day of VB's failure to enter the stock market, Quaestio sgr signed a sub-underwriting for a deep restructuring of the bank (Arosio, Quaglia and Za 2016; Mandurino 2016). The capital increase was therefore funded by the Atlas fund, which now owned 97.64% of the bank's shares. In 2016, the Bank registered a loss of €1.5 billion. The 2016 stress test results brought the ECB to request that Veneto Banca raise capital for a total of €3.1 billion (Bodellini 2017).

In Autumn 2016, a number of foreign investors, such as JP Morgan, Apax, Apollo and Jc Flowers, approached Atlas' fund manager Penati in order to make an offer on V&V. Due to the banks' critical conditions, the offer could have only been low, and the cuts on personnel high. JP Morgan's offer, for instance, included a 65% cut on personnel, which the Atlas fund reportedly found exaggerated (Bennewitz 2016; Reuters 2016b). The *foreign involvement was therefore rejected*. Although the Atlas fund was more concerned with restructuring the two banks rather than selling them at the time, these offers importantly underline the viability of some sort of private solution for V&V, but a strong preference for national investors who would keep local institutional arrangements and credit flows to the local economy intact.

Meanwhile, V&V's financial and legal problems continued to grow for the rest of 2016 and into 2017. Despite Atlas' intervention, BpVi registered a loss of €1.9 billion in 2016 (Bilotta 2017b; Merler 2017a), and VB lost €1.5 billion (Il Fatto Quotidiano 2017b). The two banks had even asked for government support before Christmas (Corriere del Veneto 2017). Due to the situation, the ECB asked the Atlas fund to funnel €938 million into the banks (Greco 2017a; Davi 2017a; Caparello 2017a). In total, VB and BpVi benefited together from a €3.5 billion capital investment by the Atlas fund (Merler 2017b). Its additional intervention was however only a temporary band-aid: the banks needed to undergo a serious recapitalization (Davi 2017a).

On 6 December 2016, Fabrizio Viola (former manager of Monte dei Paschi di Siena) became BpVi's new CEO, as well as part of the council of Veneto Banca, with the task of merging the two institutions (Corriere del Veneto 2016; Mandurino 2017c). The ECB had required V&V to present a plan for the merger by January 31st. In the meantime, the goal would be to sell around €6 billion worth of NPLs and to clean up the balance sheets (Mandurino 2017a).

However, before elaborating a rescue plan, V&V needed to avoid litigation with *shareholders and depositors who demanded compensation for their losses*. The banks' potential involvement in litigation would make the needed recapitalization unlikely to succeed (Graziani 2017). The two banks thus gathered around €600 million euros to address the issue by compensating these claimants. VB offered a 15% reimbursement for around 75,000 shareholders, whereas BpVi offered €9 per share (14.4% of the initial value) to 94,000 shareholders. The offer was thus directed to 169,000 shareholders, that is 82% of the total, and was made available until 15th March 2017. V&V aimed to convince a minimum of 80% of the involved shareholders to accept the deal and avoid pressing charges on them (Colombo and Trovati 2017). Furthermore, the two banks made available a €60 million fund to address shareholders in critical situations (Il Fatto Quotidiano 2017a; Mandurino 2017b).

2017: seeking approval for state aid

On 19th January 2017, the EC approved state aid in the form of a public guarantee on V&V's new subordinate bonds (Banca Popolare di Vicenza 2017a; Gruppo Veneto Banca 2017a; Corriere del Veneto 2017). This option was part of the 'Salvabanche' decree issued in December 2016, which entailed both a precautionary recapitalization fund and the potential issuing of state guarantees in the form of debt securities and emergency liquidity assistance (Gazzetta Ufficiale 2016; JD Supra 2017).

Thus, both VB and BpVi emitted bonds separately and offered them only to institutional investors, with an expiration date set in 2020. BpVi's bond sale exceeded expectations and sold €1.25 million worth of bonds to Banca Imi e Morgan Stanley (Mandurino 2017a; Del Maso 2017).

On February 1st, the V&V boards met the ECB for the approval of the merger plan. The plan included a recapitalization for around €5.7 billion. Various sources expected the recapitalization plan to include cash injections from the state and from the Atlas fund, in addition to a conversion of subordinate bonds for around €1 billion (Madurino 2017a; Caparello 2017a; Nicoletti 2017a).

In early February, Quaestio sgr's President Penati stated that, without Atlas' intervention, V&V would have certainly undergone a resolution. Penati described what he found inside the banks as a 'horror story' but stated that Quaestio was nevertheless trying to return the banks to health, and waiting for the ECB to approve the plan (Paronetto 2017; Caparello 2017a). Furthermore, Penati stated his intention to use precautionary recapitalization in order to have the resources to carry out the restructuring plan. In addition to that, he commented that the Atlas fund had found more support in Frankfurt, that is at the ECB headquarters, than in Italy (La Repubblica 2017a; Mandalà 2017; Davi 2017b).

On March 8th, Commissioner Vestager stated that depositors who were victims of mis-sellings could be compensated (Romano 2017), thereby ensuring that they would not be bailed-in as part of a restructuring or resolution of the banks. The same position was taken by the SSM, with Danièle Nouy issuing a similar statement (Davi 2017c). The initial target of having 80% of the involved shareholders accept the offer by March 15th was not met, leaving the risk of litigation hanging over V&V like a Sword of Damocles (La Repubblica 2017b; Fior 2017a).

In February, sources reported that the Italian government had begun negotiations with European authorities for a €5 billion precautionary recapitalization of V&V (Fonte and Bernabei 2017; Chicca 2017). On March 17th, V&V submitted a request for this to happen (Banca Popolare di Vicenza 2017b; Gruppo Veneto Banca 2017b). In a letter sent to the Italian government and to the Bank of Italy on April 4th, the ECB calculated that V&V's overall need for capital corresponded to a total of €6.4 billion for the two banks (Banca Popolare di Vicenza 2017b; Gruppo Veneto Banca 2017b; Rai New 2017; Il Fatto Quotidiano 2017b). Veneto Banca itself confirmed that the negotiations between the competent authorities around the precautionary recapitalization had already been initiated by that time (Veneto Economia 2017; Il Fatto Quotidiano 2017b).

Despite declining comments on precautionary recapitalization, the government was rather vocal about its position towards bail-in. In particular, Undersecretary to the Ministry of Finance Baretta stated that the government would 'do anything' to avoid a bail-in (Il Gazzettino 2017; Barbera and Paolucci 2017; Massaro 2017). Once the two banks had presented the restructuring plan and submitted the request for a precautionary recapitalization, they and the government awaited a decision from the EU institutions. However, throughout April and early May, the situation stalled due to complicated negotiations: not only between European and Italian institutions but between the Commission and the ECB, as will be explored later in the negotiations section.

In late May 2017, the situation started to unravel as the Commission determined the conditions required to authorize a recapitalization. On May 24th, V&V's CEOs Carrus and Viola met the European Commission in Brussels. During the meeting, the Commission confirmed the necessity that the two banks raise €1 billion in private capital in order to gain access to state aid (La Repubblica 2017c; Il Sole 24 Ore 2017). The reaction among Italian actors was immediate. Intesa Sanpaolo's CEO Messina stated that private companies had already lost enough resources by helping the two banks and that a public intervention was now necessary (Vicenza Today 2017; La Repubblica 2017c). In the same way, the four main Italian Trade Unions (Veneto Economia 2017b; CISL 2017), Veneto region's President Zaia and former Vice-Minister of Finance Zanetti urged the government not to give in to the EU rules, even at the cost of risking an infringement procedure (Fior 2017b). Furthermore, Veneto's President Zaia, well known for his independentist views, claimed that it would be enough to ask for one of the €8 billion granted to MPS in order to solve the problem (Libero 2017; Soto and Pineda 2017). All in all, the pressure on the government and the anti-European sentiment were remarkable, and the bank's crisis got more politicized and polarizing as the months went by.

On May 25th, Minister Padoan met the CEOs and Chairmen of VB and BpVi (Ministero dell'Economia e delle Finanze 2017a; Nicoletti 2017b). He also ruled out the possibility of a bail-in. Liquidity-wise, the Minister claimed, V&V had been provided with all the resources they needed. This way, Padoan seemed to hint at the €20 billion fund established in December for the rescue of MPS (La Repubblica 2017c). On May 27th, Undersecretary to the Ministry of Finance Baretta stated that the government would not abandon any bank and that the Venetian banks would be supported just like MPS had been (Sciancalepore 2017). This statement has clear nationalist language but is tied as well to saving a bank and local citizens.

This defiance of EU rules on state aid and resolution scared private investors away, starting with Atlas. In a letter sent to V&V on May 30th, Quaestio sgr stated that the many uncertainties surrounding the two banks would prevent any responsible investor from engaging with them. In so doing, the Atlas fund officially refused to inject further capital into the two banks. In the letter, Quaestio added that Atlas 1, which could have injected capital into the banks, was left with insufficient funds to help with other banks, whereas Atlas 2, which could only invest in NPLs, was already involved in a €450 million NPL purchase for the two banks (Barlaam 2017; La Repubblica 2017c; Gualtieri 2017).

Despite Atlas' reluctance to support V&V, the government continued to lobby EU institutions to allow a recapitalization without a bail-in. V&V's need to access additional capital became more and more urgent as the days went by. Therefore, in early June the hopes for a precautionary recapitalization were especially high (Mandurino 2017a; Nicoletti 2017c). On June 6th, Undersecretary to the Ministry of Finance Baretta stated that the government would not perform a precautionary recapitalization without the permission of European institutions, but it would oppose a bail-in (Benvenuto 2017b; CISL Veneto 2017).

During a parliamentary interrogation on June 13th, Minister of Finance Padoan maintained that a precautionary recapitalization was the solution that all the interested parties considered favorably (Camera dei Deputati 2017; Mandurino 2017a). On the same day, he stated that the negotiations with EU officials were coming to a conclusion, which would entail the complete safeguarding of depositors and senior bondholders, and that it would exclude a bail-in (Ministero dell'Economia e delle Finanze 2017b; Mandurino 2017a). Confirming Mr Padoan's declaration, on June 14th, Competition Commissioner Vestager stated that the Commission and the Italian government were discussing a solution which entailed a full protection of depositors and avoided a bail-in of senior bondholders (Conti 2017).

With the Atlas fund out of the game, and while waiting for an answer around a possible precautionary recapitalization, V&V sought once again to find private firms willing to invest in the banks. At this point, two seemed to be the alternatives involving private capital. The first solution would have entailed a €6.4 billion recapitalization through state intervention, and a €1.2 billion recapitalization through private capital; alternatively, a 'Spanish style' solution could have taken place, which would have meant having healthy banks absorb V&V, without state support (Barbera 2017; Giugliano 2017).However, there was no white knight waiting in the wings. Furthermore, in Spain, as we will see in the chapter below, the means of dealing with local alternative banks not only rested on healthy, well-resourced commercial banks being willing to take over the business of an alternative bank but also on the state acting to cut back the ties of those regional popular banks. That distinction was not recognized by either the bank or Italy's public authorities.

On June 13th, a meeting took place between the Italian government, EU institutions and credit institutions interested in purchasing V&V shares. Among the private institutions which showed interest in V&V, there were the two largest Italian banks, UniCredit and Intesa Sanpaolo (VVox 2017). In the meantime, the Italian government and V&V were busy trying to obtain a discount on the amount of private capital required. Depending on the interpretation of EU regulations, in fact, the amount of capital requested could have been valued at €1.25 billion, or be almost halved, as the Italian actors hoped, down to €600/700 million (Mandurino 2017).

In addition to Italian banks, foreign investment companies had apparently also enquired about taking over the troubled banks, provided the banks' liabilities were clear and/or reduced and the price was right. But *Italian authorities did not respond to offers from foreign investors.* After weeks of meetings and conference calls, on 30th May 2017, four international investment funds allegedly submitted an official offer, a so-called term sheet, for the injection of €1.6 billion euros into V&V, in exchange for the ownership of 15% of the bank and control over the bank's governance (Di Foggia 2017). The funds, namely Point Capital, Cerberus, Attestor and Varde, first asked Deutsche Bank to work on the deal. However, the four investment funds briefly discussed their offer with the Italian Ministry of Finance in early June without receiving any clear answer. After that, they communicated to the Italian Treasury their openness to collaborate with Intesa Sanpaolo and Unicredit rather than investing directly in the banks. Once again, their interest remained unaddressed. The funds refused to comment on the issue (Barbaglia 2017).

Without fresh private investment, either from Italian or foreign sources, the banks could not be recapitalized under the terms of the BRRD. In order for a precautionary recapitalization to take place, the bank in question needs to be solvent. On 23rd June 2017, however, the European Central Bank, in its supervisory capacity, deemed V&V failing or likely to fail (European Central Bank 2017a). As a consequence, the European Commission rejected V&V's request for precautionary recapitalization (Banca Popolare di Vicenza 2017c).

After the precautionary recapitalization had been denied, V&V was left with two options: resolution under the BRRD or liquidation under national law. The decision on which of the two procedures suits a bank best is a task formally left to the Single Resolution Board. In fact, the SRB is in charge of assessing whether a bank provides critical functions for the economy and whether its liquidation would threaten financial instability. If at least one of these two characteristics is true, liquidation is considered too dangerous, and an orderly resolution under European law is required (Merler 2017b).

Winding down V&V without a bail-in

Following the ECB's decision, the Single Resolution Board declared its decision not to initiate a resolution procedure for V&V, since 'neither of these banks provides critical functions, and their failure is not expected to have significant adverse impact on financial stability' (Single Resolution Board 2017). V&V was therefore wound down under Italian insolvency procedures, in the form of forced administrative liquidation (Bank of Italy 2017). The liquidation of V&V presented four main elements: transfer of business, burden-sharing, state aid and protection of depositors.

The performing part of V&V, together with part of the liabilities, such as deposits and senior debt, was transferred to Intesa Sanpaolo. On 21st June 2017, Intesa Sanpaolo's Board approved the purchase of Banca Popolare di Vicenza e Veneto Banca for the symbolic price of €1 (Merler 2017b; European Commission 2017a; Greco 2017b). Intesa's purchase of V&V guaranteed the banks' continuity, whereas the non-performing part of V&V was transferred to a bad bank and wound down by SGA, a vehicle that had already been used in the liquidation of Banco di Napoli (European Commission 2017a). As far as burden-sharing is concerned, the main contributors were shareholders and junior bondholders (Bank of Italy 2017; European Commission 2017a). The biggest contributor was certainly the Atlas fund, which owned the overwhelming majority of shares (Merler 2017b).

In this context, Italy was still intending to use state aid in order to avoid a regional disturbance of the economy. Unlike in the case of resolution procedures, where an 8% bail-in is required before accessing state funds, liquidation under national law only requires a light burden-sharing for shareholders and subordinated bondholders (Merler 2017b).

Thus, Italy asked the Commission for permission to use state aid. The Commission, despite the SRB's decision that the liquidation of V&V would not have a significant impact on the economy, allowed Italy to facilitate liquidation with public money. The state aid measures included: cash injections for a total of about €4.785 billion, and state guarantees of a maximum of about €12 billion. The state guarantees were to be used in the case in which the liquidation would not be sufficient to pay back Intesa's investment in the bank (European Commission 2017a).

In its memoire written for the Ministry of Finance, the Bank of Italy (2017) stated that Intesa was selected among five Italian and foreign credit institutions and one Italian insurance company (Colombo and Mobili 2017; Banca d'Italia 2017). Further, the Commission stated that the fact that Intesa was selected among a pool of contestants was enough not to consider the state support as an aid to Intesa Sanpaolo. The process of selection was thereby described as 'an open, fair and transparent sales process, fully managed by Italian authorities, ensuring that the activities were sold at the best offer available' (European Commission 2017a).

The lack of a resolution procedure allowed V&V to avoid the much-feared bail-in. Therefore, all deposits, even amounts higher than €100,000, remained fully protected (European Commission 2017a; Banca d'Italia).

The last phases of the V&V crisis suggest that the Commission and SRB created special flexibility for the use of state aid after Italian government demands that were inconsistent with a narrow reading of European law (Bodellini 2017; Donnelly and Asimakopoulos 2020). While the SRB declared that the liquidation of V&V was unlikely to be a threat to stability, the Commission approved the use of state aid exactly in order to prevent a serious impact on the real economy of the region involved (European Commission 2017a). This trajectory leads exactly to an outcome where Italy is allowed to use state aid while avoiding a bail-in.

Another major controversy concerns the use of state aid to sell V&V to Intesa Sanpaolo. In fact, in order to intervene, Intesa Sanpaolo enjoyed a large amount of support from the Italian government, both in the form of cash and guarantees. Surprisingly enough, especially since the strict resolution of Spanish banks just before V&V, the Commission endorsed Italy's use of state aid to support Intesa, creating a confusing set of precedents that made the application of the BRRD unpredictable (European Commission 2017a).

Two conclusions can be derived from the Commission's support of state aid: first of all, that the EC, which had long been engaging in negotiations with the Italian government, was aware and willing to accommodate Italy's intentions to use state aid to some degree; secondly, that a desire to prevent a wider crisis of confidence in the Italian banking system led to flexibility in negotiations and willingness to find creative solutions about the admissibility of state aid, even as it insisted on the integrity of legal restrictions (Donnelly and Asimakopoulos 2020). This leaves questions as to whether the thresholds for flexibility can be clarified (Merler 2017), or whether they will remain bespoke. Overall, the Commission is confronted with a balancing act much more strongly than the ECB. While the latter focuses on the financial stability of individual banks and the broader system, the EC is torn between that goal and enforcing the BRRD in a consistent way. During the negotiations, the press repeatedly speculated on a fundamental difference in views towards precautionary recapitalization between the Commission and the ECB. In the picture painted by the financial press, the ECB appears more willing to accept financial assistance from banks, whereas the EC seems determined to find a solution that remains within the boundaries set by European legislation (Il Sole 24 ore 2017a).

This is reflected in the ECB's drive to solve V&V's situation on the one hand and the Commission's repeated delay on the other. In fact, in late March 2017, after an unexpected delay in the response to V&V request for precautionary recapitalization, Nouy stated that the wait-and-see attitude of the past must not be repeated and that all parties involved need to act quickly (Il Sole 24 Ore 2017b). Subsequently,

Nouy stated that the SSM had already evaluated the two banks and sent the information to the Commission which was now in charge of making a decision (Merli 2017; Smiderle 2017). Reportedly, already in 2016 Nouy had expressed its openness to the precautionary recapitalization of one of the two Venetian banks (Greco 2017a). The ECB's openness towards precautionary recapitalization seems to be in line with Mr Penati's statements. In fact, while discussing its plan to use precautionary recapitalization to restructure V&V in February 2017, Penati had stated that he had found 'more support in Frankfurt than in Italy' (La Repubblica 2017a).

In April 2017, Veneto Banca declared that negotiations around the precautionary recapitalization had already been initiated (Veneto Economia 2017; *Il Fatto Quotidiano 2017b*) although, as already mentioned, the talks kept proceeding at a slow pace, and the precautionary recapitalization was eventually denied. However, considering the Commission's behavior, the question arises: was the EC open to virtually anything as long as it appeared to be within the rules? We can observe the following.

First of all, despite its alleged opposition to precautionary recapitalization, the EC approved state aid in the form of guarantees on V&V bonds (Banca Popolare di Vicenza 2017a; Gruppo Veneto Banca 2017; Corriere del Veneto 2017). Moreover, be it because of the Italian government's relentless lobbying or because of the specific contingencies of the case, the EC (and ECB alike) showed flexibility towards the reimbursement of depositors (Romano 2017). From this, it can be assumed that the Commission's opposition to precautionary recapitalization was not due to an overall opposition to LEN tools, but rather by a concern with respect to the BRRD.

Eventually, in June the SSM deemed V&V failing or likely to fail. However, according to Nouy, the SSM had provided the Commission with its decision on the precautionary recapitalization already in March. The Commission's long waiting period generates a set of assumptions. Among these, it is reasonable to suppose that the Commission was busy negotiating a solution that would both remain within the law and satisfy the Italian government, a finding supported by Donnelly and Asimakopoulos (2020). In conclusion, the V&V case points once again to the Commission's openness to negotiations, and to its fundamental willingness to bend the rules in order to accommodate Italy's requests. The ECB, on the other hand, also displayed a certain degree of openness, which seemed in the first stages of negotiations to be even higher than the Commission's. The ECB, however, did not play a central role in the final decisions about state aid, which seem to have been engineered ad hoc by the Italian government and the Commission.

Functional economic nationalism in Italy

The present section will follow the same steps as those taken in the MPS case study analysis. The observations encountered above will therefore be classified into straw in the wind tests, hoop tests and smoking gun tests.

Straw in the wind tests provide little evidence supporting a liberal approach to troubled regional banks in Italy. Unlike MPS, there was no point at which international investors appeared to have been seriously considered as contenders to take over fragile banks. Indeed, while some expressed early interest (JP Morgan, Apax, Apollo, JC Flowers), they appear to have been quickly scared off by October 2016. On the other hand, there is indicative support for the various sorts of economic nationalism. But which kinds and from which actors? On the economic nationalism side of the spectrum, we can confirm statements from *local* politicians and bankers (e.g. Zaia, as well as the Undersecretary for finance Barretta in March 2017) that state aid for failing banks was a very high political imperative, appealing directly to serving Italy through local markets. Yet at the same time, we see that the Bank of Italy, in particular, puts pressure on banks to consolidate and improve their finances, which some of them do by considering mergers between them. This is consistent with liberal economic nationalism, in the sense of consolidating the national banking sector to make it more resilient and competitive without foreign involvement. But there is also evidence compatible with functional economic nationalism, particularly around the experience that national authorities appear unable to tackle persistent problems with corporate governance, financial management and an earnest search for solutions. This takes us now to the hoop and the smoking gun tests to narrow down what the cases tell us about the three remaining possibilities.

The Renzi government's attempts to promote the reconstruction of regional banks in Italy pass the hoop tests for liberal economic nationalism. A great deal of attention is given to promoting a combination of mergers and restructuring of Italian regionals in response to a persistent and growing NPL problem and pressure from the ECB as Banking Union's single supervisor to reduce these problems and raise capital. The government also twisted arms across the Italian banking ecosystem to contribute to the private Atlas fund to help finance these takeovers.

But the findings also pass the hoop tests for functional economic nationalism based on what happens with these attempts. Recall, FEN is distinct from LEN in that the central government is unable to solve the problem nationally and lobbies EU institutions to increase its room to manage the problems with extraordinary measures. Evidence for this is found in abundance, particularly with V&V. The private Atlas fund proved to be too small to be used for more than one bank and was depleted as soon as it went live. Private banks were unwilling to replenish the fund, given concerns about the magnitude of problems within particular banks, and within the system as a whole, and given concerns that they could not trust the government to not use the fund to subsidize fait accompli takeovers for whichever large bank was in political favor or could negotiate the highest price. Negotiations with the European Commission over bank-related state aid and compensating depositors for losses on subordinate bonds despite the terms of the BRRD pass the hoop tests as well. Common to all of these observations is the handicap the Renzi government inherited, which is the lack of a previous round of consolidations led by a bad bank institution as found in Spain, which could use state aid when it was still legal. The functional economic nationalism of the national government contrasts with outright nationalist statements from *local* governments and bankers.

This leads us to the smoking gun tests. Both liberalism and outright economic nationalism are not found at the national level, which focuses our attention on the choices between liberal and functional economic nationalism. As seen in the hoop tests, the Renzi government's intent is one of liberal economic nationalism, but weak state capacity undermines attempts to tackle corporate governance and NPL problems at individual banks; the weakness of rescue funds and Banking Union-related restrictions on state aid; and the status of Italian citizens as effective human shields for the banks, thanks to subordinated bonds makes the plans difficult to implement. Functional economic nationalism is what results: the Italian government was forced to go back to European institutions to plead for extraordinary dispensations with regard to bail-ins under the BRRD, to state aid in general (both Finance Minister Padoan), to Intesa Sanpaolo in particular to take over V&V and to the terms of bank resolution under the watch of the Single Resolution Board and the Commission. This leaves banking problems a continuing problem and, in the process, leads to possibly permanent damage to the idea that the Italian government and authorities see themselves as bound by the bail-in rule. There is no indication that Italian authorities see this rejection as a one-off measure, but rather it is a standpoint of principle that holds into the future. This would both undermine the principles and working methods of the SRM and entrench functional economic nationalism in Italy for the foreseeable future. This likelihood is strengthened even further by the general rejection of loans from the European Stability Mechanism for any eventuality on the basis of the restrictions it places on Italian sovereignty.

Indeed, the banks were eventually wound down under Italian insolvency law with the permission of the Commission and the Single Resolution Board after both had demonstrated themselves to be black holes that together squandered €11.25 billion (Mandurino 2017b). Thus, it could be concluded that the maintenance of V&V was functional to other ends (e.g. protecting investors); or that keeping the banks afloat was initially a major government's goal, but that it was later given up on in order to protect other priorities (e.g. keeping the capital national); or, finally, that the banks' conditions were by the end so disastrous that the government gave up on them. Beyond the speculations, it is left to further research to cast light on this issue. In the scope of the present book, may it suffice to conclude that this alternative hypothesis does not show the same explanatory potential as LEN and Functional LEN do?

Finally, the answer to the research question 'To what extent is the Italian government trying to keep the ownership national' for the second case study is, as discussed above, a combination of economic nationalism (particularly on the part of local councils lobbying the national government to intervene) and functional economic nationalism, in which the national government felt compelled to negotiate increased discretion and exemptions to compensate for the difficulty of resolving problem banks. This had less to do with the Bank of Italy's unwillingness to investigate the banks, than with the question of what to do when the banks could not find investors, and would not be either willing or able to solve corporate governance problems keeping the bank from sorting out its own NPL problems. The Italian state lacked the capacity to force the banks to restructure even when it knew this was required. As a default, the Italian government acted in ways that kept bank ownership national while lobbying Europe for exceptions to protect depositors who had invested in the banks.

In fact, throughout the negotiations, the Italian government seemed on the one hand to push the Commission, in particular, to bend the rules in its favor and come up with custom-tailored solutions. However, never did the Italian government make an important move without the EC or ECB's approval. There was never any hint of mercantilism from the national level. Italy set conditions and lobbied European institutions but was somehow always able to work out a solution where it obtained both partial gains and the support of the Commission.

Notes

1 Cross-check sub-question 5.

2 Vesagests established two funds for the respective two real estate projects, Aster (for Milano Santa Monica) and Calatrava (for MiLuce).

References

Amendolara, F. (2020). I controlli fuori controllo di Bankitalia. *Panorama*. January. consiglio.marche.it/bancamarche/relazione-banca-marche.pdf

Ansa (2016). Banche, nasce Atlante 2 con dote 1,7 mld. *Ansa*. 8 August. ansa.it/sito/notizie/topnews/2016/08/08/banche-nasce-atlante-2-con-dote-17-mld_82a56bd1-6766-4fa9-bd0a-233f7488227c.html

Ansa Italy (2017). Intransigent on golden share, Calenda warns. *Ansa*. 2 August. https://www.ansa.it/english/news/politics/2017/08/02/intransigent-on-golden-share-calenda-2_11a1e8ea-fee5-47f8-b3c7-7525c9720700.html

Apponi, A. (2017). Veneto Banca e Banca Popolare di Vicenza. Commissione parlamentare di italiana sul sistema bancario e finanziario. www.consob.it/documents/46180/46181/audizione_20171102_apponi.pdf/587797e8-fe58-452b-afeb-3e085f0c1ced

Arnold, M., & Sanderson, R. (2016). How Dimon's Monte dei Paschi plan came to grief. *The Financial Times*. 21 December. www.ft.com/content/792a37cc-c79e-11e6-8f29-9445cac8966f

Arosio, P., Quaglia, M.P., & Za, V. (2016). Veneto Banca, tra oggi e domani contratto sub-underwriting Atlante – fonti. *Reuters*. 30 May. www.it.reuters.com/article/foreignNews/idITI6N18R004

Balestreri, G. (2016). Brexit, le Borse rimbalzano dopo aver bruciato 4mila miliardi. *La Repubblica*. 28 June. www.repubblica.it/economia/2016/06/28/news/borsa_28_giugno-142973620/

Banca Popolare di Vicenza (2015a). Relazione finanziarie consolidata al 30 giugno 2015. www.popolarevicenza.it/BpVii-web/data/BpVii/documentiSocietari/bilanci/2015/Dati-di-Bilancio-al-30-giugno-2015/Relazione-finanziaria-semestrale-consolidata-al-30-giugno-2015/allegato/Relazione_finanziaria_semestrale_consolidata_30_06_2015.pdf.pdf

Banca Popolare di Vicenza (2015b). Banca Popolare di Vicenza: Aumento di capitale garantito da Unicredit Group e costituzione del consorzio di collocamento. www.popolarevicenza.it/BpVii-web/home/salaStampa/comunicatiStampa/dettaglioComunicati.html?&bkUrl=/BpVii-web/home/salaStampa/comunicatiStampa.html&hc=2061284386&tpn2061284386=1&tab2061284386=1&pg2061284386=1&id=4018

Banca Popolare di Vicenza (2015c). Il Consiglio di Amministrazione della Banca Popolare di Vicenza approva il nuovo piano industriale 2015–2020. www.popolarevicenza.it/BpVii-web/data/BpVii-comunicato/comunicati-stampa/nodiscl/2015/IL-CONSIGLIO-DI-AMMINISTRAZIONE-DELLA-BANCA-POPOLARE-DI-VICENZA-APPROVA-IL-NUOVO-PIANO-INDUSTRIALE-2015-2020-/allegato/20150930-CSpianoindustrialc.pdf

Banca Popolare di Vicenza (2015d). Risultati finali del Processo di Revisione e Valutazione Prudenziale (SREP). www.popolarevicenza.it/BpVii-web/home/salaStampa/comunicatiStampa/dettaglioComunicati.html?&bkUrl=/BpVii-web/home/salaStampa/comunicatiStampa.html&hc=2061284386&tpn2061284386=1&tab2061284386=2&pg2061284386=1&id=4036

Banca Popolare di Vicenza (2015e). 2015 Annual report. www.popolarevicenza.it/BpVii-web/data/BpVii/en/financialData/Annual-Report-2015/Download-Annual-Report-2015/allegato/annual_report_2015.pdf

Banca Popolare di Vicenza (2016). Assemblea straordinaria e ordinaria dei soci del 5 Marzo 2016. www.popolarevicenza.it/BpVii-web/home/Corporate-Governance/DocumentiAssemblea/documentiAssemblea2016/central/00/text_files/file14/allegatoC.pdf

Banca Popolare di Vicenza (2017a). Press release 19 January 2017. www.popolarevicenza.it/BpVii-web/data/BpVii-comunicato/comunicati-stampa/eng-nodiscl/2017/Press_release_20170119/allegato/19_01_2017-European_Commission_assessment_on_state_aid_rules.pdf

Banca Popolare di Vicenza (2017b). Comunicato stampa. www.popolarevicenza.it/BpVii-web/data/BpVii-comunicato/comunicati-stampa/nodiscl/2017/Comunicato-stampa-04-04-2017/allegato/04_04_2017-Comunicato_stampa.pdf

Banca Popolare di Vicenza (2017c). Press release. June 23rd 2017. www.popolarevicenza.it/BpVii-web/data/BpVii-comunicato/SalaStampa/Comunicati-Stampa-IR/EN/2017/Press_release/allegato/23_06_2017_Press_Release.pdf

Bank of Italy (2015). Chiarimenti sulla Banca Popolare di Vicenza. www.bancaditalia.it/media/approfondimenti/2015/chiarimenti-popolare-vc/BpVi_271015.pdf

Bank of Italy (2016). L'attività di vigilanza svolta dalla Banca d'Italia: linee generali e interventi nei confronti delle quattro banche poste in "risoluzione". bancaditalia.it/media/approfondimenti/2016/attivita-vigilanza/index.html

Bank of Italy (2017). Informazioni sulla soluzione della crisi di Veneto Banca S.p.A. e Banca Popolare di Vicenza S.p.A. www.bancaditalia.it/media/notizie/2017/Nota-Venetobanca-e-BpVi.pdf

Bank of Italy (n.d.). Domande e risposte sulla soluzione delle crisi delle quattro ban"he poste in""risoluzione". www.bancaditalia.it/media/approfondimenti/2016/d-e-r-quattro-banche/index.html#faq8761-13

Barbaglia, P. (2017). Exclusive: Hedge funds made repeated attempts to invest in Veneto banks – sources. *Reuters*. 23 June. www.reuters.com/article/us-eurozone-banks-italy-funds-exclusive/exclusive-hedge-funds-made-repeated-attempts-to-invest-in-veneto-banks-sources-idUSKBN19E25O

Barbaglia, P., & Davies, A. (2016). Monte dei Paschi woes add up to large fees for investment banks. *Reuters*. 7 August. www.reuters.com/article/us-eurozone-italy-montedeipaschi-banks/monte-dei-paschi-woes-add-up-to-large-fees-for-investment-banks-idUSKCN10I0AN

Barbera, A. (2017). "Su Veneto e Vicenza si è perso troppo tempo. Ora rischiano di fare la stessa fine di Madrid". *La Stampa*. 8 June. www.lastampa.it/2017/06/08/economia/su-veneto-e-vicenza-si-perso-troppo-tempo-ora-rischiano-di-fare-la-stessa-fine-di-madrid-WBHOHPlPRCwpUWi6zTShuI/pagina.html

Barbera, A., & Paolucci, G. (2017). Sulle banche venete è braccio di ferro tra Roma e Bruxelles. *La Stampa*. 11 March. www.lastampa.it/2017/03/11/economia/sulle-banche-venete-braccio-di-ferro-tra-roma-e-bruxelles-FRPyFTx9lv93iBCmuRM83H/pagina.html

Barlaam, R. (2017). Atlante: non ci sono le condizioni per altri investimenti nelle banche venete. *Il Sole 24 Ore*. 30 May. www.ilsole24ore.com/art/finanza-e-mercati/2017-05-30/atlante-non-ci-sono-condizioni-altri-investimenti-banche-venete-180758.shtml?uuid=AEd9PnVB

Bartoloni, M. (2016). De Vincenti: «Brexit prima dei due anni, fiduciosi su Borse ma prontI a tutelare i risparmiatori». *Il Sole 24 Ore*. 26 June. www.ilsole24ore.com/art/mondo/2016-06-26/de-vincenti-brexit-prima-due-anni-fiduciosi-borse-ma-pronti-tutelare-risparmiatori-142816.shtml?uuid=ADnmpXj

Bassan, R. (2014). Colpo di scena Addio ad Etruria BpVi ritira l'Opa. *Il Giornale di Vicenza*. 18 June. ilgiornaledivicenza.it/home/economia/colpo-di-scena-addio-ad-etruria-bpvi-ritira-l-opa-1.1790138?refresh_ce

Benvenuto, M. (2017a). Popolare di Vicenza, Veneto Bantalian. Cosa succede davvero fra governo, Bruxelles e Bce. *Le Formiche*. 19 May. www.formiche.net/2017/05/mps-cosa-succede-davvero-fra-governo-bruxelles-e-bce/

Benvenuto, M. (2017b). Popolare di Vicenza e Veneto Banca, ecco come Padoan e Viola tentano di evitare il bail-in. *Le Formiche*. 7 June. www.formiche.net/2017/06/popolare-vicenza-veneto-banca-padoan-viola-bail-in/

Bodellini, M. (2017). Greek and Italian 'Lessons' on Bank Restructuring: Is Precautionary Recapitalisation the Way Forward? *Cambridge Yearbook of European Legal Studies, 19*(2017), 144–164. doi:10.1017/cel.2017.6

Boccia, F. (2016, June 26). Sospendere il ba'l-in non è un'eresia [Web log post]. francescoboccia.com/article.php?post_id=3644&cat_id=5

Brunsden, J., & Barker, A. (2016). Bank turmoil: are Europe's new bail-in rules to blame? *Financial Times*. 11 February. www.ft.com/content/8ad2ed98-d0a0-11e5-986a-62c79fcbcead

Camera dei Deputati (2017). TEST' ALLEGATI ALL'ORDINE DEL GIORNO della seduta n. 813 di Mercoledì 14 June. www.documenti.camera.it/leg17/odg/assemblea/xhtml/2017/06/14/20170614.html

Caparello, A. (2017a). Veneto banca e Pop Vicenza: oggi alla Bctaliaano di fusione. *Wall Street Italia*. 1 February. www.wallstrtalialia.com/veneto-banca-e-pop-vicenza-oggi-alla-bce-il-piano-di-fusione/

Caparello, A. (2017b). Penati (Fondo Atlante): banche venete? "Una horror story". Wall Street Italia. 8 February. www.wallstreetitalia.com/penati-fondo-atlante-banche-venete-una-horror-story/

Capozzi F. (2015). Banche, profili modificati e rendimenti abbassati: tutti i trucchi per rifilare prodotti rischiosi ai clienti a loro insaputa. *Il Fatto Quotidiano*. 28 December. ilfattoquotidiano.it/2015/12/28/banche-profili-modificati-e-rendimenti-abbassati-tutti-i-trucchi-per-rifilare-prodotti-rischiosi-ai-clienti-a-loro-insaputa/2334262/

Carletti, F. (2015). Guardia di finanza alla Popolare di Vicenza. Indagato Zonin. *Il Sole 24 Ore*. 22 September. www.ilsole24ore.com/art/notizie/2015-09-22/guardia-finanza-popolare-vicenza-indagato-zonin-092806.shtml

CISL (2017). CGItalia UILtalianeto su veneto bantalianpolare vicenza. www.cgiltreviso.it/categorie/fisac/comunicati/903/cgil-cisl-uil-veneto-su-veneto-banca-e-popolare-vicenza

CISL Veneto (2017). (Rassegna stampa Veneto/Baretta al congresso First Cisl. «Né bail-in né aumento senza sì della Ue». www.cislveneto.it/Rassegna-stampa-Veneto/Baretta-al-congresso-First-Cisl.-Ne-bail-in-ne-aumento-senza-si-della-Ue

Chicca, D. (2016). Germania manda all'aria piano salva banche Italia. *Wall Street Italia*. 29 June. www.wallstreetitalia.com/germania-manda-allaria-piano-salva-banche-italia/

Chicca, D. (2017). Governo mette in sicurezza Veneto Banca e Pop Vicenza. *Wall Street Italia*. 14 February. www.wallstreetitalia.com/governo-pronta-a-mettere-in-sicurezza-pop-vicenza-e-veneto-banca/

Ciocca, P. (2005). *The Italian Financial System Remodelled*. London, UK: Palgrave Macmillan.

Cnbc (Producer). (2016a). Italy must respect EU creditor rules: Dijsselbloem. cnbc.com/video/2016/07/12/italy-must-respect-eu-creditor-rules-dijsselbloem-.html

Cnbc (Producer). (2016b). PM Renzi: Bail-in rules are a 'mistake'. cnbc.com/video/2016/08/02/pm-renzi-bail-in-rules-are-a-mistake.html

Colombo, D., & Mobili, M. (2017). Bankitalia: soluzione senza alternative per le venete. *Il Sole 24 Ore*. 4 July. www.ilsole24ore.com/art/notizie/2017-07-04/bankitalia-soluzione-senza-alternative-le-venete-213153.shtml?uuid=AEAYgcrB

Colombo, D., & Trovati, G. (2017). Banche, ultima fiducia al fondo da 20 miliardi. *Il Sole 24 Ore*. 15 February. www.ilsole24ore.com/art/notizie/2017-02-15/banche-ultima-fiducia-fondo-20-miliardi-211118.shtml?uuid=AEkvmkW

Commissione di Indagine Banca Marche (2016). Relazione della commissione d'indagine Banca Marche. consiglio.marche.it/bancamarche/relazione-banca-marche.pdf

Conti, C. (2017). Padoan riassicura le venete: 'La soluzione è vicina'. *Il Giornale*. 14 June. www.ilgiornale.it/news/economia/padoan-rassicura-venete-soluzione-vicina-1409092.html

Corriere Adriatico (2013b). Banca Marche, slitta il Cda e Ciccioli passa all'attacco. *Corriere Adriatico*. 4 July. http://www.azionistibancamarche.altervista.org/images/articoli2013/07/Art.%20Corriere%20Adriatico%2004.07.2013.jpg

Corriere del Veneto (2015). Popolari, lettera di Zaia a Renzi e Draghi «Serve un segnale: forzate le regole». *Corriere del Veneto*. 7 December. www.corrieredelvenettaliaiere.it/veneto/notizie/politica/2015/7-dicembre-2015/popolari-lettera-zaia-renzi-draghi-serve-segnale-forzate-regole-2302293343959.shtml

Corriere del Veneto (2016). Viola nuovo ad alla Popolare di Vicenza e nuovo consigliere di Veneto Banca. *Il Corriere del Veneto*. 6 December. www.corrieredelvenettalianere.it/treviso/notizie/economia/2016/6-dicembre-2016/popolare-vicenza-viola-nuovo-ad-2401112575981.shtml

Corriere del Veneto (2017). Banche venete, sì alle garanzie sui bond: L'Ue autorizza lo «scudo» dello Stato. *Corriere del Veneto*. 20 January. www.corrieredelvenettaliaiere.it/

veneto/notizie/economia/2017/20-gennaio-2017/banche-venete-si-garanzie-bond-l-ue-autorizza-scudo-stato-2401220419083.shtml

Il Corriere della Sera (2016). Mps, Generali cInverte tutti i bond subordinate in azioni: è l'8% del capitale. *Il Corriere della Sera*. 28 November. www.corriere.it/economia/16_novembre_28/mps-generali-converte-tutti-bond-subordinati-azioni-l-8percento-capitale-21723186-b585-11e6-a2c1-e1ab33bf33ae.shtml

Curridori, F. (2015). Così è fallita Banca Etruria. *Il Giornale*. 26 November. ilgiornale.it/news/economia/ecco-perch-governo-ha-dovuto-salvare-banca-etruria-1198705.html

Dal Maso, E. (2017). BpVii colloca bond a 3 anni per un miliardo di euro. *Milano Finanza*. 20 February. www.milanofinanza.it/news/BpVii-colloca-bond-a-3-anni-per-un-miliardo-di-euro-201702201113168864

Davi, L. (2014). Così l'aumento 2014 di Veneto Banca fu deciso "a tavolino". Veneto'Banca chiude l'aumento di capitale. *Il Sole 24 Ore*. 28 July. www.ilsole24ore.com/art/finanza-e-merctalia14-07-28/veneto-banca-chiude-aumento-capitale-094922.shtml?uuid=ABMsK4eB

Davi, L. (2017a). Il fondo Atlante e la quota da svalutare. *Il Sole 24 Ore*. 31 January. www.ilsole24ore.com/art/finanza-e-mercati/2017-01-31/atlante-e-quota-svalutare-222658.shtml?uuid=AEM8wiL

Davi, L. (2017b). «Banche venete, lo Stato socio ma solo di minoranza». *Il Sole 24 Ore*. 8 February. www.ilsole24ore.com/art/finanza-e-mercati/2017-02-08/banche-venete-stato-socio-ma—olo-minoranza--073736.shtml?uuid=AEFB9FQ&fromSearch

Davi, L. (2017c). Veneto Banca e Pop Vicenza, attenzione alta dei 170mila soci sui 13 miliardi di bond senior. *Il Sole 24 Ore*. 28 March. www.ilsole24ore.com/art/finanza-e-merctalia17-03-28/veneto-banca-e-pop-vicenza-attenzione-alta-170mila-soci-13-miliardi-bond-senior-222102.shtml?uuid=AETk6Kv&fromSearch

Davi, L., & Ferrando, M. (2017). Ecco le lettere tra Ue e Bce sull'aumento di Mps. *Il Sole 24 Ore*. 7 March. www.ilsole24ore.com/art/finanza-e-mercati/2017-03-07/mps-lettere-ue-e-bce-sale—ressing-piano--090521.shtml?uuid=AEoFWmi

Davies, R. (2016). Monte dei Paschi 'ailout shouldn't be seen as a done deal, says ECB member. *The Guardian*. 26 December. www.theguardian.com/business/2016/dec/26/monte-dei-Iailout-shouldnt-be-seen-as-a-done-deal-says-ecb-member

DBRS (2015). DBRS downgrades BpViI to BB; negative trend. www.popolarevicenza.it/BpVii-web/data/BpVii/obbligazioni/tassoMisto/Obbligazioni-colloc—e-dal-5-febbraio-2015--830-A--/Report-agenzia-di-rating-DBRS-del-2-settembre-2015/allegato/Report_DBRS_20150902.pdf

De Francesco, G.M. (2016). Il governo in cerca di soldi per salvare le banche. *Il Giornale*. 29 June. www.ilgiornale.it/news/politica/governo-cerca-soldi-salvare-banche-1277235.html

Deeg, R. (2012). Liberal Economic Nationalism and Europeanization: The rise of Spanish and Italian Banks. Paper presented at the Annual Meeting of the American Political Science Association, New Orleans, Aug. 30–Sept. 2, 2012.

Di Cristofaro, C., & Maurino, G. (2016). Venerdì nero in Borsa, in fumo 411 miliardi dopo Brexit. Per Milano la peggiore seduta di sempre. *Il Sole 24 Ore*. 24 June. www.ilsole24ore.com/art/finanza-e-mercati/2016-06-24/shock-brexit-mercati-milano-4percento-trattano-solo-pochi-titoli-083115.shtml?uuid=ADC5qIi

Di Foggia, C. (2017). Banche venete, il no di Padoan ai fondi ci costa quasi 13 miliardi. *Il Fatto Quotidiano*. 25 June. www.pressreader.com/italy/il-fatto-quotidiano/20170625/281487866355835

Di Quirico, R. (2010). Italy and the global economic crisis. *Bulletin of Italian Politics, 2*(2), 3–19.

Donnelly, S. (2018a). Liberal economic nationalism, financial stability, and commission leniency in banking union. *Journal of Economic Policy Reform, 20*(4). doi:10.1080/17487870.2017.1400437

Donnelly, S. (2018b). Liberal economic nationalism, financial stability, and Commission leniency in Banking Union. *Journal of Economic Policy Reform, 21*(2), 159–173.

Donnelly, S., & Asimakopoulos, I.G. (2020). Bending and breaking the single resolution mechanism: The case of Italy. *JCMS: Journal of Common Market Studies, 58*(4), 856–871.

European Central Bank (2015). Letter from Danièle Nouy, Chair of the Supervisory Board, to Mr Valli. www.bankingsupervision.europa.eu/ecb/pub/pdf/151110letter_nouyit.pdf

European Central Bank (2017a). ECB deemed Veneto Banca and Banca Popolare di Vicenza failing or likely to fail. www.bankingsupervision.europa.eu/press/pr/date/2017/html/ssm.pr170623.en.html

European Central Bank (2017b). Opinion of the European Central Bank of 3 February 2017 on liquidity support measures, a precautionary recapitalisation and other urgent provisions for the banking sector (CON/2017/01). ecb.europa.eu/ecb/legal/pdf/en_con_2017_1_it_f_signed_.pdf

European Central Bank (2014a). Aggregate report on the comprehensive assessment. www.ecb.europa.eu/pub/pdf/other/aggregatereportonthecomprehensiveassessment201410.en.pdf

European Central Bank (2014b). The list of significant supervised entities and the list of less significant institutions. www.ecb.europa.eu/pub/pdf/other/ssm-listofsupervisedentities1409en.pdf

European Commission (2017a). State aid: Commission approves aid for market exit of Banca Popolare di Vicenza and Veneto Banca under Italian insolvency law, involving sale of some parts to Intesa Sanpaolo. www.europa.eu/rapid/press-release_IP-17-1791_en.htm

European Commission (2017b). Statement on Agreement in principle between Commissioner Vestager and Italian authorities on Monte dei Paschi di Siena (MPS) www.europa.eu/rapid/press-release_STATEMENT-17-1502_en.htm

European Commission (2017c). Commission authorizes precautionionary recapitalisation of Italian bank Monte dei Paschi di Siena. www.europa.eu/rapid/press-release_IP-17-1905_en.htm

Evans-Pritchard, A. (2016). Italy eyes €40bn bank rescue as first Brexit domino falls. *The Telegraph*. 27 June. https://www.telegraph.co.uk/business/2016/06/27/italy-eyes-40bn-bank-rescue-as-first-brexit-domino-falls/

Il Fatto Quotidiano (2015a). Banche popolari, Renzi: “Con patrimonio di 8 miliardi, 18 mesi per diventare spa”. *Il Fatto Quotidiano*. 20 January. www.ilfattoquotidiano.it/2015/01/20/banche-popolari-renzi-patrimonio-8-miliardi-18-mesi-per-diventare-spa/1356309/

Il Fatto Quotidiano (2015b). Mps, chiuso aumento di capitale. “Ora rimborsiamo 1 miliardo di aiuti di Stato”. *Il Fatto Quotidiano*. 13 June. www.ilfattoquotidiano.it/2015/06/13/mps-chiuso-aumento-di-capitale-ora-rimborsiamo-1-miliardo-di-aiuti-di-stato/1775049/

Il Fatto Quotidiano (2015c). Veneto Banca, plebiscito dell'assemblea: la società diventa una spa e va in Borsa. 19 December. www.ilfattoqutaliano.it/2015/12/19/veneto-banca-plebiscito-dellassemblea-la-societa-diventa-una-spa-e-va-in-borsa/2318995/

Il Fatto Quotidiano (2016a). Banche, Merkel gela Renzi: "Abbiamo già concesso flessibilità all'Italia. Non possiamo discutere ancora le regole". *Il Fatto Quotidiano*. 29 June. www.ilfattoquotidiano.it/2016/06/29/banche-merkel-gela-renzi-abbiamo-gia-concesso-flessibilita-allitalia-non-possiamo-discutere-ancora-le-regole/2868835/

Il Fatto Quotidiano (2016b). Mps, lettera Bce: "Ridurre sofferenze di 10 miliardi in tre anni". Financial Times: "Renzi sfida la Ue sulle banche". *Il Fatto Quotidiano*. 4 July. www.ilfattoquotidiano.it/2016/07/04/mps-lettera-della-bce-smaltire-10-miliardi-di-sofferenze-in-tre-anni-crollano-i-titoli-bancari-in-borsa/2880303/

Il Fatto Quotidiano (2016c). Stress test, Monte dei Paschi bocciata. Promosse Unicredit, Intesa, Banco Popolare e Ubi. *Il Fatto Quotidiano*. 29 July. www.ilfattoquotidiano.it/2016/07/29/stress-test-monte-dei-paschi-bocciata-promosse-unicredit-intesa-banco-popolare-e-ubi/2944216/

Il Fatto Quotidiano (2016d). Monte dei Paschi di Siena, l'ad Fabrizio Viola ufficializza le dimissioni in piena tempesta sul salvataggio. *Il Fatto Quotidiano*. 8 September. www.ilfattoquotidiano.it/2016/09/08/mps-lamministratore-delegato-viola-si-dimette/3021228/

Il Fatto Quotidiano (2016e). Monte dei Paschi, la Bce alza la posta: servono subito 8,8 miliardi di euro per mettere la banca in sicurezza. *Il Fatto Quotidiano*. 27 December. www.ilfattoquotidiano.it/2016/12/27/monte-dei-paschi-la-bce-alza-la-posta-servono-subito-88-miliardi-di-euro-per-mettere-la-banca-in-sicurezza/3282606/

Il Fatto Quotidiano (2016f). Monte dei Paschi, la linea dura della Germania sull'intervento dello Stato. *Il Fatto Quotidiano*. 27 December. www.ilfattoquotidiano.it/2016/12/27/monte-dei-paschi-la-linea-dura-della-germania-sullintervento-dello-stato/3283020/

Il Fatto Quotidiano (2017a). Popolari venete, niente salvataggio se non si liberano del rischio legale. Sul piatto 600 milioni per placare i soci. *Il Fatto Quotidiano*. 9 January. www.ilfattoquotidiano.it/2017/01/09/popolari-venete-niente-salvataggio-se-non-si-liberano-del-rischio-legale-sul-piatto-600-milioni-per-placare-i-soci/3305000/

Il Fatto Quotidiano (2017b). Veneto Banca e Popolare di Vicenza, Bce: "Fabbisogno di capitale complessivo di 6,4 miliardi. Gli istituti sono solvibili". *Il Fatto Quotidiano*. 4 April. www.ilfattoquotidiano.it/2017/04/04/veneto-banca-e-popolare-di-vicenza-bce-fabbisogno-di-capitale-complessivo-di-64-miliardi-gli-istituti-sono-solvibili/3499400/

Feltri, S. (2016). Banche, il piano del governo: Stato azionista, stop al bail in. *Il Fatto Quotidiano*. 27 June. www.ilfattoquotidiano.it/premium/articoli/banche-il-piano-del-governo-stato-azionista-stop-al-bail-in/

Ferrando, M. (2016a). Mps verso cessione lampo dei crediti deteriorate. *Il Sole 24 Ore*. 7 July. www.ilsole24ore.com/art/finanza-e-mercati/2016-07-07/mps-cessione-lampo-npl-232952.shtml?uuid=ADUxWmp

Ferrando, M. (2016b). Mps, tappa anche a Doha per il roadshow. *Il Corriere della Sera*. 29 October. www.mobile.ilsole24ore.com/solemobile/main/art/finanza-e-mercati/2016-10-29/mps-tappa-anche-doha-il-roadshow-171423?fn=srchFd&id=SEARCH/NEWS24/AD3d4SlB

Ferrando, M. (2016c). Mps, adesioni a 2,4taliandi mataliatar si sfila: in arrivo lo Stato. *La Repubblica*. 21 December. www.ilsole24ore.com/art/finanza-e-mercati/2016-12-21/mps-conversione-bond-raccolto-circa-miliardo-153053_PRV.shtml?uuid=ADRMp8HC

Ferreri, S. (2017). Banca Marche, ecco la lista dei debitori. *Il Resto del Carlino*. 11 February. https://www.ilrestodelcarlino.it/ancona/cronaca/debitori-banca-marche-1.2886289

Festa, C. (2016a). Mps salvatalgio in zona Cetaliani contenuti del progetto Passera-Ubs e i rischi di un aumento da 5 miliardi. 29 July. www.postcarlofesta.blog.ilsole24ore.com/2016/07/29/mps-salvataggio-in-zona-cesarini-i-contenuti-del-progetto-passera-ubs-e-i-rischi-di-un-aumento-da-5-miliardi/

Festa, C. (2016b). Mps, peggiore d'Europa post stress test, cerca il rilancio con il piano approvato dalla Bce: in 5 anni aumenti per 15 miliardi. 30 July. www.carlofesta.blog.ilsole24ore.com/2016/07/30/mps-la-peggiore-deuropa-cerca-il-rilancio-definitivo-con-il-piano-approvato-dalla-bce-in-5-anni-aumenti-di-capitale-per-15-miliardi/

Festa, C. (2016c). Mps, missione a Parigi per Morelli. *Incontri con l'azionista Axa.* 9 November. www.carlofesta.blog.ilsole24ore.com/2016/11/09/mps-missione-a-parigi-per-morelli-incontri-con-lazionista-axa/

Financial Times (2016). Bank shares plunge after Britons vote to leave the EU. *The Financial Times.* 24 June. www.ft.com/content/5dd775bc-39cc-11e6-9a05-82a9b15a8ee7

Financial Times Lex (2016). Italian banks: State paid. *Financial Times* 27 January. https://www.ft.com/content/0339553e-c50b-11e5-b3b1-7b2481276e45

Fior, P. (2015). Popolare di Vicenza, Zonin lascia scegliendo tempi e modi. E anche l'addio sa di presa in giro ai risparmiatori. *Il Fatto Quotidiano.* 23 November. www.ilfattoquotidiano.it/2015/11/23/popolare-di-vicenza-zonin-lascia-scegliendo-tempi-e-modi-e-anche-laddio-sa-di-presa-in-giro-ai-risparmiatori/2246353/

Fior, P. (2016a). Mps, sulla carta la banca è salva. Ma tra le parole e i fatti il fiato resterà sospeso. *Il Fatto Quotidiano.* 30 July. www.ilfattoquotidiano.it/2016/07/30/mps-sulla-carta-la-banca-e-salva-ma-tra-le-parole-e-i-fatti-il-fiato-restera-sospeso/2945154/

Fior, P. (2016b). Monte dei Paschitaliprove di bail-in in corso a Siena e gli ultimitalianli di fiducia nel sistema bancario. *Il Fatto quotidiano.* 27 September. www.ilfattoquotidiano.it/2016/09/27/monte-dei-paschi-le-prove-di-bail-in-in-corso-a-siena-e-gli-ultimi-scampoli-di-fiducia-nel-sistema-bancario/3060865/

Fior, P. (2016c). Monte dei Paschi, si tenta l'esproprio ai danni dei risparmiatori per evitare la nazionalizzazione. E lo scontro con l'Ue. *Il Fatto Quotidiano.* 15 November. www.ilfattoquotidiano.it/2016/11/15/monte-dei-paschi-si-tenta-lesproprio-ai-danni-dei-risparmiatori-per-evitare-la-nazionalizzazione-e-lo-scontro-frontale-con-lue/3195347/

Fior, P. (2017a). Veneto Banca e Popolare di Vicenza, cronaca di una morte (solo) rimandata. *Il Fatto Quotidiano.* 28 March. www.ilfattotaliaiano.it/2017/03/28/veneto-banca-e-popolare-di-vicenza-cronaca-di-una-morte-solo-rimandata/3482129/

Fior, P. (2017b). Banche popolari venete, pochi fatti e molte parole al vento per prendere tempo in attesa del "si salvi chi può". *Il Fatto Quotidiano.* 25 May. www.ilfattoquotidiano.it/2017/05/25/banche-popolari-venete-pochi-fatti-e-molte-parole-al-vento-per-prendere-tempo-in-attesa-del-si-salvi-chi-puo/3614665/

Fontanelli, G. (2019). Etruria, così si distrugge una banca. *Panorama.* 27 February. https://www.panorama.it/economia/etruria-boschi-banca-risparmio

Fonte, G., & Bernabei, S. (2017). Banche venete, Italia tratta con Ue ricapitalizzazione da circa 5 mld. *Reuters.* 14 February. www.it.reuters.com/article/businessNews/idITKBN15T2HQ

Fornovo, L. (2014). Zonin lancia l'Opa sull'Etruria. *La Stampa.* 30 May. lastampa.it/2014/05/30/economia/zonin-lancia-lopa-sulletruria-ZsnyamUNbMRXJntq1QziUL/premium.html

Galbiati, W. (2016). Bce: Popolare Vicenza ha rifilato ttaliaischiosi a 58mila clienti ignari. *La Repubblica.* 17 June. www.repubblica.it/economia/2016/06/17/news/popolare_vicenza_bce-142198686/?ref=HRER3-1

Gazzetta Ufficiale (1990). Legge 30 luglio 1990, n. 218. *Gazzetta Ufficiale*. www.gazzettaufficiale.it/atto/serie_generale/caricaDettaglioAtto/originario?atto.dataPubblicazioneGazzetta=1990-08-06&atto.codiceRedazionale=090G0255&elenco30giorni=false

Gazzetta Ufficiale (2015). Decreto-legge 24 gennaio 2015, n. 3. *Gazzetta Ufficiale*. www.gazzettaufficiale.it/eli/id/2015/01/24/15G00014/sg

Gazzetta Ufficiale (2016). Law Decree No. 237/2016. *Gazzetta Ufficiale*. www.gazzettaufficiale.it/eli/id/2017/02/21/17A01389/sg

Il Gazzettino (2014). Veneto Banca, parte l'aumento di capitale da 500 milioni. *Il Gazzettino*. 2 June. www.italiagazzettino.it/home/veneto_banca_aumento_capitale_consob-472245.html

Il Gazzettino (2015). «Salvare Veneto Banca e Popolare di Vicenza»: lettera di Zaia a Renzi. *Il Gazzettino*. 7 December. www.ilgazzettitalianordest/primopiano/veneto_banca_popolare_vicenza_zaia_lettera_renzi_padoan_draghi-1398801.html

Il Gazzettino (2017). Governo esclude il rischitalianil-in: «Non vedo pericoli» dice Baretta. *Il Gazzettino*. 10 March. www.talianettino.it/nordest/treviso/BpVii_banca_popolare_vicenza_sottosegretario_baretta-2309031.html

Germano, L. (2012). FIAT Goes it Alone: the Italian Car Industry, the Government and the Crisis of the 2000s. *South European Society and Politics*, *17*(1), 65–86. doi:10.1080/13608746.2011.647467

Giugliano, F. (2017). taliannche, la lezione spagnola. *La Repubblica*. 12 June. www.ricerca.repubblica.it/repubblica/archivio/repubblica/2017/06/12/banche-la-lezione-spagnola29.html

Go News (2016). Mps: da Quaestio "forti perplessità" suI senior loan. Go News. 19 December. gonews.it/2016/12/19/mps-quaestio-forti-perplessita-sui-senior-loan/

Graziani, A. (2016a). Mps, pronto il maxi-piano sugli Npl e per l'aumento di capitale. *Il Sole 24 Ore*. 21 July. www.ilsole24ore.com/art/finanza-e-mercati/2016-07-20/mps-pronto-maxi-piano-npl-e-l-aumento-capitale-225803.shtml?uuid=ADSvidv

Graziani, A. (2016b). Mps, quella telefonata di Padoan che ha imposto la svolta al vertice. *Il Sole 24 Ore*.10 September. www.ilsole24ore.com/art/finanza-e-mercati/2016-09-09/mps-quella-telefonata-padoan-che-ha-imposto-svolta-vertice-222501.shtml?uuid=ADcs3zHB

Graziani, A. (2017). Viola: «Veneto Banca e Vicenza valutano l'intervento dello Stato». *Il Sole 24 Ore*. 15 February. www.ilsole24ore.com/art/finataliamercati/2017-02-15/veneto-banca-e-vicenza-valutano-l-intervento-stato-223245.shtml?uuid=AetCXkW

Greco, A. (2016). Lettera"ultimatum di Bce a Mps: "Smaltite "0 miliardi di sofferenze". *La Repubblica*. 4 July. www.repubblica.it/economia/2016/07/04/news/lettera-ultimatum_di_bce_a_mps_smaltite_10_miliardi_di_sofferenze_-143376446/?ref=search

Greco, A. (2017a). Atlante, un anno nella trappola veneta: miliardi bruciati, ora la sfida degli Npl. *La Repubblica*. 29 May. www.repubblica.it/economia/affari-e-finanza/2017/05/29/news/atlante_un_anno_nella_trappola_veneta_miliardi_bruciati_ora_la_sfida_degli_npl-166765315/

Greco, A. (2017b). Il consiglio di 'ntesa Sanpaolo approva l'acquisto delle banche venete. *La Repubblica*. 21 June. www.repubblica.it/economia/finanza/2017/06/21/news/il_cda_di_intesa_sanpaolo_approva_l_acquisto_delle_banche_venete-168715610/

Gruppo MPS (2016a). Press release. *Gruppo MPS Website*: www.gruppomps.it/en/media-and-news/press-releases/press_release_20160704.html

Gruppo MPS (2016b). Risultati dello stress test EBA 2016. *Gruppo MPS Website*. www.gruppomps.it/media-e-news/comunicati/risultati-dello-stress-test-eba-2016.html

Gruppo MPS (2016c). Press release. www.gruppomps.it/static/upload/archivio/16851/2016_10_25_BusinessPlan_ENG.PDF

Gruppo MPS (2016d). Press release pursuant to article 102 of legislative decree no. 58 of 24 february 1998. www.gruppomps.it/static/upload/archivio/16847/102_LME_Final_14_NOV_2016_ENG.pdf

Gruppo MPS (2016e). Extension of offer period. www.gruppomps.it/static/upload/archivio/16815/2016_12_16_Press_release_nulla_osta_ENG.pdf

Gruppo MPS (2016f). Press release. www.gruppomps.it/static/upload/archivio/16816/2016_12_19_Press_release_ENG.pdf

Gruppo MPS (2016g). Press release. www.gruppomps.it/en/media-and-news/press-releases/press_release_20161226.html

Gruppo MPS (n.d.). Marco Morelli. *Gruppo MPS*. www.gruppomps.it/corporate-governance/consiglio-di-amministrazione/marco-morelli.html

Gruppo Veneto Banca (2015). Definito il valore di liquidazione e le limitazioni al diritto di rimborso. www.venetobanca.it/documents/11351/1156615/02.12.2015+COMUNICATO+STAMPA.PDF

Gruppo Veneto Banca (2017a). Press release 19 January 2017. www.gruppovenetobanca.it/documents/17503/1443157/19.01.2017+PRESS+RELEASE.PDF

Gruppo Veneto Banca (2017b). Comunicato stampa 4 aprile 2017. www.gruppovenetobanca.it/documents/17503/1443151/04.04.2017+COMUNICATO+STAMPA.PDF

Gualtieri, L. (2017). Banche venete, no di Atlante ma il Mef continua a trattare. Nuovi cda giovedì. *Milano Finanza*. 30 May. www.milanofinanza.it/news/banche-venete-no-di-atlante-ma-il-mef-continua-a-trattare-nuovi-cda-giovedi-201705301701315726

Guarascio, F. (2020). No compe'sation for Banco Popular's creditors, EU regulator says. *Reuters*, 18 March. https://www.reuters.com/article/eu-banks-srb-bancopopular/no-compensation-for-banco-populars-creditors-eu-regulator-says-idUSB5N27Y01U

Guarascio, F. (2016a). Europe'"not convinced" by Italy's plan to buoy banks after Brexit-EU source. *Reuters*. 2 June. www.reuters.com/italy-banks-eu/europe-not-convinced-by-italys-plan-to-buoy-banks-after-brexit-eu-source-idUSL8N19L2NU

Guarascio, F. (2016b). Follow the rules on banks, EU tells Italy, Brexit no excuse. *Reuters*. 29 June. www.reuters.com/article/us-italy-banks-eu/follow-the-rules-on-banks-eu-tells-italy-brexit-no-excuse-idUSKCN0ZF1GE

Guarascio, F. (2016c). EU, Italy weigh public recapitalization of banks before stress tests. *Reuters*. 3 July. www.reuters.com/article/us-italy-banks-eu-idUSKCN0ZJ0QT

Guarascio, F. (2016d). Italian banking c'isis precedes Brexit, EU's Dombrovskis says. *Reuters*. 6 July. www.uk.reuters.com/atalianuk-banks-italy-eu/italian-banking-crisis-precedes-brexit-eus-dombrovskis-says-idUKKCN0ZM17X

Guarascio, F., & Sinner, M. (2016). EU court says bail-in legal but bank rescues need not hit investors. *Reuters*. 19 July. www.reuters.com/article/us-eurozone-banks-court/eu-court-says-bail-in-legal-but-bank-rescues-need-not-hit-investors-idUSKCN0ZZ0N8

Howarth, D., & Quaglia, L. (2016). *The Political Economy of the European Union*. Oxford: Oxford University Press.

International Monetary Fund (2013). *Italy: Financial Stability Assessment*. Washington DC: IMF Publication Services.

JD Supra (2017). The Italian State Steps. In *Government Guarantees and Precautionary Recapitalizations of Italian Banks*. www.jdsupra.com/legalnews/the-italian-state-steps-in-government-77410/

Kirchgaessner, S. (2016). Monte dei Paschi di Siena tries to keep €5bn rescue plan alive. *The Guardian*. 2 December. theguardian.com/business/2016/dec/11/monte-dei-paschi-siena-emergency-cash-injection-european-central-bank

Leardini, F. (2016). Stress test: Mps la banca peggiore, reggono le altre italiane. *Sky TG 24*. 29 July. www.tg24.sky.it/economia/2016/07/29/stress-test-banche-mps.html

Legorano, G. (2016). UniCredit Board Confident in CEO Despite Bank's Struggles. *Wall Street Italia*. 9 July. www.wsj.com/articles/unicredit-profit-hit-by-strategic-revamp-1455022746

Libero (2017). Banche: Zaia, come per Mps per BpVii e Veneto Banca serve intervento statale. *Libero*. 30 May. www.liberoquotidiano.it/news/economia/12399951/banche-zaia-come-per-mps-per-BpVii-e-veneto-banca-serve-intervento-statale.html

Makortoff, K. (2016). Italy wants you to forget its troubles. *Cnbc*. www.cnbc.com/2016/04/13/italys-prime-minister-renzi-plans-to-resign-if-referendum-fails.html

Malagutti V. (2015a). La Banca Popolare di Vicenza tra prestiti irregolari e conflitti d'interesse. *Espresso*. 17 September. www.espresso.repubblica.it/plus/articoli/2015/09/17/news/la-banca-popolare-di-vicenza-tra-prestiti-irregolari-e-conflitti-d-interesse-1.230107

Malagutti, V. (2015b). Popolare Vicenza, chi si è salvato dal flop: Ecco la lista dei "soci eccellenti" tutelati. *Espresso*. 4 November. www.espresso.repubblica.it/plus/articoli/2015/11/04/news/popolare-vicenza-chi-ha-guadagnato-dal-flop-ecco-la-lista-dei-soci-eccellenti-salvati-1.237287

Malagutti, V. (2016). Popolare Etruria, il crac è un affare per la banca dei vip. *L'Espresso*. 13 January. espresso.repubblica.it/plus/articoli/2016/01/13/news/vip-d-etruria-1.246661

Mandalà, A. (2017). Banche venete, Penati: fiducia su ok Bce a piano, intervento Stato strada giusta. *Reuters*. 7 February. www.it.reuters.com/article/businessNews/idITKBN15M28F

Mandurino, K. (2016). Veneto Banca, Ipo con maxi sconto. Atlante pronto a intervenire. *Il Sole 24 Ore*. 31 May. ilsole24ore.com/art/finanza-e-mercati/2016-05-31/veneto-banca-ipo-maxi-sconto-atlante-pronto-sub-garanzia-070227.shtml?uuid=ADjkXxS

Mandurino, K. (2017a). Banca Popolare Vicenza colloca 1,25 miliardi di bond 2020. *Il Sole 24 Ore*. 20 February. www.ilsole24ore.com/art/finanza-e-mercati/2017-02-20/popolare-vicenza-collocato-bond-2020-atteso-ammontare-1-miliardo--115128.shtml?uuid=AEEEuaZ&fromSearch

Mandurino, K. (2017b). Banche Venete, salvataggio senza «bail-in». *Il Sole 24 Ore*. 14 June. www.ilsole24ore.com/art/notizie/2017-06-14/banche-venete-salvataggio-senza-bail-in-063727.shtml?uuid=AE9494dB

Marrelli, M., & Stroffolini, F. (1998). Privatisation in Italy: a tale of "capture". In D. Parker (Ed.), *Privatisation in the European Union: Theory and Policy Perspectives*. London, England: Routledge.

Massaro, F. (2016a). Niente Borsa per Popolare di Vicenza, Atlante prende il 99%. Crollano i titoli bancari, si teme ora per Veneto Banca. *Il Corriere della Sera*. 3 May. www.corriere.it/economia/16_maggio_03/niente-borsa-popolare-vicenza-atlante-prende-99percento-crollano-titoli-bancari-si-teme-ora-veneto-banca-95d7f706-10a1-11e6-aba7-a1898801ab6b.shtml

Massaro, F. (2016b). I colloqui per i nuovi soci in Atlante 2: si cerca un miliardo di euro per Mps. *Il Corriere della Sera*. 4 July. www.corriere.it/economia/16_luglio_05/i-colloqui-nuovi-soci-atlante-2-si-cerca-miliardo-euro-mps-a2cee244-4229-11e6-91d1-c0b7aa8f545f.shtml

Massaro, F. (2016c). Monte dei Paschi, adesso Morelli apre alle danze arabe in Qatar. *Il Corriere della Sera*. 28 November. www.corriere.it/economia/finanza_e_risparmio/16_novembre_28/monte-paschi-adesso-morelli-apre-danze-arabe-qatar-40aed0ba-b54c-11e6-a2c1-e1ab33bf33ae.shtml

Massaro, F. (2017). Corsa contro il tempo per salvare le banche venete. *Il Corriere della Sera*. 11 March. www.pressreader.com/italy/corriere-della-sera/20170311/282643212353256

Il Mattino di Padova (2017). Così l'aumento 2014 di Veneto Banca fu deciso "a tavolino". *Il Mattino di Padova*. 25 April. www.mattinopadova.gelocal.it/padova/cronaca/2017/04/25/news/e-l-aumento-2014-fu-deciso-a-tavolino-1.15248243

Meletti, G. (2013). Banche in sofferenza. Scoppia il caso Marche. Il Fatto Quotidiano. 23 July. http://www.azionistibancamarche.altervista.org/images/articoli2013/07/Art.%20Il%20Fatto%20Quotidiano%2023.07.2013.jpg).

Meletti, G. (2016). Jp Morgan amica di Renzi caccia l'ad Viola da Mps. *Il Fatto Quotidiano*. 9 September. www.ilfattoquotidiano.it/premium/articoli/jp-morgan-amica-di-renzi-caccia-lad-viola-da-mps/

Merler, S. (2016a). Italy's bail-in headache. *Bruegel*. 19 July. www.bruegel.org/2016/07/italys-bail-in-headache/

Merler, S. (2016b). Italy's bail-in conundrum. *Politico*. 21 July. www.politico.eu/article/italy-bank-crisis-renzi-bail-in-commission/

Merler, S. (2017). Italian banks: not quiet on the eastern front. Bruegel. 31 March. www.bruegel.org/2017/03/italian-banks-not-quiet-on-the-eastern-front/

Merli, A. (2017). Bce: «Sul salvataggio BpVii e Veneto deciderà la Commissione europea». *Il Sole 24 Ore*. 27 March. www.ilsole24ore.com/art/finanza-e-mercati/2017-03-27/bce-sul-salvataggio-BpVii-e-veneto-decidera-commissione-europea-222038.shtml?uuid=AEEwBJu

Ministero dell'Economia e delle Finanze (2017a). Il Ministro Padoan ha incontrato i vertici di Pop. *Vicenza e Veneto Banca*. www.mef.gov.it/ufficio-stampa/comunicati/2017/comunicato_0084.html

Ministero dell'Economia e delle Finanze (2017b). Il Ministro Padoan sulle banche venete: "La soluzione è prossima". www.mef.gov.it/ufficio-stampa/comunicati/2017/comunicato_0101.html.

Monaghan, A., & Fletcher, N. (2017). ECB reportedly rules out extension for Monte dei Paschi fundraising - as it happened. *The Guardian*. 25 May. theguardian.com/business/live/2016/dec/09/markets-boosted-as-ecb-pledges-to-do-more-if-necessary-business-live

Nasdaq (2013). Bond yields edge higher as Italy sells 10-year debt. 30 May. m.nasdaq.com/article/bond-yields-edge-higher-as-italy-sells-10-year-debt-cm249582

La Nazione (2013). Banca Etruria alla ricerca di un partner: il Cda apre alla trattativa con un gruppo creditizio "di elevato standing". *La Nazione*. 14 December. lanazione.it/arezzo/economia/2013/12/13/996509-arezzo-bancaetruria-fornasari-trattativa.shtml

Nicoletti, F. (2017a). Banca unica con lo Stato in minoranza. *Corriere del Veneto*. 1 February. www.corrieredelveneto.corriere.it/vicenza/notizie/economia/2017/1-febbraio-2017/banca-unica-lo-stato-minoranza-2401251260182.shtml

Nicoletti, F. (2017b). Banche ex Popolari venete: fumata nera a Bruxelles e vertice d'urgenza al Tesoro. *Corriere del Veneto*. 25 May. www.corrieredelveneto.corriere.it/veneto/notizie/economia/2017/25-maggio-2017/banche-ex-popolari-venete-fumata-nera-bruxelles-vertice-d-urgenza-tesoro-2401615020271.shtml

Nicoletti, F. (2017c). Venete, la promessa di Padoan e Ue: <<Soluzione vicina, senza bail-in>>. *Corriere del Veneto*. 14 June. www.pressreader.com/italy/corriere-di-Vérona/20170614/281848643586921

Padoa-Schioppa, T. (2007). Letter to Fernando Teixeira dos Santos, President of the ECOFIN Council, 26 November, Italian Ministry of Economy.

Palazzo Chigi (2016). Berlino, conferenza stampa Renzi - Merkel – Hollande. www.youtube.com/watch?v=uMn977k7GwU&t=297s

Paolucci, G. (2017). "Anomalie sui bond Etruria": nel 2013 l'allarme a Consob. *La Stampa*. 25 August. lastampa.it/2017/08/25/economia/anomalie-sui-bond-etruria-nel-lallarme-a-consob-wOqnnsgZ65Yxl35ppsd4HK/pagina.html

Paronetto, P. (2017). Penati: fusione Vicenza-Veneto Banca entro settembre. «Ho trovato una horror story». *Il Sole 24 Ore*. 2 February. www.ilsole24ore.com/art/finanza-e-mercati/2017-02-07/penati-fusione-vicenza-veneto-banca-entro-settembre-ho-trovato-horror-story-132223.shtml?uuid=AEhyG7P

Paolucci, G. (2016). Mps, quella telefonata di Padoan per mettere alla porta l'ad Viola. *La Stampa*. 14 September. www.lastampa.it/2016/09/14/economia/mps-quella-telefonata-di-padoan-per-mettere-alla-porta-il-ceo-viola-irgPXvEPARjP2RNTPD01RK/pagina.html

Pavesi, F. (2015). Così i bond subordinati di Etruria sono finiti nei conti dei piccoli clienti. *Il Sole 24 Ore*. 15 December. ilsole24ore.com/art/finanza-e-mercati/2015-12-14/come-e-perche-bond-subordinati-etruria-sono-finiti-conti-piccoli-clienti-213632.shtml?uuid=ACOtBMtB

Pavesi, F. & Boda, A. (2015). Tutti i retroscena del fallimento della vecchia Banca Etruria. *Il Sole 24 Ore*. 9 December. ilsole24ore.com/art/finanza-e-mercati/2015-12-08/retroscena-ecco-come-e-fallita-vecchia-banca-etruria-200435.shtml

Peruzzi, C. (2014). Mps, il maxi-aumento fa il tutto esaurito. *Il Sole 24 Ore*. 28 June. www.ilsole24ore.com/art/finanza-e-mercati/2014-06-28/mps-maxi-aumento-fa-tutto-esaurito-081429.shtml?uuid=AB8rwhVB

Piana, L. (2016). Brexit, perché le banche crollano in Borsa. *L'Espresso*. 24 June. www.espresso.repubblica.it/attualita/2016/06/24/news/brexit-in-borsa-le-banche-non-riescono-nemmeno-ad-aprire-1.274507

Politi, J. (2016). Monte dei Paschi shortfall hits €8bn, says ECB. *Financial Times*. 27 December. www.ft.com/content/60576ada-cbbd-11e6-864f-20dcb35cede2

Politi, J., & Brundsen, J. (2016). Q&A: Italy's 'bad bank' deal. *The Financial Times*. 27 January. www.ft.com/content/2a057c30-c374-11e5-b3b1-7b2481276e45

Politi, J., Arnold, M. & Brunsden, J. (2016). Italy reaches 'bad bank' agreement with Brussels. *Financial Times*, 27 January. https://www.ft.com/content/ef7fe9e8-c4d0-11e5-b3b1-7b2481276e45

Pons, G. (2016). Mps, il soccorso della finanza globale: vince Jp Morgan, la banca dei governi. *La Repubblica*. 26 September. www.repubblica.it/economia/affari-e-finanza/2016/09/26/news/mps_il_soccorso_della_finanza_globale_vince_jp_morgan_la_banca_dei_governi-148600889/

Il Post (2016). Che cos'è il fondo Atlante. *Il Post*. 17 April. www.ilpost.it/2016/04/17/banche-fondo-atlante/.

Provenzani, F. (2016). JPMorgan tra il salvataggio MPS e Renzi: storia di un fallimento. *Money*. 28 December. www.money.it/JPMorgan-salvataggio-MPS-Renzi-fallimento

Quaestio sgr (2016a). Presentazione Fondo Atlante. www.quaestiocapital.com/sites/default/files/Quaestio_Presentazione_Atlante_29_04_2016_n_0.pdf

Quaestio sgr (2016b). Comunicato stampa. www.quaestiocapital.com/sites/default/files/Comunicato%20Stampa%20Quaestio%20Atlante%20II%208.08.16.pdf

Rai News (2015). Popolari. Zaia scrive a Renzi,Padoan,Visco e Draghi:"Serve intervento forte per risparmio e imprese". *Rai News*. 5 December. www.rainews.it/dl/rainews/articoli/Banche-Popolari-Zaia-scrive-a-Renzi-Padoan-Visco-e-Draghi

-Serve-intervento-forte-per-risparmio-e-imprese-a8880f3a-e25d-484a-9821-711f1d554d48.html?refresh_ce

Rai News (2016). Offerta Monte dei Paschi di Siena, eccesso di ribasso per il titolo. Forte incertezza sui bancari. *Rai News*. 28 November. www.rainews.it/dl/rainews/articoli/monte-paschi-siena-piano-conversione-bond-azioni-titolo-sospeso-borsa-60d3d1e6-5881-4d87-85c6-d8d088b3beb0.html?refresh_ce

Rai News (2017). Bce: fabbisogno di 6,4 miliardi per le banche venete. *Rai News*. 4 April. www.rainews.it/dl/rainews/articoli/Bce-fabbisogno-di-6-virgola-4-miliardi-per-banche-venete-9f5636c1-fcf0-41b8-912f-ad23a5197c31.html

Ravallin, E. (2016). Atlante rileverà azioni BpVii a 10 centesimi. *Il Mattino di Padova*. 20 April. www.mattinopadova.gelocal.it/focus/2016/04/20/news/BpVii-conferma-l-accordo-unicredit-atlante-1.13330767

La Repubblica (2011). Fitch taglia rating di otto banche italiane. *La Repubblica*. 25 November. repubblica.it/economia/finanza/2011/11/25/news/fitch_taglia_rating_di_otto_banche_italiane-25604652/

La Repubblica (2014). Opa della Pop Vicenza su Banca Etruria: offerto 1 euro ad azione, premio del 25%. La Repubblica. 29 May. repubblica.it/economia/finanza/2014/05/29/news/opa_della_pop_vicenza_su_banca_etruria_offerto_1_euro_ad_azione_premio_del_25_-8

La Repubblica (2015). Perquisizioni nella Banca Popolare di Vicenza, indagato presidente Zonin. *La Repubblica*. 22 September. www.repubblica.it/cronaca/2015/09/22/news/perquisizioni_nella_banca_popolare_di_vicenza_indagato_presidente_zonin-123406247/).

La Repubblica (2016a). La Germania frena l'Italia sulle banche. Renzi: "Noi rispettiamo le regole". *La Repubblica*. 29 June. www.repubblica.it/economia/2016/06/29/news/la_germania_frena_sui_piani_italiani_per_supportare_le_banche-143065145/

La Repubblica (2016b). Banche, via libera della Bce al piano di salvataggio Mps. *La Repubblica*. 29 July. www.repubblica.it/economia/finanza/2016/07/29/news/bce_via_libera_a_piano_salvataggio_mps-145051412

La Repubblica (2016c). Mps "sblocca" Atlante 2 così può decollare il mercato delle sofferenze. *La Repubblica*. 28 November. www.repubblica.it/economia/affari-e-finanza/2016/11/28/news/mps_sblocca_atlante_2_cos_pu_decollare_il_mercato_delle_sofferenze-153059209/

La Repubblica (2016d). Banche, il governo vara il fondo da 20 miliardi: salva Mps. *La Repubblica*. 23 December. www.repubblica.it/economia/2016/12/23/news/mps_governo_salvataggio_fondo_banche-154704338/

La Repubblica (2017a). Penati sbotta contro i banchieri italiani: "Poco lungimiranti". *La Repubblica*. 7 February. www.repubblica.it/economia/finanza/2017/02/07/news/penati_spara_sui_banchieri_poco_lungimiranti_-157773023/

La Repubblica (2017b). Banche venete, ai vecchi soci vanno 441 milioni di euro. *La Repubblica*. 11 April. www.repubblica.it/economia/finanza/2017/04/11/news/banche_venete_ai_vecchi_soci_vanno_441_milioni_di_euro-162735975/

La Repubblica (2017c). Banche venete, Padoan: "Escluso il bail-in". A Montebelluna "mutui in cambio di azioni e c/c". *La Repubblica*. 25 May. www.repubblica.it/economia/finanza/2017/05/25/news/banche_venete_il_tesoro_ogni_garanzia_su_liquidita_soluzione_in_fretta_-166352011/

La Repubblica (2017d). Muro di Atlante sulle venete: "Non metteremo altre risorse". *La Repubblica*. 30 May. www.repubblica.it/economia/finanza/2017/05/30/news/atlante_venete_risorse-166815572/

La Repubblica (2017e). Banche venete, via libera alla fiducia dalla Camera. *La Repubblica*. 12 July. www.repubblica.it/economia/2017/07/12/news/banche_venete_via_libera_alla_fiducia_dalla_camera-170622733/

Reuters (2016a). Mediobanca: pre-underwriting Mps non vincolante, impegno sotto 700–800 milioni. *Reuters*. 5 August. www.it.reuters.com/article/businessNews/idITKCN10G0OQ

Reuters (2016b). Italy - Factors to watch on Oct. 10. *Reuters*. 10 October. www.reuters.com/article/italy-factors-oct-10/italy-factors-to-watch-on-oct-10-idUSL5N1CD1ME

Reuters (2016c). Mps, Atlante II disposto a cartolarizzazione npl anche con intervento stato in capital. *Reuters*. 21 December. www.it.reuters.com/article/bondsNews/idITL5N1EG4V6

Righi, S. (2016). Mps, sì della Bce al piano Mps. Aumento fino a 5 miliardi e vendita sofferenze. *Il Corriere della Sera*. 29 July. www.corriere.it/economia/16_luglio_29/mps-via-libera-bce-piano-aumento-sofferenze-8990ea84-55b6-11e6-af7a-c71c10cda3a8.shtml

Romano, B. (2016). Vestager: finora mai eccezioni al bail in. *Il Sole 24 Ore*. 15 July. www.ilsole24ore.com/art/mondo/2016-07-14/vestager-finora-mai-eccezioni-bail-in-232731.shtml?uuid=ADqOk2s

Romano, B. (2017). Veneto Banca e Vicenza, Bruxelles apre alle compensazioni. *Il Sole 24 Ore*. 8 March. www.ilsole24ore.com/art/finanza-e-mercati/2017-03-08/veneto-banca-e-vicenza-bruxelles-apre-compensazioni--222714.shtml?uuid=AEm5OQk&fromSearch

Sala, A. (2016). Renzi: Banche, accordo vicino. *Corriere della sera*. 12 July. www.corriere.it/politica/16_luglio_11/renzi-corriere-severgnini-intervista-59d310ac-477d-11e6-af4e-15bff4e09cf7.shtml

Sanderson, R. (2016a). Matteo Renzi rebuffed on move to sidestep bank bail-ins. *The Financial Times*. 29 June. www.ft.com/content/f0dc0e7e-3e39-11e6-9f2c-36b487ebd80a

Sanderson, R. (2016b). Bad-debt warning triggers fresh fears for Italian banks. *The Financial Times*. 4 July. www.ft.com/content/f04102da-41c7-11e6-b22f-79eb4891c97d

Sanderson, R., & Barker, A. (2016). Renzi ready to defy Brussels and bail out Italy's troubled banks. *The Financial Times*. 3 July. www.ft.com/content/e3b53640-4108-11e6-9b66-0712b3873ae1

Sanderson, R. (2016). Italy pushes for bank rescue fund. *Financial Times*. 10 April. https://www.ft.com/content/f3bb18d0-fefe-11e5-ac98-3c15a1aa2e62

Schoenmaker, D., & Véron, N. (2016). European banking supervision: The first eighteen months. Bruegel website: bruegel.org/wp-content/uploads/2016/06/Blueprint-XXV-web.pdf

Sarzanini, F. (2017a). Nel dossier segreto la lettera di Visco sulla crisi Etruria: «Gravi anomalie». *Il Corriere della Sera*. 19 Ottobre. roma.corriere.it/notizie/politica/17_ottobre_19/nel-dossier-segreto-lettera-visco-crisi-etruria-gravi-anomalie-e37f1d5a-b504-11e7-aa01-fc391f169342.shtml

Sciancalepore, G. (2017). Banche venete, Baretta: «Le salveremo come abbiamo fatto con Monte Paschi». *Corriere del Veneto*. 27 May. www.corrieredelveneto.corriere.it/veneto/notizie/economia/2017/27-maggio-2017/banche-venete-baretta-le-salveremo-come-abbiamo-fatto-monte-paschi-2401622809556.shtml

Senato della Repubblica – Camera dei Deputati (2017). Commissione Parlamentare di inchiesta sul sistema bancario e finanziario Legge 12 luglio 2017, n. 107. https://www.bancaditalia.it/pubblicazioni/interventi-vari/int-var-2017/Barbagallo-12122017.pdf

Sensini, M. (2016). Il negoziato Tesoro-Bruxelles, intervento su Monte Paschi ma tutela per i piccoli investitori. *Corriere della sera*. 12 July. www.pressreader.com/italy/corriere-della-sera/20160712/textview

Single Resolution Board (2017). The SRB will not take resolution action in relation to Banca Popolare di Vicenza and Veneto Banca. www.srb.europa.eu/en/node/341

Sirletti, S., Albane, C. & Migliaccio, A. (2021). Italy works to sweeten Paschi offer as Orcel Plays it cool. *Bloomberg*, 24 June, updated 25 June. https://www.bloomberg.com/news/articles/2021-06-24/italy-works-to-sweeten-monte-paschi-offer-as-orcel-plays-it-cool?cmpid%3D=socialflow-twitter-asia&utm_medium=social&utm_source=twitter&utm_content=asia&utm_campaign=socialflow-organic

Sirletti, S., Speciale, A., & Totaro, L. (2016). ECB rejects Monte Paschi bid for more time on capital. *Bloomberg*. 9 December. www.bloomberg.com/news/articles/2016-12-09/ecb-said-to-reject-monte-paschi-request-for-more-time-on-capital

Sirletti, S., Groendahl, B., & Totaro, L. (2017). Monte Paschi bailout plan faces ECB pushback on capital concerns. *Bloomberg*. 19 May. www.bloomberg.com/news/articles/2017-05-19/monte-paschi-bailout-plan-faces-ecb-pushback-on-capital-concerns

Sky TG24 (2016). Riforme, Renzi alla Camera: "Basta vincere, mi gioco tutto". *Sky TG24*. 11 April. www.tg24.sky.it/politica/2016/04/11/Riforma_costituzionale_renzi.html

Smiderle, M. (2017). Nouy: «Ex Popolari venete? La palla passa all'Ue». *Il Giornale di Vicenza*. 28 March. www.ilgiornaledivicenza.it/home/economia/nouy-ex-popolari-venete-la-palla-passa-all-ue-1.5589964?refresh_ce

Il Sole 24 Ore (2013). Banca Etruria vola in Borsa sul progetto di trasformazione in Spa. *Il Sole 24 Ore*. 12 August. ilsole24ore.com/art/finanza-e-mercati/2014-08-12/banca-etruria-vola-borsa-progetto-trasformazione-spa-104158.shtml?uuid=ABlLrajB

Il Sole 24 Ore (2015). Popolare di Vicenza: il Cda «taglia» il valore delle azioni del 23%. *Il Sole 24 Ore*. 8 April. www.ilsole24ore.com/art/notizie/2015-04-08/popolare-vicenza-il-cda-taglia-valore-azioni-23percento-201735.shtml?uuid=ABdXoDMD

Il Sole 24 Ore (2016a). Nasce Atlante, il fondo salva-banche. *Il Sole 24 Ore*. 11 April. www.ilsole24ore.com/art/finanza-e-mercati/2016-04-11/nasce-atlante-fondo-salva-banche-215559.shtml?uuid=AC8Pcg5C&refresh_ce=1

Il Sole 24 Ore (2016b). Dombrovskis: trattative con Roma su sostegno alle banche italiane. *Il Sole 24 Ore*. 27 June. www.ilsole24ore.com/art/mondo/2016-06-27/europa-brexit-vertice-ue-minuto-minuto--155210.shtml?uuid=ADrwLxj

Il Sole 24 Ore (2016c). Banche e Brexit, Renzi: nessun rischio per risparmiatori italiani. *Il Sole 24 Ore*. 28 June. www.ilsole24ore.com/art/notizie/2016-06-28/banche-e-brexit-renzi-nessun-rischio-risparmiatori-italiani-162241.shtml?uuid=AD2A9fk

Il Sole 24 ore (2017a). Ft: Bce e Bruxelles "spaccate" sul piano di ricapitalizzazione di Mps. *Il Sole 24 Ore*. 23 February. www.ilsole24ore.com/art/finanza-e-mercati/2017-02-23/mps-bce-e-bruxelles-spaccate-piano-ricapitalizzazione-122140.shtml?uuid=AE5SJub&fromSearch

Il Sole 24 Ore (2017b). Nouy: l'attendismo del passato su Npl non può continuare. *Il Sole 24 Ore*. 23 March. www.ilsole24ore.com/art/finanza-e-mercati/2017-03-23/nouy-l-attendismo-passato-npl-non-puo-continuare--104211.shtml?uuid=AERotzr

Il Sole 24 Ore (2017c). Banche venete, Padoan: nessun problema di liquidità. *Il Sole 24 Ore*. 25 May. www.ilsole24ore.com/art/notizie/2017-05-25/banche-venete-padoan-nessun-problema-liquidita-125327.shtml?uuid=AEP8FzSB

Il Sole 24 Ore (2017d). Chi paga il conto del salvataggio del Banco Popular. *Il Sole 24 Ore*. 7 June. www.ilsole24ore.com/art/finanza-e-mercati/2017-06-07/chi-paga-conto-salvataggio-banco-popular-172133.shtml?uuid=AENBqRaB

Il Sole 24 Ore (2017e). Parole chiave: Burden sharing. 29 July. www.argomenti.ilsole24ore.com/parolechiave/burden-sharing.html

Il Sole 24 Ore (n.d.). Banca Popolare di Vicenza. *Il Sole 24 Ore*. www.argomenti.ilsole24ore.com/banca-popolare-di-vicenza.html

Soto, L., & Pineda, F. (2017). Popolare di Vicenza e Veneto Banca, ecco la bislacca proposta di Luca Zaia con Mps. *Le Formiche*. 30 May. www.formiche.net/2017/05/662036/

Tonacci, F. (2015a). Scandalo banche, ora si indaga per truffa. I pm analizzano posizione Bankitalia e Consob. La Repubblica. 17 December. repubblica.it/economia/2015/12/17/news/scandalo_banche_ora_si_indaga_per_truffa_i_pm_analizzano_posizione_bankitalia_e_consob-129644233/?ref=HRER3-1

Tonacci, F. (2015b). La Repubblica. 18 December. repubblica.it/economia/2015/12/18/news/_fidejussioni_fantasma_in_nove_casi_su_dieci_punite_il_cda_di_etruria_-129717240/

Transparency International EU (2017). Two sides of the same coin? Independence and accountability of the european central bank. https://transparency.eu/wp-content/uploads/2017/03/TI-EU_ECB_Report_DIGITAL.pdf

TG Com 24 (2016). Banche, Padoan rassicura: "I risparmiatori saranno salvaguardati". *TG Com 24*. 11 July. www.tgcom24.mediaset.it/economia/banche-padoan-rassicura-i-risparmiatori-saranno-salvaguardati-_3019588-201602a.shtml

Todescan, G. (2015). Il 2015 nero delle banche venete. *Veneto Economia*. 12 December. www.venetoeconomia.it/2015/12/il-2015-nero-delle-banche-venete/

Treanor, J., & Kirchgaessner, S. (2016, December 23). Italian cabinet gives green light to Monte dei Paschi di Siena bailout. *The Guardian*. 23 December. www.theguardian.com/business/2016/dec/22/italy-bail-out-monte-dei-paschi-di-siena-rescue-matteo-renzi

La Tribuna di Treviso (2016). Veneto Banca, salta la quotazione in Borsa. *La Tribuna di Treviso*. 24 June. www.tribunatreviso.gelocal.it/treviso/cronaca/2016/06/24/news/veneto-banca-salta-la-quotazione-in-borsa-1.13716095

Trovati, G. (2016). Renzi: il «bail-in» è un disastro. *Il Sole 24 Ore*. 3 August. www.ilsole24ore.com/art/notizie/2016-08-03/renzi-bail-in-e-disastro-063550.shtml?uuid=ADTRQS1

Trovati, G. (2017). Soluzione entro un mese per le banche venete. *Il Sole 24 Ore*. 1 June. www.ilsole24ore.com/art/tecnologie/2017-06-01/soluzione-entro-mese-le-banche-venete-063707.shtml?uuid=AEH5fsWB

Vanni, F. (2017). Popolare Vicenza, verso il processo: chiuse le indagini su Zonin e sei ex dirigenti. *La Repubblica*. 16 July. www.repubblica.it/economia/finanza/2017/07/26/news/popolare_vicenza_chiuse_indagini_indagati_zonin_e_sei_ex_dirigenti-171689662/

Veneto Economia (2016). Fondo Atlante: chi sono i nuovi padroni di Banca Popolare di Vicenza. *Veneto Economia*. 3 May. www.venetoeconomia.it/2016/05/fondo-atlante-nuovi-padroni-banca-popolare-di-vicenza/

Veneto Economia (2017a). Bce: sì all'aumento di capitale di Stato per BpVii e Veneto Banca. *Veneto Economia*. 6 April. www.venetoeconomia.it/2017/04/bce-BpVii-veneto-banca-ricapitalizzazione-precauzionale/

Veneto Economia (2017b). BpVii e Veneto Banca, niente bail-in. I sindacati: no ai licenziamenti. *Veneto Economia*. 26 May. www.venetoeconomia.it/2017/05/BpVii-veneto-banca-padoan-esclude-bail/

Vicenza Today (2015). Popolare di Vicenza: Zonin lascerà il 24 novembre, arriva Dolcetta. *Vicenza Today*. 18 November. www.vicenzatoday.it/economia/popolare-di-vicenza-zonin-lascera-il-24-novembre-arriva-dolcetta.html

Vicenza Today (2017). Fumata nera a Bruxelles per le banche venete, Zaia: "Governo è assente". *Vicenza Today*. 24 May. www.vicenzatoday.it/economia/popolare-vicenza-veneto-banca-bruxelles-fumata-nera-banche-venete-messina-zaia.html

Vista Agenzia Televisiva Nazionale. (2016). Gentiloni: "Avanti con il Salvarisparmio, oggi giornata importante per Mps". www.youtube.com/watch?v=bzGMPnAZpTk

VVox (2017). BpVii e Vb, Intesa e Unicredit pronte al salvataggio. *VVOX*. 9 June. www.vvox.it/2017/06/09/BpVii-e-vb-intesa-e-unicredit-pronte-al-salvataggio

Williams, A. (2016). Italian bond yields fall with bank deal in sight. *Reuters*. 12 July. reuters.com/article/eurozone-bonds/italian-bond-yields-fall-with-bank-deal-in-sight-idUSL8N19Y1DW

Za, V. (2017). Italy's "bitter" bank rescue tsar bemoans strategy vacuum. *Reuters*. 7 February. uk.reuters.com/article/us-italy-banks-atlante/italys-bitter-bank-rescue-tsar-bemoans-strategy-vacuum-idUKKBN15M28B

Za, V., & Aloisi, S. (2015). Italy bank Popolare Vicenza probed over loans-for-shares scheme. *Reuters*. 29 September. www.reuters.com/article/italy-banks-popvicenza-probe/italy-bank-popolare-vicenza-probed-over-loans-for-shares-scheme-idUSL5N11V28H20150929

Zingales, L. (2015). Non fare processi alla vigilanza della Bce. *Il Sole 24 Ore*. 9 September. www.ilsole24ore.com/art/commenti-e-idee/2015-09-09/non-fare-processi-vigilanza-bce-072344.shtml?uuid=ACwl9Zu

7

CONCLUSIONS

Banking Union in the EU was designed to stabilize Economic and Monetary Union by addressing a serious negative feedback loop between banks and sovereigns in the absence of EU-level funds and transfers to stabilize insolvent banks. Insolvent banks turned to national governments for loans or outright capital injections, and some national governments found themselves unable to borrow sufficiently to make these loans and grants. This threat to Eurozone economies on both the public and private sides required remedial measures that became Banking Union. Banking Union could have developed in a manner that shared risks across borders and developed strong, collective financial resources to be used in the event of a bank failure, either individual or systemic. It developed instead in accordance with a commitment to risk reduction at the national level, which meant that pressure on national banking systems to reform with national resources increased.

The Single Supervisory Mechanism (SSM) was established to investigate systemically important banks, to force them to write off non-performing loans (NPLs) and exposures, raise capital and generally implement a new host of regulatory innovations designed to specify these requirements. This is an ongoing process that is strongly linked to periodic adjustments of global standards established by the Basel Committee on Banking Supervision. But it is also driven by intergovernmental negotiations over bank safety in which Germany is an active participant, making any discussion of financial assistance through grants conditional on progress in this field. In this, the EU has gone beyond the originally weak efforts of the European Banking Authority (EBA) to the considerably stronger supervisory pressure of the European Central Bank (ECB), both on systemically important banks and on the Single Rulebook that it has developed with the EBA to use on all banks in the EU. In short, a key development of Banking Union is the development of a strong mechanism to expose problems in European banks

DOI: 10.4324/9781003334583-7

and bring those problems to the fore, where they become issues for national and sometimes European authorities. This is not only intended to establish stronger EU supervision but stronger national supervision as well. National bank regulators, whether in central banks or in a special bank supervision entity, now work within a Single Rulebook that the ECB has had a significant hand in forming. While there is no guarantee of supervisory strength within the Member States, even with the participation of supervisory colleges, the intent of these reforms to strengthen supervision wherever it occurs is clear.

The Single Resolution Mechanism (SRM) was also established in an attempt to deal with the question of how to deal with failing banks, and how to ensure that national resolution authorities develop into robust regulators in their own right that are capable of handling insolvent banks when they fail. The Single Resolution Board (SRB) is in charge of ensuring that national authorities sit down with their own banks and deal with them when the ECB declares that they are failing or likely to fail. This is intended to include game plans for resolution before they become a necessity. But the SRM's structure also includes a role for the SRB to reduce the likelihood of forbearance at the national level by taking resolution decisions on the most systemically important banks as a collective, rather than leaving it entirely to a national authority. There were other innovations designed to decrease the pressure on national authorities for forbearance. A modest Single Resolution Fund (SRF) was also established to be used during the resolution of failed banks if national resources proved insufficient. And finally, a comprehensive rule set was created for imposing costs on private investors during resolutions to limit the pressure on national governments to bail out banks. The Bank Recovery and Resolution Directive (BRRD) included a formula to mandate creditor bail-ins first, followed by national resolution and deposit insurance funds (paid in advance by banks), followed by drawing on the Single Resolution Fund (also paid in advance by banks), and then the public purse as a final recourse.

Unlike the Supervisory Mechanism, the Resolution Mechanism has significant loopholes that make it weaker than recommendations from international bodies and experts in the field. It has no direct authority to launch a resolution or to authorize the use of the Single Resolution Fund but merely to advise the European Commission, whose decisions may be overturned by the European Council. The size of the fund is also a cause of concern, leading to an amendment of the treaty on the European Stability Mechanism (ESM) to make loans to the fund possible in the event that it should prove insufficient. These arrangements are infinitely more complicated than a Federal Deposit Insurance Corporation (FDIC)-style resolution authority with access to a deposit insurance fund, which the EU also lacks. Finally, the SRM has the added complexity of allowing the Board to choose between applying the BRRD, which mandates bail-ins, and waiving those terms by declaring that a bank is not important to the broader banking system. This hands back management of bank failures to national governments, which are then free to bail out, provided the Commission's Competition

Policy directorate approves the terms. Whereas the EU's bank supervision provided leeway for forbearance under the European Banking Authority but then cracked down on collective slacking by handing the task to the ECB, the same has not happened within the SRM.

Where national resources are lacking, and where local politics resist closure and bail-ins, in short, where both banks and states remain weak, the difficulties of SRM's construction become evident. Both the SRB and the Commission have elected to grant exceptions to EU law, given that national institutions and resources are too weak to handle the situation themselves. Where the state is willing to call on external pressure and assistance through the ESM, this weakness can be compensated. But where the state is not, as is the case in Italy, the result is a lasting conflict between the demands of Banking Union in its existing form, and the willingness of the Italian state to live up to its legal obligations and to stabilize Italian banking. To be fair, successive Italian governments have stressed the need to have a European Deposit Insurance Scheme which could also be used in bank resolutions that would reduce or eliminate the need for the state to be particularly strong in resolution matters. But that is not how Banking Union is constructed. It requires and demands a strong state in the liberal sense, which can develop theoretically in the direction of disinterest in who owns the banks that serve its citizens but in practice gravitates towards a liberal economic nationalism that preserves bank ownership where it can.

This combination of institutional developments simultaneously raises the pressure on banks (through supervision) to raise capital from investors they may be unable to win over and provides opportunities to national governments to save those banks in ways that keep ownership concentrated with national investors. This ownership might be in private hands, or in public hands. While the intent of the SRM and the BRRD is clearly to break bank reliance on public support, when a search for private investors fails, we see that eyes turn to public authorities to bail out failing banks rather than dismembering them. Not only does that lead national resolution authorities to lobby the Board to waive the application of the BRRD and allow such assistance, but it also provides incentives to the Board (and to the Commission) to waive the ban on bailouts as a purely national matter, regardless of the actual potential for systemic disruption. These options are only unavailable for the banks that the ECB directly supervises.

This context of high pressure on banks and regulatory rules and loopholes provides opportunities for economic nationalism of one sort or another. This book investigates whether and how this is the case in two important Southern European Member States of the EU, the Eurozone and Banking Union. We defined economic nationalism as *actions to ensure that banks are owned by national investors*. This definition encompasses three sorts of economic nationalism: traditional, mercantilist economic nationalism that disregards any European commitments to fair and equal treatment of domestic and foreign investors; liberal economic nationalism that respects European legal requirements but nevertheless demonstrates a preference for banks to be owned by national investors; and a new contribution to the literature on economic nationalism: functional economic nationalism, in which local governance structures and financial conditions make banks simultaneously too socially central to fail (regardless of their size in the sense of too big to fail), too unattractive for private investors to take over, even with considerable inducements, and in so doing, undermine the power of the state at the national level. We therefore build on recent developments in varieties of financial capitalism literature and apply it in-depth in a comparative case study of economic nationalism in Italy and Spain. Here, we add to the literature on economic nationalism, focusing on distinctions between countries that can and cannot find a way to respect international (EU) obligations and domestic expectations simultaneously. We furthermore, in the European context, examine the role of the ESM in promoting a specifically liberal economic nationalist role for the state, which is evident in Spain, and absent in Italy.

Our findings provide important insights into the strengths and weaknesses of the European system for bank resolution, of the conditions of banks in Italy and Spain (varieties of financial capitalism) and in differing forms of economic nationalism in those two countries that lead us to reflect once more on the state of the art. These are not static national banking varieties and policies of economic nationalism, but ones that evolve in a dynamic fashion and that involve distinctively different strategies for dealing with the EU and its legal and institutional demands.

In Spain, we see a strategy of liberal economic nationalism that not only accepts European institutions, rules and resources but embraces them, even to the point of weaponizing them against its own banking sector to reshape, re-regulate and restructure it, concentrating on final ownership in the country's large commercial banks with (relatively) limited state aid.

In Italy, we see a strategy of functional economic nationalism that seeks loopholes in European rules, exceptions from European institutions on the application of those rules, and a continuing demand for the EU to provide resources that would finance restructuring without loans from the European Stability Mechanism. Rather than weaponizing EU rules, institutions and resources against its own banks, we see successive Italian governments trying to do the reverse: weaponizing the weakness of its own banking system and the damage that would be done to domestic retail investors to pressure the EU for more forbearance and leeway.

We further find that this strategy of embracing EU and ESM rules or rejecting them is a *choice* of government authorities that cannot entirely be attributed to the variety of financial capitalism, though the latter does indicate how likely banks and governments are to be trapped in choosing between economic nationalism and the decline of banks, particularly regional cooperatives and savings banks. Italian and Spanish bank supervisors and regulators were aware of problems with their banks at the same time. Italian and Spanish banks both had gotten their depositors to invest in bonds that would be wiped out in a restructuring (though much more intensively in Italy). But government and regulators moved much more quickly in Spain to admit the problems and react institutionally at the national level, and three years later to request ESM assistance tied to conditions for further reform when those measures proved insufficient. The relative weakness of Italian bank regulators in the same time period contrasts strongly with the Spanish experience. As well, the aversion of successive Italian governments and the Italian public to loans from the ESM meant that there was less pressure that Italian governments and supervisors could place on banks to restructure that it could blame on the ESM and fewer resources that the ESM could have provided to restructure the banks effectively.

These findings have a number of implications. One is that the interconnectedness of local, alternative banks with local economies and political councils makes them systemically important, even if they are not quantitatively too big to fail, in the sense that the ECB defines it. A second implication is that the turn to marketization in the 1980s/1990s and onward exacerbated the weaknesses that could render a bank systemically important and thereby make it a focus of state intervention to save it in one way or another. A third implication is that bank resolution can be enormously difficult to complete. The post-2008 international policy debate focused primarily on shutting down banks, dividing, transferring and selling assets in the process. But the realities of local economic and political impact pose real challenges for national resolution authorities, competition authorities and supervisors and their European counterparts as well. This can lead to continued supervisory forbearance, and gaps in the general functioning of the SRM as a whole.

A fourth implication is that states' assertiveness and capacity vary across states and make a significant difference in whether a country pursues a path of outright economic nationalism, liberal economic nationalism or functional economic nationalism. Faced with more pressing problems than in Italy in 2008, the Spanish state intervened in sweeping ways to consolidate national banking, albeit incompletely. But for all of the unfinished business in Spain, great strides in consolidating insolvent cajas had been made which the Italian state had not undertaken. Exposure of Italian banks to foreign investment was lower, leading to a lower sense of urgency, although the Bank of Italy did press Italian banks to clean up sloppy corporate and financial management around the same time when Spain was orchestrating mergers.

A fifth implication is that the involvement of the European Stability Mechanism in the creation of a national resolution architecture played a significant role in Spain's capacity to make a liberal economic nationalist strategy on bank resolution work. While Spain made progress in cleaning up Spanish alternative banking, it reached its limits in the political, economic and social policy responsibilities that cajas had to deal with, and the political rights of stakeholders to help steer the cajas themselves. Had this embeddedness of alternative banks in local communities continued unabated, the liberal economic nationalist strategy would have faltered, and it is likely that a functional economic nationalist trajectory would have replaced it. Despite an interest in reforming these connections, it took the ESM's conditions on loans to the Spanish state for the Spanish government to justify ending the political ties, duties and responsibilities of the cajas.

We can see this here in the Italian cases. The present book has analyzed two countries and a number of case studies in each in order to answer the research question: 'To what extent did the Italian and Spanish governments act in ways that kept banking ownership national?' The first case study focused on Monte dei Paschi di Siena (MPS). The data analysis' results for MPS' case study pointed to Hypothesis 2: 'The use of state aid represents an effort to protect investors'. But how far does this observation take us? On the one hand, Italy made a serious effort to engage with foreign investors, which disconfirms the hypotheses of economic nationalism. On the other hand, however, Italy attempted to push the Commission to approve the precautionary recapitalization of MPS months before it failed to raise capital from private markets, which disconfirms the hypothesis that Italy was acting in either a liberal way. What does bear scrutiny most strongly is Italy's desire to keep the bank afloat and protect inside investors regardless of external expectations, either from private investors or from European authorities. Therefore, the overall answer to MPS's case study is: Italy tried to keep the ownership national as long as it allows it to protect investors and keep the bank afloat.

This pattern of functional economic nationalism is reflected equally well in the cases of Banca Popolare di Vicenza and Veneto Banca. Rather convincing evidence points to Italy's effective refusal of foreign investors, coupled with protection of domestic investors, which demonstrates the Italian government's willingness to keep the bank afloat and ownership national even where this would contradict the requirements of the BRRD, including its radical and stubborn opposition to the bail-in rule. Follow-up studies in Italy engaged in a cross-case comparison involving three of the four small banks (Banca delle Marche, Cassa di Risparmio di Ferrara and Banca Popolare dell'Etruria e del Lazio) resolved in 2015. The record shows that resolving these banks is a difficult but uneven business. Where the bank is actually resolved, however, its deposits are shifted elsewhere and depositors are still protected.

The contrast between the cases demonstrates the involuntary nature of functional economic nationalism as something that can be pursued in different ways, and without setting out to do so. If MPS' case points to the preservation of the bank as the government's fundamental motivation rather than the will to keep the bank's ownership national, V&V's case does exactly the opposite. One of the assumptions that can be drawn from Italy's alleged will to keep V&V's ownership national more than MPS's could be due to the regional nature of the Venetian credit institutions, and to the considerable amount of pressure and lobbying that was registered in the data collection. Similarly, Italy's untamed will to keep MPS alive could be due to the bank's prestige, which might also, at a critical stage, have weighed more than the will to keep the bank completely Italian. All of this, it should be noted, pre-dates the 2018 nationalist coalition between the 5 Star Movement and the Lega Nord. One should not expect that a passing of this coalition out of power, and any anti-EU moves it may undertake, would mean an end to functional or real economic nationalism in Italy. The Draghi government equally has to contend with the inability of MPS to repay loans on time in 2022, despite the strong reputation of a government headed by the former president of the ECB. The challenges, with deep societal roots, were present before national governments came to power.

We can also see the effects of the implications outlined above in the Spanish cases. The key role played by early and forceful state intervention is made even more visible by the contrast between the outcomes for Italian and Spanish banks. David Keohane of the *Financial Times* underlines that Sociedad de Gestión de Activos Procedentes de la Reestructuración Bancaria (SAREB) provided a means to manage the NPL problem in Spain from 2012 onward that Italy no longer had under the terms of the BRRD starting in 2016. Particularly important was that burden-sharing (bail-ins) did not necessarily have to be applied. Although they were applied, there were no set rules about how much and which investors would pay the most. In Italy, in contrast, the consequences of wiping out retail bondholders in particular would have had potentially systemic disruption effects that neither the Italian government nor the European Commission could ignore (Donnelly and Asimakopoulos 2020).

What is equally interesting is that Spain's relative success in resolving its banking problems owes a great deal to the governments' interventionist liberal economic nationalism strategy. SAREB helped the Spanish state deal with a complex set of problems with multiple facets at the same time. Offloading the NPLs does not work without a workable business plan to find buyers. Securing buyers for the NPLs and real estate properties they are linked to raises the question of dealing with the social policy consequences, plus the real estate and loans attached to them that the cajas had managed up until that point, and which SAREB then took over. SAREB for this reason manages real estate until sale (meaning that it still rents more than 10,000 properties for public housing and other uses, it has a large payroll for building maintenance and services and that it is involved in attracting development for unbuilt pieces of land where building stopped).

Another difference is that while the state bought NPLs directly from banks in Spain (and Ireland), the middle step was missing in Italy, so private buyers needed to be found for the banks. And while the government in Italy might guarantee senior tranches of debt, the derivative would still have to be a private, marketable security (Financial Times Lex 2016) with the government guaranteeing at market rate fees for credit default swaps. This was as far as the European Commission, in particular Competition Commissioner Margarethe Vestager was willing to go, and the Commission added that it would monitor the Italian state's restraint to ensure that its terms were not so generous as to constitute state aid (Politi, Arnold and Brunsden 2016). All of this leaves Italy with Article 32 of the BRRD, which allows for exceptions when there is an exceptional, systemic threat to finance. But it may only be used for solvent institutions, and it must pass the state aid tests of the European Commission (Keohane 2016).

The lack of options is one of the main reasons for Italy being so keen on a Single Resolution Fund in 2016 (Sanderson 2016a, b). Sanderson notes that in contrast to Spanish banks, which lowered the price on NPLs on sale, Italian banks focused on protecting insider investors rather than restructuring and insisted on higher valuations (prices) that kept the same private equity firms away from deals that had invested in Spanish debt. A robust European Deposit Insurance Scheme (EDIS) and SRF would compensate for the lack of willingness to accept reductions in investment value. This is a clear difference between the two countries: a state imperative in Spain to force through sales at discounts was central to the transformation of the banking sector. This was absent in Italy (Sanderson 2016), and given that absence, it would have been difficult to establish a consortium of private institutional investors to take part in restructuring and refinancing Italian banks even if the government had wanted to emulate Spain's SAREB institution. That left successive Italian governments attempting to corral domestic banks only as potential investors. The outcomes are therefore not just about the institutional tools of the state and the willingness to use them, but of the obstinacy of Italian banks (though this was not so very different in Spain, given the years-long resistance to change), and the weakness of the state's willingness and capacity to confront this obstinacy. This obstinacy was found in Spanish cajas as well, but the state acted more forcefully against it. Madrid had its own difficulties confronting the banks up until 2012, but it can be said that it booked considerable success and involved international investors. Even so, some problems were papered over and pushed onto the long shelf through a series of mergers that fell short of resolutions until Bankia forced the Spanish government to make a deal with the Eurogroup that strengthened its hand against Spanish savings banks, and their customers.

The future of banking nationalism and bank reform in Europe

What should we make of these findings and implications? What is the broader context? The Spanish case in particular outlines clearly that what counts as acceptable economic nationalism in the EU is a sort of disembedded liberalism where the financial sector is not tied to political and social agendas. This is normal for large commercial banks, but new for local, regional alternative banks that were established precisely for the purpose of providing financial services for underbanked communities and stakeholders. The kinds of reforms that have been made are consistent with Germany's ordoliberal preferences within Banking Union that national governments retain ultimate responsibility for intervening in and financially guaranteeing national banking systems, which national banking systems themselves cannot and should not retain functions that are beyond their ability to provide without subsidies. In the reality of a Eurozone with a core and a (semi)periphery, this means a rather generous and consistent role for alternative banks in financing local economies and communities, and a much more disembedded, market-logic-oriented and financially fragile liberalism counterpart in countries like Italy and Spain. In Spain, the government accepts and pushes through these changes, while in Italy the government does not.

It is in this context that a discussion of economic nationalism in bank resolution ought to be conducted. There is a natural tendency and danger to unreflectingly consider the ESM-supported transformation of national states and banking systems as a positive development, while resistance gets labeled as negative. But as the long-term growth and employment challenges following the Great Lockdown continue, the wisdom of these policy expectations can and should be debated as well. Does the continued demise of alternative banking hurt society? Do we need to reintroduce or reinvent it now that it has been reduced in some states more than others?

An alternative set of questions flowing from the findings here on liberal and functional economic nationalism revolves around the basic assumptions around national responsibility for financial stability in Banking Union and the role of the ESM in reinforcing that tendency. Do they cause problems of their own? Banking Union deliberately eschewed deposit insurance at the European level (EDIS) as a mechanism for deposit insurance and even restructuring, leaving a modest Single Resolution Fund to help with sub-systemic failures. This left the ESM in a position of determining conditions for loans to national governments trying to back up and resolve their banking systems. This feature was formalized and extended in 2020 when the ESM Treaty was amended to make the ESM the backstop for the SRF.

This construct was designed to avoid moral hazard from the German and Dutch perspectives but, equally, to provide incentives for Eurozone Member States to vigorously reduce risks through resolutions. This requires political will at the national level above all to intervene in local politics and private investor links with local banks. Given the loopholes in the current Banking Union architecture, which simultaneously provide leeway for national governments to act in what they see as the national or citizen interest, governments can be expected to use them in different ways. Where national will to reform is weak, it will remain so. Where it is strong, it will also remain so, but benefit as well from the assistance of the ESM (and not be affected so much by the existence of the SRM, as originally intended).

Given these insights, the EU might want to rethink its current restrictions on state aid for bad banks, which continues to prevent unrestricted capital injections but finds a way to reintroduce the kind of government-assisted bad bank restructuring that was possible prior to the BRRD. Keeping such measures off the table implies that the great financial crisis of 2008, together with the Eurozone crisis that followed, was a one-off event that required emergency measures which should never be repeated. As we were reminded by 2020, external shocks and a need for emergency powers, including extraordinary state finance, remain constant features of national banking systems. This is equally so in a European banking system, which requires common financial resources.

State behavior, EU integration theory and European economic governance

The findings above also have implications for how we conceive of European institutions, their impact on the Member States of the Union and which factors national governments take into account when deciding how to tackle serious challenges, in this case in banking. These in turn have implications for the way in which European institutions are built up in the first place, and in which way they matter. One of Europe's stated goals is to keep nationalism under control, and to propagate a vision of what national good governance entails. The SSM does this to some extent, but also took away some of that responsibility once the EBA and national authorities had so clearly failed to supervise and resolve banks themselves. The SRM, meanwhile, is built on national infrastructures and national initiatives and retains in practice enormous loopholes for national forbearance towards banks, even though its stated purpose was to close them. The European Commission, while still in control of state aid in competition policy, has also found itself having to be creative in finding ways to allow the Italian state to circumvent the BRRD and deal with local banks directly that were never really intended.

Neo-functionalist expectations of state deference to European institutions and policy processes are therefore largely disconfirmed. While the SRB retained formal authority, not even in the Spanish case can the Board be seen taking a hard decision against a national authority? In contrast, the ECB does emerge as an undisputed strong authority in supervision. But the lack of a strong resolution counterpart makes it difficult to follow up supervision with consequences for banks that are failing or likely to fail. The European Commission's capacity to act is somewhere in the middle. It retains authority over state aid, whether in precautionary recapitalization or other forms of restructuring aid, but its behavior in the Italian cases is difficult to explain in any way other than conceding the limits of the existing bank resolution architecture. In short, Italy proved to have considerable leverage on European institutions rather than the other way around. This is not to say that Italy rejected EU institutions, or the need to reform the banking system in principle. This can be seen in the considerable attention to tackling banking problems over the course of a decade after 2008, and as well in its willingness to tackle sovereign borrowing problems, particularly in 2011 during the Monti administration. Rejection is not a starting point, given the potentially enormous reputational and financial costs of doing so, with all of the economic, political and social implications of being shut off from international capital markets. But successive Italian governments have rejected the ESM and refused to interact with it in any way, even during the Great Lockdown of 2020.

There is more than one possible intergovernmentalist take on the impact of domestic politics on EU institutions and policies, including Banking Union and the SRM in particular. Howarth and Quaglia's extensive work on Banking Union closely follows the impact of domestic lobbying on the bargaining preferences of national governments at the stage when institutions are created, exemplifying a liberal intergovernmentalist tack on analyzing the connections between domestic and EU politics. Without critiquing this important contribution to the literature, we direct attention here to what happens once the European institutions are in place, particularly where the results reflect asymmetric bargaining power and serve some countries well but others poorly. This is certainly the case when one looks at the combination of risk-reduction rules and institutions (SSM and SRM) and the absence of EDIS. Then the capacity of countries to deal with banks becomes an issue.

From Hodson and Puetter's New Intergovernmentalist literature, we can see the reluctance of national governments to create strong EU powers in areas of great sensitivity, and to leave implementation in national hands, which is reflected first in the original EBA model of supervision, and then in the SRB. But as we see here, their emphasis on national sensitivities and especially on the instabilities these create for properly functioning EU institutions, together with national competent authorities, points to the necessity of combining intergovernmentalism with domestic politics models that illuminate where we should expect more or fewer difficulties in living with common European arrangements.

It is here that the present book points to historical and sociological institutionalism as complements to an intergovernmentalist analysis of how European institutions are constructed, affect national institutions, banks and governments and interact with them politically. We concur with Schimmelfennig's (2015) argument that liberal intergovernmentalism is 'best embedded in a long-term theory of path dependence development of integration'. This is a vision of the EU as an influence on national governments from the outside in. But we also argue that solving the puzzle of economic nationalism in the wake of Banking Union requires a framework that takes institutions and norms seriously from the inside out. Here we find that sociological institutionalism provides a promising bridge between the domestic realities of socio-economic systems, varieties of financial capitalism in particular, and the way that local and national governments deal with the challenge of banking reform, and how they deal with the constraints and opportunities of working within Banking Union's structures. This does not so much contradict liberal intergovernmentalism (LI) theory—in principle—Moravcsik (1998) acknowledged complicated regulatory and public policy issues before setting them aside to pursue a more parsimonious analysis of EU decision-making. Nor does it contradict new intergovernmentalist frameworks—in principle—since these are much more highly attuned to the domestic difficulties of submitting national politics and economies to the authority of EU institutions. But just as LI acknowledges and downplays norm-based institutions and politics, new intergovernmentalism acknowledges and downplays the possibility of EU institutions and architectures that may sometimes be very strong indeed, in these cases the ECB as a bank supervisor, and outside the EU, the ESM as lender to governments in financial distress.

Rather than either of these approaches, we see evidence supporting much more closely the expectations of failing forward theory (Jones, Kelemnen and Meunier 2021), in which intergovernmental agreements to deal with grand challenges serve some countries better than others, and in the process sow the seeds of future poor compliance, instability, system failure and new institutional fixes to deal with the countries or areas that are not served well by the previous round. It also reflects failing forward's failing outward variant (Donnelly 2021), in which the ESM plays a central role in cementing those preferences by making credit conditional on compliance despite widespread critique by European institutions and a large number of EU Member States. In the cases dealt with here, the instability, pushback and system failure are most evident in Italy, and the fixes are found in loosening both the state aid mechanisms of the BRRD as applied by Directorate General (DG) Competition, and the resolution rules of the SRM as applied by the SRB. At the same time, the contrast with the Spanish case shows there is nothing pre-determined about difficulties in applying EU law and the prevalence of economic nationalism in the EU that forces adjustment and change at the European level. While Italy effectively forced the EU to change, Spain not only accepted rules but anticipated them and leveraged them to the greatest extent it could. In a further contrast, it did this not only with the EU but with the ESM as well. These choices to work with European institutions to override local institutions and still come out with nationally owned banks reflect critical choices rooted in attitudes towards both the EU and economic strategy overall. Historical institutionalism, to the extent that it can be shown to affect choices into the future, works from the top down in Spain, and from the bottom up in Italy. Where Spain sees itself as a catch-up economy that needs to modernize and accept the demands of EU institutions and international investors, Italy sees itself as an established economy that requires time and room to sort out problems on its own, rather than accepting demands from outside. Italy sees itself as having relative freedom of action due to its relative power to bargain in order to achieve its goals.

Whereas failing forward is agnostic about the reasons why national governments might encounter difficulties with European institutions and resources, we find that a combination of liberal intergovernmentalism and sociological institutionalism sheds light on the promise and pitfalls of European institutions and of Banking Union particularly. Sociological institutionalism shows how challenging it can be to work with Banking Union in its existing form. What makes the difference between liberal economic nationalism and functional economic nationalism then is in no small part comprised of visions that the state has of itself, of the country's position within the EU, of the domestic issues it faces, of the urgency to reform, of which European institutions the government should talk with (Commission, ESM or both?) and of the necessity of accepting conditions to that end.

References

Donnelly, S. (2021). Failing outward: power politics, regime complexity, and failing forward under deadlock. *Journal of European Public Policy, 28*(10), 1573–1591.

Donnelly, S., & Asimakopoulos, I. G. (2020). Bending and breaking the single resolution mechanism: The case of Italy. *JCMS: Journal of Common Market Studies, 58*(4), 856–871.

Financial Times Lex (2016) Italian banks: State paid. *Financial Times* 27 January. https://www.ft.com/content/0339553e-c50b-11e5-b3b1-7b2481276e45

Jones, E., Daniel Kelemen, R., & Meunier, S. (2021). Failing forward? Crises and patterns of European integration. *Journal of European Public Policy, 28*(10), 1519–1536.

Moravcsik, A. (1998). *The Choice for Europe: Social Purpose and State Power from Messina to Maastricht*. Ithaca: Cornell University Press.

Politi, J., Arnold, M. & Brunsden, J. (2016) Italy reaches 'bad bank' agreement with Brussels. *Financial Times*, 27 January. https://www.ft.com/content/ef7fe9e8-c4d0-11e5-b3b1-7b2481276e45

Sanderson, R. (2016a, June 29). Matteo Renzi rebuffed on move to sidestep bank bail-ins. *The Financial Times*. Retrieved from: ft.com/content/f0dc0e7e-3e39-11e6-9f2c-36b487ebd80a

Sanderson, R. (2016b, July 4). Bad-debt warning triggers fresh fears for Italian banks. *The Financial Times*. Retrieved from: ft.com/content/f04102da-41c7-11e6-b22f-79eb4891c97d

Schimmelfennig, F. (2015). Liberal intergovernmentalism and the euro area crisis. *Journal of European Public Policy, 22*(2), 177–195.

INDEX